Salt Marshes
A Natural and Unnatural History

Judith S. Weis
and Carol A. Butler

Rutgers University Press
New Brunswick, New Jersey, and London

Library of Congress Cataloging-in-Publication Data

Weis, Judith S.
Salt marshes : a natural and unnatural history / Judith S. Weis and Carol A.
Butler.
p. cm.
Includes bibliographical references and index.
ISBN 978–0–8135–4548–6 (hardcover : alk. paper)
ISBN 978–0–8135–4570–7 (pbk. : alk. paper)
1. Salt marshes. I. Butler, Carol A. II. Title.
QH87.3.W43 2009
578.769—dc22

2008043710

A British Cataloging-in-Publication record for this book is available from
the British Library.

Silent Spring by Rachel Carson. Copyright © 1962 by Rachel L. Carson.
Under the Sea-Wind by Rachel Carson. Copyright © 1941 by Rachel L.
Carson. Reprinted by permission of Frances Collin, Trustee

Visit our Web site: http://rutgerspress.rutgers.edu

Manufactured in the United States of America

Contents

Illustrations

Acknowledgments

First of all, I, Judith S. Weis, would like to express my thanks to Mike Bottini, who had the idea for this book originally and was initially supposed to be the co-author, until other obligations prevented him from doing so. Secondly, my husband, Peddrick Weis, has been a research colleague in salt marshes for decades and a strong supporter throughout the development of this book. Pete also is responsible for taking (and re-taking) many of the photographs included here as well as preparing the photos that were originally taken by others for publication. I thank all those contributors of photos, including family members Michael Horn and Mandy Jordan, friend Bernie Klempner, and others. I am also grateful to Elaine Evans for finding the hermit crab that we needed to photograph.

Some early experiences helped to develop my interest in this field. As a seven-year-old, spending the summer on Shelter Island, New York, I found a large hermit crab crawling in shallow water. It was living in a whelk shell that was covered with algae and barnacles and other attached forms—a whole collection of living things, all walking along the bottom. I thought this was absolutely wonderful and fascinating, though few others on the beach shared my enthusiasm. I still think it is fascinating and wonderful. I am grateful that my parents (now deceased) gave me this formative opportunity.

I am grateful to Dr. Evelyn Shaw, who, so many years ago, took me on as an undergraduate research assistant for a summer research project at Woods Hole, where I first became exposed to salt marshes and their inhabitants. The following year, the Marine Biological Laboratory's course Marine Ecology, with its amazing faculty, including Eugene Odum, Howard Sanders, and Larry Slobodkin, greatly expanded my knowledge of coastal ecology. Sadly, this course is no longer offered by the MBL.

I thank our offspring, Jennifer Weis Miner and Eric Weis, for their enthusiasm on field trips as children and their continued support, advice, and interest in nature as adults. The current enthusiasm of our granddaughters, Emily and Jessica Miner, for paddling around the Accabonac salt marshes and looking at wildlife is also greatly appreciated.

I appreciate the hospitality of two institutions that are no longer with us for enabling me to become familiar with the salt marshes on the East End of Long Island. During the 1970s, the New York Ocean Science Laboratory in Montauk hosted us during the summers. After they closed, we moved the base of summertime research operations for about twenty years to the Marine Science division of Southampton College, part of Long Island University. This campus is now part of SUNY Stony Brook.

The graduate students in the lab at Rutgers University during the development of this book also provided stimulation, interesting new information in salt marsh and estuarine ecology, and insight—Celine Santiago Bass, Lauren Bergey, Tish Robertson, Craig Woolcott, James MacDonald, Jessica Reichmuth, and Allison Candelmo—thank you for all your good work and good company. The same is true for research associate Terry Glover, whose insights into animal behavior and statistical prowess have been invaluable. I thank former post-doctoral student Lisamarie Windham for her knowledge of plant biology and ability to take the lead on our salt marsh plant research projects comparing *Phragmites* and *Spartina*. I appreciate the excellent research of all the other marsh scientists I have cited in this book, as well as those who I neglected to cite (sorry!).

I also acknowledge the Estuarine Research Federation (now called the Coastal and Estuarine Research Federation), a scientific society that has provided me with a professional home for many years and a network of colleagues with interests in salt marshes and their inhabitants. I am grateful to funding agencies, including the National Science Foundation, National Oceanic and Atmospheric Administration, Environmental Protection Agency, U.S. Geological Survey Water Resources Research Institutes, New Jersey Sea Grant Program, New Jersey Department of Environmental Protection, and the Meadowlands Environmental Research Institute, for supporting our research.

Historian Stephen Marshall and the staff at the Hackensack Riverkeeper organization, especially Hugh Carola, were most helpful in getting accurate historical information as well as a great photograph of the Meadowlands (see chapter 8). I am also grateful to Bill Sheehan and the rest of the staff of the Hackensack Riverkeeper organization for their tireless advocacy on behalf of this embattled marshland and their role in battle against the Mills Mall and the eventual turn-around of the Meadowlands Commission. I thank Robert Ceberio, then Executive Director of the commission, for his courage and wisdom in reversing the pro-development stance of the Meadowlands Commission.

I am grateful to various environmental groups: the Group for the East End, led by Robert DeLuca; the Nature Conservancy, led by Nancy

Kelley; and the Accabonac Protection Committee, especially Cile Downs and Jorie Latham, for their advocacy in protecting and maintaining the beautiful marshes of the East End of Long Island, most particularly Accabonac Harbor. Accabonac appears in many of the illustrations in this book. Larry Penny, the Natural Resource Director of the town of East Hampton, for many years has been a strong advocate for protection as well. I appreciate the work of Jim Ash and Carol Crasson of the South Fork Natural History Museum for their work in educating the community in Eastern Long Island about their natural resources and for their knowledge, assistance, and encouragement. I am grateful to all the other conservation organizations that are working to protect marshes, wherever they are.

Finally, I am grateful to the reviewer of the draft of this book, Scott Warren, for his incisive comments and recommendations that have improved the book considerably, and to our editor, Doreen Valentine, for all her help and work on this project and for finding Carol A. Butler as a co-author to turn my dull prose into more interesting reading.

Introduction

Salt marshes have been among my favorite places for many years, both for the experiences of tranquility and peace they provide and as places to study. In addition to being fascinating biologically (as we hope to convey in this book), they are easy to get to and don't require long trips on ships to reach, like habitats other marine biologists study. They are great places to take students, provided you go during the right part of the tidal cycle. If you go at high tide, you probably won't see much!

Because salt marshes used to be viewed as wastelands, they have been mistreated and abused by people for centuries. In recent decades we've learned so much more about their ecology and the free "services" they provide to us. As a result they have been given some protection. We felt there was a need for a book aimed at students and members of the general public who are amateur naturalists, birders, and nature lovers, to provide information about salt marshes and to increase their understanding of these under-appreciated and vital habitats. The first three chapters provide basic information on the ecology of salt marshes and describe the plants and the animals found there, covering the East Coast and the West Coast of the United States. Numerous photographs should help readers to identify species that they may come across while visiting a salt marsh.

The scope of the book goes beyond the physical limits of the marsh proper to describe animals such as fishes that live in the shallow estuarine waters that are next to the marshes and cover them at high tide. The scope also goes beyond strictly "salt" marshes to cover those lower salinity marshes further upstream that have more freshwater input and are officially called "brackish" marshes.

The second part of the book (the "unnatural" history part) deals with ways that humans have altered marshes over the years. We examine physical alterations such as filling and ditching, chemical alteration by environmental pollution, and biological alterations—the introduction of non-indigenous or alien species into native habitats. These three chapters describe how the ecology of the marshes and estuaries has been affected by these changes. In the seventh chapter we cover two different aspects of ecological improvement: marsh restoration and the construction and use of marshes for water or soil treatment (cleanup). The final chapter tells the story of the Hackensack Meadowlands, a vast landscape across the Hudson River from New York City. We trace a history of many years of degradation and decline, followed by a tale of recent ecological recovery. Although this story has a happy ending for today, when one deals with environmental issues, nothing ever really ends. The battles for preservation and conservation must continue as the threats to our salt marshes ebb and flow.

I Natural History

1 Salt-Marsh Basics

To stand at the edge of the sea, to sense the ebb and the flow of the tides, to feel the breath of a mist moving over a great salt marsh, to watch the flight of shore birds that have swept up and down the surf lines of the continents for untold thousands of year, to see the running of the old eels and the young shad to the sea, is to have knowledge of things that are as nearly eternal as any earthly life can be.

—Rachel Carson, *Under the Sea Wind,* 1941

What is it about marshland that evokes sensations of muck, salt, and sweet decaying matter? In our imaginations the salt marsh stands as a boundary between solid ground and the watery world, a place where mollusks, fishes, and grasses meet. It is a place of mosquitoes, herons, and hermit crabs—neither fully land nor fully water. A biologist might describe salt marshes as coastal wetlands that are transitional zones between the aquatic and terrestrial worlds. Some of the plants and animals living in these areas have origins as land species, for example, grasses, insects, birds, and mammals. Others, such as mollusks, crabs, and fishes, come from the sea. Since marshes are flooded by the flowing tides, the resident species must be hardy. The plants must be able to live in salt water and in soil that tends to be waterlogged and low in oxygen. And twice a day, many of the sea animals that are under water during high tide must survive being exposed to the air, sun, wind, and possibly rain when the waters run out at low tide. These are harsh conditions, where drastic change occurs in regular cycles.

In some places, salt and fresh waters combine directly. Bays, inlets, harbors, and sounds are all places where fresh water from rivers and streams mixes with salt water from the ocean, and these areas are called "estuaries." Salt marshes are found throughout the world on protected shorelines and on the edges of estuaries. In the United States, they span the entire East Coast and are extensive along the Gulf of Mexico but are less common on the West Coast.

There was once a vast wetland in New York harbor consisting of three great marshes: Jamaica Bay, the New Jersey Meadowlands, and the coast of Staten Island. Salt marshes are most extensive between New Jersey and northern Florida, particularly along the coasts of the Carolinas and Georgia. Further south in Florida, they are replaced by mangrove swamps, which are the tropical equivalents of salt marshes. On the Pacific Coast, most of the shoreline tends to be rocky, and salt marshes are relatively scarce except in the major marsh-estuary systems of California's San Francisco Bay and Washington's Puget Sound. They are also found in other coastal regions from the Arctic tundra to the tropics and on every continent except Antarctica. Countries with large salt-marsh areas include China, Argentina, and Brazil.

Among wetlands that are broadly called salt marshes, the ratio of salt water to fresh water predicts the diversity of habitat and resident species. A brackish marsh, for example, occurs in the portion of an estuary where the salt water is more diluted with fresh water. Further up the estuary there is a transition to freshwater marshes that are still somewhat affected by the tides, although the concentration of salt is low. Still further upstream are freshwater marshes that are untouched by the tidal ebb and flow. There is a parallel transition to less salt-tolerant plants as the water in the marsh becomes fresher, and the community of animals changes as well.

Salt and brackish marshes are also called tidal marshes because they occur in the *intertidal* zone between low and high tides. The lower portions of marshes on the East Coast of the United States are alternately flooded and drained twice a day by the tides. The regular cycling of the tides is caused by the gravitational pull of the sun and the moon on the earth's water. The term *flood tide* refers to the incoming tide, while *ebb tide* indicates the falling, receding tide.

The moon, being relatively close to us, exerts a strong pull on the earth so that water on the side of the earth facing the moon at any given time is pulled up, creating a high tide. As the earth rotates every twenty-four hours, the bulge moves through different points around the earth, creating high and low tides approximately every six hours throughout the day. Because the moon also moves, circling the earth every twenty-eight days, the timing of high tide each day is about an hour later than it was the day before. Let's say on this particular day, your local salt marsh at noon will be at high tide (at point A) (see fig. 1.1). Six hours later it will be low tide there, the earth having made a quarter turn to point B. At midnight it will be high tide again at point C, then at six o'clock in the morning it will be low tide, at point D. The next high tide will not be exactly at noon; it will

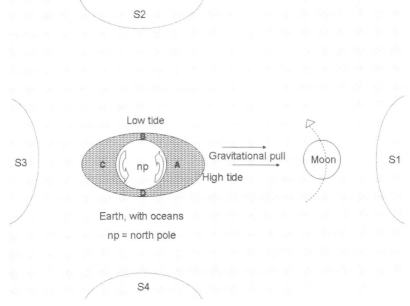

Fig. 1.1. Effects of the moon on the earth's tides. Arrows show direction of earth's rotation, from the perspective of looking down at the north pole, and direction of the moon revolving around the earth. When a point on the earth is at A or C, it is experiencing high tide. Six hours later, when it is at B or D it is experiencing low tide. If the sun is at S1 or S3 (full or new moon), the gravitational pulls of the sun and moon are added, causing especially high and low spring tides. If the sun is at S2 or S4 (first and third quarters), the sun is counteracting the moon and reducing the difference between high and low tide (neap tides). *Diagram by J. Weis.*

be about an hour later because the moon will have moved 1/28th of the way around the earth.

When the sun and moon are in line with each other and the earth (when the sun is at S1 or S3), their gravitational pull in combination is greater than at any other time of the month, so the flood tides rise higher and ebb tides fall lower than at any other time. These especially high and low tides are called "spring" tides (there is no connection with the springtime season), and they happen every two weeks at the time of the full moon and new moon. On the weeks in between, the pull of the sun and moon are at right angles to each other (when the sun is at S2 or S4), so they oppose each other. During those periods, the high tides do not rise very high and the low tides do not fall very low. These tides, when the tidal range is minimal, are referred to as "neap" tides.

The exact height and timing of the tides at any given place is determined by many other factors, such as the shape of the shoreline and the strength and direction of the wind. One extreme case is the Bay of Fundy in Nova Scotia, where there is a difference of almost fifty feet in the depth of the water between high and low tides. In some places in the Caribbean, the difference between high and low water is less than one foot.

The environmental conditions in a salt marsh are highly variable because the incoming fresh water and ocean water are always mixing in the estuary. If a marsh is located right on the ocean, its water will be quite a bit more saline than the water in a marsh located further upstream in an estuary that receives lots of fresh water. Salinity also fluctuates depending on the phase in the tidal cycle and the amount of recent rainfall. The same salt marsh may experience salinities ranging from almost freshwater to full-strength seawater, and anything that lives there must be able to tolerate these wide swings in environmental conditions. The amount of dissolved oxygen undergoes similar swings as water alternately covers and uncovers the marsh. Temperature also varies widely across the seasons. The air in summer is much warmer than the water, but in winter the water is warmer than the air. Plants and animals must cope with these variations on a daily basis, yet despite these inhospitable and inconsistent conditions, salt marshes are thriving ecosystems.

Certain species of grasses, which are actually flowering plants, are found only in the shallow intertidal areas and are highly specialized to deal with salt water and salty soil. They are called *halophytes,* from the Greek *hals,* meaning "salt," and *phyton,* the Greek word for "plant." Because they have to deal with being submerged in water part of the time, they are also considered *hydrophytes,* with *hydro* being the Greek word for "water." In addition to having to tolerate the salt and the water, the lack of oxygen in the waterlogged marsh soil is another factor that makes the environment stressful to plants. The diversity of plants is lowest at the more stressful lower elevations of a marsh and generally increases as one moves higher in the marsh to areas that are only affected by the salt water during very high tides. In the high marsh one can find grasses, rushes, herbs, and shrubs. The lower marsh zone in regions of Europe and along the Pacific Coast of the United States frequently lacks vegetation altogether.

Marine animals also must cope with a stressful environment due to the dramatic fluctuations in the marsh to which they must constantly adapt. They must find a way to keep moist during low tide, and when the tide is out there is no food for those that obtain their food directly from the water. Most of these animals are inactive during the low tide, with a few exceptions. Fiddler crabs forage at low tide and remain in their burrows at high tide, safe from predatory fish. Smaller crustaceans, called amphipods and isopods, may also remain active on the marsh surface during low tide, and the salt-marsh mussel frequently "air gapes" at low tide.

Virtually all residents of the salt marsh time their lives and especially their reproductive cycles according to the tides and the phases of the moon. On the highest tides at the full and new moon, fiddler crabs release their young where tidal currents can carry them out to the ocean. Horseshoe crabs come up onto the beach to lay their eggs at the high tides before the full moon.

Salt marshes develop gradually when certain geological conditions occur. Marsh formation begins when the tides carry and deposit sediments (soil, fine-grained clay, sand, and silt) across low-lying land, creating wet mudflats or sand flats. The sediments are carried to the estuary from freshwater rivers and eroding shorelines. Salt marshes develop in sheltered areas that are flat and slow draining, where mats of microscopic algae and bacteria form. These mats stabilize the sediment so that it stays put and its elevation can increase. This process speeds up when the salt-marsh plants take root as the marsh ecosystem develops.

Salt-tolerant grasses enter the scene when plants raft in on the tides and seeds are carried in by the air or water. The plants slowly take hold and spread, usually by means of underground horizontal stems or *rhizomes,* further stabilizing the sediment through the growth of dense root systems and adding volume, helping to raise elevations. Once the grasses are in place, the force of wave action is reduced, thus permitting additional layering and settling of the sediment to occur. As the plants decay, fine sediment builds up, causing marsh accretion and creating an even richer habitat. As sea levels rise, the marsh pushes landward and seaward, and freshwater plants on the land get replaced by marsh grasses that can tolerate the salt.

Underneath the marsh, peat accumulates from the below-ground (root and rhizome) plant debris. Peat formation eventually raises the elevation of the sediment surface so that it is flooded less of the time. At that point, other somewhat less salt- and flood-tolerant plant species are able to survive. Eventually, this leads to the development of high marsh areas that are flooded less often by the incoming ocean tides than the lower areas. Indeed, marshes must continually grow vertically through layer upon layer of sediment to keep up with rising sea levels. The bulk volume of roots and rhizomes contributes to both sediment deposition and marsh accretion. The equilibrium rate that matches marshland growth to changing sea level has been about four to ten inches per century, under conditions that have been prevalent for as long as we have been keeping records. With climate change causing thermal expansion of water and melting of glaciers along many coastlines, sea level is rising faster than the sedimentation rate. Unless marsh accretion is able to keep pace with sea level rise, marshes may be drowned and replaced by open water.

The end result of the natural sedimentation process is a general spreading of the entire marsh system with a pattern of *zonation* of plants, in which particular species are located in bands at different elevations. A fully developed marsh includes creeks that form a network over the marsh. These creeks are the routes used by tidal water as it enters and leaves the marsh, and they are the primary link of the estuary to the land.

Whether we are talking about the salt marshes of San Francisco or Iraq or New Jersey, general principles and themes emerge. The general ecology of salt marshes, the roles played by different species of animals and plants, and the ways in which humans have destroyed or harmed the marshes are applicable worldwide. Early settlers in America, for example, found marshes important for raising livestock, but when agriculture moved inland due to expanded settlement, salt marshes were regarded as useless wastelands. In the past several decades, though, people have begun to understand wetlands, to appreciate the "ecosystem services" they provide to us, free of charge. Indeed, salt marshes are important for many reasons.

Many species of migratory shorebirds and ducks depend on having wetland areas as stopovers during their migration between summer and winter habitats, and some birds winter in the marsh. Wading birds such as egrets and great blue herons feed in the productive salt marshes during the summer months. They can also feed there during the winter thaw.

Animals in various stages of life can be found among the salt-marsh plants. The marsh surface is covered with water at high tide, and juveniles of small fish move up and swim among the stems of the marsh grasses, where they are protected from larger predators that can't penetrate the shallow waters of the creeks. Studies have shown that more than two-thirds of the commercially harvested fish on the East Coast spend some portion of their life cycle in the marsh-estuary ecosystem. Oysters, quahogs, scallops, soft-shelled clams, blue crabs, and winter flounder are among the important species taken from these habitats.

Salt marshes are called *nurseries,* where many species of fish and shellfish live during the early stages of their lives, depending on the marsh for food and shelter. The plants provide shelter for spawning, and they protect the juveniles of many different species of commercial and ecological importance, including blue crabs, croakers, flounders, and spot. Bluefish spawn out in the ocean, for example, but the juveniles (snappers) move into estuaries in the spring and remain there through the summer, feasting on the smaller fish that live in the marsh-estuary system.

Salt marshes also serve to shield and protect coastal areas from storms and floods. They are important shoreline stabilizers because they can take the brunt of storm waves, buffering the shoreline from flood and storm damage. One common source of flood damage occurs following storms when runoff from the land hits the coastal plain. Marshes are natural sponges that can absorb much of this runoff, reducing its impact on coastal environments and real estate. Established marsh grasses are also very effective against erosion. The roots and rhizomes of marsh plants help the sediments cohere and consolidate, resulting in less erosion in vegetated areas. When marshes are removed, the effects of storms on coastal communities are much more severe and devastating, and therefore more costly.

We can look at the most powerful storms in recent years and see a pattern. Where marshes were strong, functional systems, the damage to the land and to costal communities was much less severe. In Sri Lanka, for example, the Indian Ocean tsunami in December 2004 caused much less devastation in areas where mangroves were present than in areas where they had been removed. Hurricane Katrina in August 2005 produced a catastrophe in New Orleans in part because of the loss of tidal wetlands.

Since the 1950s, an average of over 25 square miles per year of Louisiana's coastal wetlands has been lost due to a number of factors, including development and oil and gas exploration and production. The loss during the summer of Hurricanes Katrina and Rita was several-fold greater. The engineering of channels and the system of levees along the Mississippi River prevented regular tidal flooding, stopping the flow and process of salt-marsh sedimentation and vertical growth. The normal accumulation of sediments washing down into the marsh did not occur. If the area had been undisturbed, accumulated sediments would have elevated the marshes and reduced the effects of the storm surge. As it was, the hurricanes caused the additional loss of 215 square miles of salt marsh, an order of magnitude greater than the average annual loss. According to the Army Corps of Engineers, for every 3 square miles of wetlands, a storm surge can be reduced by a foot. Imagine thousands of families being spared the devastation of Katrina. Among many other lessons, Hurricane Katrina and its aftermath demonstrate the importance that wetlands play in protecting communities from floods.

Marshes also purify water, cleaning and filtering out excess pollutants, sediments, and nutrients from the water that washes down from the land.

Aftermath

It's not the storm itself—wind and rain lashing shore,
uprooting trees, toppling poles and dousing lights,
flooding cellars and roads, capsizing boats—
but the aftermath—the bright calm, the pair
of drowned cats crumpled against the picket fence,
the parlor of Izzy's shack open for inspection,
the walls fallen flat on all sides, your own
roof filling the front yard, covering your car,
and your own twin daughters dazed by Nature's
petulance—that makes you reconsider
your life and weigh your possessions and the cost
of putting down stakes too near the coast
as the globe warms, and storms grow worse.

(From *Grounded,* by George Held. © Finishing Line Press, 2007.
Reprinted with permission.)

Marshes along the shore slow the movement of runoff from land into the estuary while they increase sedimentation and the removal of wastes. The salt-marsh sediments retain or sequester many kinds of toxic contaminants, helping to reduce the degree of contamination of the coastal waters. Wetlands also intercept nutrients that arrive in runoff from the land, protecting adjacent estuarine areas from excess nutrients which can be harmful at high concentrations. Resident microbes in marshes can remove wastes from the water. They break down and process waste products and other pollutants in their normal metabolism. In some areas, engineers have constructed wetlands specifically to treat wastewater, a process that capitalizes on this natural ability.

Marshes are highly productive habitats. Most people do not know that salt marshes rival tropical rainforests in producing the most basic food energy per acre. They are highly productive because they are rich in nutrients and they cycle the nutrients very efficiently. They also have a variety of different types of plants that perform photosynthesis: rooted grasses, seaweeds, and microscopic algae both in the water (plankton) and living on the surface of the mud.

There have been some attempts to attach a dollar value to the services provided by salt marshes and other natural areas. However, monetizing the benefits of salt marshes to a region and then making decisions about the conservation or destruction of that region in purely economic terms is an overly simplistic approach. Many of the important functions of a marsh are intangible and its benefits accrue to everyone, so fixing its value is unrealistic if not impossible.

Marshes can be disturbed by both natural factors and human activities. Natural disturbance by ice and floating debris can cause significant damage to temperate marshes, particularly in the colder northern areas of New England. Tidal action can lift up pieces of marsh and deposit them on higher areas, where they literally suffocate the underlying vegetation. We call the floating masses of dead plant material *wrack,* and it is produced in the fall when some plants die and collapse and then are swept away by the tides. Depending on the conditions that promote aggregation of the drifting wrack, the wetland can become stagnant, encased by a barrier of debris, or winter ice can amass and destroy large chunks of low marsh vegetation. Fire and overgrazing by large animal populations, like geese, can also destroy large areas of marshes. But these effects are minor compared with the damage that results from human activities.

As more and more people choose to live in coastal areas, the human impact on tidal marshes has increased. By the turn of the twentieth century, 42 percent of the United States population lived in coastal counties. Marshes have been filled, drained, diked, ditched, grazed, and harvested. They will continue to be lost to sea-level rise. They have become depositories for pollutants, wastes and fertilizers that wash into streams and rivers from the land, as well as for contaminants introduced from coastal waters. They have been sprayed with wide-spectrum insecticides for mosquito control, chemicals that have a wide range of negative effects on the ecology of marsh and estuarine animals and plants. They have also been invaded by a range of non-native species that have altered their ecology.

Over the past two hundred years, a lot of marsh has been lost, but we now know that salt marshes should be nurtured and treasured. Throughout much of our history in the United States, policies and people have destroyed coastal habitats. Today, most of our larger coastal cities and towns hug the shores of estuaries, continuing to encroach on these vital habitats. Cities developed early in these locations because they were ideal sites for trade when most goods were carried by ships. Forest products like timber and agricultural production like wheat and corn could be easily moved down river to a coastal port where ships were waiting to transport the goods to markets worldwide. Ports were often dredged out of marshes, and networks of roadways and railroads were built that cross the marshes in every direction. Such construction has disrupted the flow of water, impeded tidal exchange, and strangled the marshes by degrees.

Salt marshes have been treated as something to be despised and "re-claimed," that is, converted to a use that is considered to have more value. In the past, there was a widespread perception that wetlands were waste-lands and pestilent swamps. They were drained, dredged, and filled with dredge materials for urban development. In other cases, they were fenced in for livestock grazing or polluted through use as garbage dumps.

Mud flats and salt marshes lack the public appeal and mystique of tropical rain forests and coral reefs, even though in their own way they are just as interesting and ecologically as valuable. While protective legislation in the 1970s slowed the rate of loss, marshes are still being degraded by the invasion of exotic species, poor management practices, development of urban and suburban areas, and the rise in sea level, concomitant with climate change. As marshes are destroyed and altered, even if at a slower rate than in the past, our vulnerability to floods and storms, the purity of our water systems, the vitality of our communities, and the health of our population are all at risk. A myriad of plant and animal species face dire consequences if marshlands continue to be lost or exploited. To fully appreciate all of these repercussions, it is important to understand their functioning so we may be able to better conserve and restore them.

Wetlands have become a major battleground in disputes between developers and environmentalists. With increased appreciation of their value, the scale of their loss and its ecological consequences are finally being recognized, prompting greater efforts for conservation. Concerned individuals and dedicated groups both within and outside of government are now mobilizing to stop and perhaps even reverse the trend.

In the late 1980s, it was estimated that about sixty thousand acres of wetlands were lost per year. Since President George H. W. Bush estab-lished a national policy of no net loss of wetlands in 1989, the overall rate of loss has been slowing down. Numerous conservation and restoration projects, both simple and complex, have taken place with varying degrees of success. The practice of creating new salt-marsh habitats to replace ones that have been destroyed elsewhere is widespread in key regions. But in many of these cases, there has been little, if any, follow-up to measure the success of the project. The situation is slowly improving with the growing realization that we can learn a lot from both our successes and failures. Despite the increased public awareness of the value of wetlands, we are still losing them to development, and some people still view them merely as obstacles in the way of urban expansion.

Putting all the ecological and economic interests aside, we can simply enjoy the marshland, relish in its cyclical wonder, its example of harsh extremes where life thrives nonetheless. Salt marshes provide us with unique opportunities for fishing, canoeing and kayaking, walking, hunting, and educational field trips. In addition, they are fascinating places to study biology. Marshes are valued for their beauty and the sense of peace and tranquility they provide. They offer visitors beauty, rest, and a taste of wilderness. They are places worth saving.

2 Primary Producers
The Plants

Salt marshes . . . are glorious places, bugs and all. With their green and brown grasses producing nutrients for the sea, they are among the richest and most productive environments on earth. Able to withstand salt water, the grasses stand eternally as a buffer between the murky estuaries and bays and the high green forests, exuding life and energy.

—Jack Rudloe, *The Wilderness Coast,* 1988

Almost all life on earth ultimately depends on plants. The term *food web* describes the feeding relationships among species in an ecosystem, and plants are at the base of the food web because they are the only organisms that create food using the energy from the sun. Using *photosynthesis* (from the Latin *photo,* meaning "light," and *synthesis,* meaning "to put together"), plants convert energy from sunlight, carbon dioxide, and water into glucose and other nutrients.

Next in the web are herbivores, which are animals that obtain their nutrition and energy by eating the plants. Carnivores eat other animals, typically those that have eaten plants. Bacteria and fungi are also part of the food web. These microbes consume dead plants and animals, obtaining energy and causing decomposition (breakdown) and recycling of the nutrients that were in the organism.

Marsh plants are essentially land plants that have adapted to being periodically covered with salt water. Because of the harsh conditions created by being submerged in salt water, there are relatively few species of plants that can survive both the salt water and the high salt content of the marsh soil. Water-related (*hydrologic*) factors such as water velocity, wave energy, and tidal regime (depth, duration, frequency, and timing of flooding) play a large part in determining which plants will survive.

As tides rise and fall, plants are exposed to wave action and currents, and the movement of the water influences the amount of sediments, pollutants, and salinity that the plants must be able to endure. Established vegetation is usually able to tolerate the movement of the water, but young plants without well-developed root systems are vulnerable to erosion and may be washed away. Very high spring tides can be especially stressful to the marsh plants because the low marshes remain flooded for longer periods of time than usual. Even the highest zones in the marsh that are rarely under water become submerged.

Environmental Conditions

The dominant species in salt marshes throughout the world tend to be grasses, especially cordgrass (*Spartina*) and species of rushes (*Juncus*). The salt wort (*Salicornia*), a succulent hydrophyte that can store water, is also found in many salt marshes. These plants are able to survive in a salty environment because the salt is excreted (cordgrass), stored (salt wort), or excluded by the roots (various other salt-tolerant plants that have a barrier in the roots limiting salt uptake). The plants are more stressed at lower tidal elevations where they are in the water a greater amount of time. Most flowering plants (Angiosperms) have a very low tolerance for salt, so there is less diversity of plants in salt marshes as compared to freshwater marshes where a staggering variety of flowering plants flourish.

Some salt marshes include bare areas, called *pans,* which are slight depressions in the marsh surface. Seawater from spring tides becomes trapped in these depressions and evaporates, causing the soil to become increasingly salty, and in some cases a salty crust forms over the soil surface. These high-salinity conditions limit the germination of seedlings and may be high enough to kill some of the less hardy halophytes.

Plants growing in the intertidal zone, which is the area between the water levels at high and low tides, must obtain oxygen from roots that are sitting in wet (*hydric*) soil that is usually poorly drained, waterlogged, and lacking in oxygen (*anoxic*). At high tide, the soil is covered by water, and the limited amount of oxygen in tidal water is quickly used up by bacteria in the soil. Low levels of oxygen in the soil stress or even kill most angiosperms. It takes special adaptations of structure and physiology to thrive in anoxic soils.

Plants in the low marsh have developed a way to deal with the lack of oxygen. They transport oxygen down to their roots in specialized tissue called *aerenchyma,* which in turn leaks some of the oxygen into the soil. The roots of the plant come close to the surface of the soil to obtain oxygen when it is available, and some have a barrier that keeps some of the salt out when they are under water. All of these mechanisms act in concert to allow the plants to live in this difficult environment.

Another effect of low oxygen in salt-marsh soils is the formation of sulfide. Sulfur is abundant in seawater and combines with oxygen as sulfate. When sulfate comes in contact with anoxic (low-oxygen) marsh soils, bacteria convert it to sulfide (a process called sulfate reduction), which bonds with iron in the soil to form insoluble iron sulfide. If there is not enough iron available, the sulfide will bind instead with hydrogen, forming hydrogen sulfide, which is quite toxic to marsh plants (and most other life forms, in fact). Hydrogen sulfide inhibits nitrogen uptake and plant productivity and gives off the familiar "rotten egg" smell at low tide. Furthermore, when tides recede and the soil is exposed to the atmosphere, the hydrogen sulfide combines with oxygen to form sulfuric acid, which can kill plants and marsh animals. These can become a problem when marshes are drained and dried and the stored sulfides oxidize. Despite the potential for chemical toxicity, the process of sulfate reduction is a very important process in marsh soils.

Sediments

Sediments are brought into marshes by river flow, tides, and storms, and organic matter is accumulated from decomposition. The roots of the marsh grasses stabilize the sediments and provide a surface onto which ribbed mussels and other animals can attach. The organic content of sediments is generally greater in high marshes than low marshes because the wave action and increased flooding in low marshes wash away some of the organic matter. The amount of organic matter in the sediments affects the amount of nutrients and metals that can be stored in the soil, and this in turn has an impact on the plant and animal communities that are able to live there.

Many factors determine the quality of the sediment. There are *geologic* factors, such as the origin of the sediments and the size of the area over which the sediment spreads, and *hydrologic* factors, including the speed of the water's currents and the volume of the water. The grain size and nutrient content of the sediments vary and are important factors for the plants that grow in them. Small-sized grains made up of silt and clay can hold more nutrients than coarse sandy soils due to their greater surface-to-volume ratio, and thus can be beneficial for plant growth. But if they are not well-drained, waterlogged fine sediments can be low in oxygen, resulting in slower plant growth.

The elevation of the marsh rises over time as the sediment accumulates, and this accretion is necessary in order to keep up with the rise in sea level, a process that is accelerating due to global warming. The processes of marsh development and accretion have been studied extensively in the Great Marsh of Barnstable on Cape Cod, where today's mature marsh overlies six meters of peat. If the overall marsh accretion rate is less than the rate of sea level rise, marshes will be submerged and cease to exist and the area will become open water.

Marsh creeks are important for the movement of water and materials between the marsh and the open water, and they facilitate the draining of the marsh during low tide, when plant roots have an opportunity to obtain essential oxygen. The more channels a marsh has, the greater the exchange of nutrients, sediments, and animals between the marsh and the downstream waters. The speed of water moving through a marsh affects primary productivity, erosion, and sediment deposition. Faster currents can carry larger sediment loads and larger particle sizes than slower currents. These large sediment loads can bury plants and smother bottom-dwelling organisms. If currents are too powerful, marsh sediments may be eroded away.

The source of the water coming into the marsh determines the amount of oxygen and various nutrients as well as the pressure put on the system from sediments and pollutants. Runoff from agricultural land may carry pesticides, large amounts of nutrients from soil fertilizers, and some sediment. In addition, runoff from urban areas may contain high concentrations of contaminants that have washed off the streets. Many less salty or brackish marshes and salt marshes also receive considerable amounts of groundwater, which is fresh water entering through marsh sediments.

The slope of the marsh surface influences the plant communities that can live there. Each plant species is adapted to living in a certain amount of water and within a certain range of salinity. Where each plant is located with regard to the slope of the marsh determines how much time it spends covered with water due to the tidal flow as well as the amount of salt to which it is exposed. On steeper slopes, plants from different marsh zones will be crammed closer together, and when the slope is very gradual you can find a very large expanse of marsh and the plants from different zones will be more spread out.

The salinity of salt and brackish marshes ranges from the salinity of the ocean (35 parts per thousand, or ppt) to almost fresh water (0.5 ppt). Salinities two to three times that of ocean water have been seen in Texas marshes in the summer when there was little freshwater inflow and high rates of evaporation. The ability to tolerate very low or very high salinity varies from species to species, and when salinity is outside the range of a particular plant, it will be stressed, its productivity will decrease, and survival will be a struggle.

Zonation of Marsh Vegetation

The general appearance of a salt marsh is a broad expanse of grasses, cut by small creeks that lead into larger creeks that lead into mud flats without vegetation or to the open waters of the estuary. A cross section of a typical marsh shows a pattern of bands of different plant species occupying different elevations. The lowest zone at the edge of the creek has plants that are under water daily for the greatest amount of time. Marsh areas at the lowest elevations that are submerged by all or most high tides are termed *low marsh*. Low marsh is occupied by essentially pure stands of smooth cordgrass on the Atlantic and Gulf coasts. Cordgrass, *Spartina alterniflora* (fig. 2.1), has a tall form that grows at the margins of the creeks and a shorter form that grows behind it. Behind this may be needle rush (*Juncus*) or salt hay (*Spartina patens*) (fig. 2.1), possibly mixed with salt wort (*Salicornia*) (fig. 2.2). The Pacific low marsh is unvegetated at higher salinities, and at lower salinities Lyngbye's sedge, *Carex lyngbyei,* may be found down the tidal slope.

The upper border of the marsh is at the highest elevation and is flooded only by occasional spring tides. This border is home to a few characteristic

Fig. 2.1. Cordgrass, in foreground; salt hay "cowlicks," behind. *Photo by Peddrick Weis.*

Fig. 2.2. Saltwort growing into bare pan. *Photo by P. Weis.*

Fig. 2.3. Marsh elder, with magnified insert showing serrated leaves. *Photo by P. Weis.*

Fig. 2.4. Groundsel, with magnified insert showing smooth leaves. *Photo by P. Weis.*

grasses, sedges, and shrubs, such as marsh elder or *Iva* and groundsel (*Baccharis*) (figs. 2.3 and 2.4), that are less adapted to salt water and can only tolerate being submerged on rare occasions. All salt marshes will show zonation, though the particular species of plants in the various zones will be different depending on geography, climate, and nutrients. The transition line between high and low marsh is generally equal to the elevation of the mean (average) water level. Differences in depth, duration, and timing of flooding affect other marsh functions such as decomposition and nutrient cycling.

Cordgrass is the only species that can survive in the frequently submerged low-marsh environment because it has evolved efficient mechanisms for dealing with the salt and the low oxygen. Zonation is maintained because other species outcompete cordgrass in the less stressful higher levels of the marsh. Some species might be able to live at a higher level of the marsh if their competitors were not present, but they could not survive at lower levels where the physical stresses are too great. In the Northeast, for example, marsh elder outcompetes needle rush at the upper edge of marshes, while needle rush displaces salt hay and then salt hay displaces cordgrass in lower marsh zones.

East Coast Marsh Grasses

Salt-marsh cordgrass (*Spartina alterniflora*) is the dominant grass in the low marsh on the East Coast. The lower part of the plant is regularly covered with water at high tide, and the excess salt that it accumulates at its roots is eliminated by glands on the underside of its leaves that excrete salt. A form that grows up to ten feet tall is found at the edge of creeks where soils are well drained, and a shorter form grows behind it in a zone with reduced drainage, oxygen-poor soils, elevated sulfide, and elevated salinity. These two forms may or may not be genetically different; the short form seems to be stunted due to the poor conditions in which it grows. However, at the University of Delaware, Jack Gallagher and Denise Seliskar transplanted tall- and short-form plants to the same plots, and nine years later, plant biomass, height, density, diameter, and flowering frequency remained quite different. Since the two forms had been living in the same environment but had retained many of their differences over time, some genetic control of the morphology and physiology seems highly likely.

Although cordgrass has pollen that is wind driven and produces seeds, its primary means of reproduction is via underground rhizomes (runners) that send up new sprouts each year, resulting in the rapid colonization of marsh areas. Its stems, which can reach more than one centimeter in diameter, range in density from ten to more than one hundred per square meter. Although the root system lives throughout the year because it is protected from the freezing weather, the above-ground portions of the plants die back in the fall in the mid-Atlantic and New England marshes. In the south, marsh grasses are functional all year round.

No other plant can compete with *S. alterniflora* in the low-marsh environment, where it is regularly submerged in seawater. It has evolved very effective mechanisms to deal with salt and low levels of oxygen. The plant's tissues contain high concentrations of salt and other dissolved chemicals that have been absorbed from the water, and when the concentration of salt in its tissues is higher than in the surrounding water, the plant draws in fluid from the saline soil rather than losing it. It also has salt glands on the underside of its leaves that excrete the excess salt that it accumulates. The physical process by which water is diffused through the cell walls is called *osmosis*. The roots concentrate the salts and allow fresher water to be sent aboveground to the leaves and stems; and, like all angiosperms,

Fig. 2.5. Salt crystals on leaf of cordgrass. *Photo by P. Weis.*

its leaves have pores, called *stomata,* for releasing water vapor. The layer of soil around the roots reddens the mud because iron sulfide in the sediments has been oxidized to iron oxide (rust) (see fig. 2.5).

Salt meadow hay (*Spartina patens*) is found behind the cordgrass, higher up in the marsh, appearing as a flat, matted patch of meadow (fig. 2.1). This plant was harvested in the past to be used as a forage crop for cattle and still is prized as a garden mulch. Shoots of salt hay are one to two feet tall, much finer and somewhat shorter than cordgrass, and they have a weak spot at the base of the stems that causes them to fall down onto the marsh surface. They often form large, characteristically swirled patterns, called *cowlicks,* which keep the ground moist. Its roots and rhizomes form a dense turf, outcompeting cordgrass at these higher, less frequently flooded elevations. The cordgrass forms a barrier between the salt hay and the creeks, and the decaying salt hay from the previous year generally remains underneath the living plants, contributing *detritus* (decaying plant material) to the marsh. While dead shoots of cordgrass wash away in the winter, salt hay litter turns brown and remains on the marsh throughout the winter.

Saltgrass or spikegrass (*Distichlis spicata*) (fig. 2.6) is often abundant in the upper regions of the marsh. It may be found along with salt hay in the meadows that are under water only during spring tides and storms. Saltgrass has greater tolerance for salt than does salt hay, and it may be found in salt-encrusted pans in the meadows, where few other plants can survive.

Salt pans (fig. 2.2) form a bare zone at intermediate levels in southern marshes, and spikegrass can invade these disturbed areas with its below-ground rhizomes. Once the plants are growing, the shade they provide reduces evaporation, thus lowering the salinity of the soil. Wiry, short, and fine, spikegrass with its light green leaves is usually scattered within the high marsh meadow, but occasionally it may occur in pure stands. It is the last of the grasses to flower in late summer and is easily recognized by its terminal flowering spike with white seeds.

Black needle rush (*Juncus roemerianus*) is a stiff, coarse grass found above the intertidal zone in salt and brackish marshes. Salt-marsh rush (*Juncus gerardii*) is often found as a belt along the upper border of the zone, particularly in more northern marshes, where it may be found on elevated creek-bank levees and near salt pans. Less tolerant of salt and flooding than salt hay, these grass-like rushes are a bit taller and darker green than salt hay, and they are not likely to form cowlicks. The reason for its common name is that the tip of the stem has a noticeably sharp point. It propagates via seeds and rhizomes and is a preferred habitat for birds known as *rails*. These slender birds, literally thin as a rail, can easily

*Fig. 2.6. Saltgrass.
Photo by P. Weis.*

Fig. 2.7. Arrowgrass.
Photo by P. Weis.

walk between and hide among the salt-marsh grasses despite the needle-sharp tips of the blades of grass.

Rushes (*Scirpus*) are grasses that are in the high marsh and have triangular stems ("sedges have edges") in cross section and relatively few leaves. These plants have lower salinity tolerance and are more common in brackish parts of the estuary or along the upper marsh border. The stems are used by muskrats for house construction, and the seeds are eaten by waterfowl.

Saltworts or glassworts (*Salicornia*) (fig. 2.2) are ankle-high succulent plants with thick stems and no obvious leaves. They are found in salt and brackish marshes in areas where salt water accumulates and is concentrated by evaporation. Many saltworts are annuals that depend on seeds to survive from one year to the next, but the perennial *S. virginica* is important throughout the Northeast marshes and the Chesapeake and Gulf coasts and is a major component of Pacific Coast marshes as well. The plant is green with segmented stems that can retain a large volume of water in isolated storage cells, helping the plant to keep its water balance. Saltworts are found in the same areas as salt hay and the short form of cordgrass. Their seeds can germinate in water that is even saltier than seawater. Jointed glasswort (*Salicornia europaea*) is often the first plant to colonize newly bare sites on the marsh. Its seeds can be transported with *wrack* (floating dead plant debris), and in the summer the plants exhibit luxuriant growth and are bright green in color. In the fall they turn a brilliant red. They are edible and can be pickled or used in salads.

Forbs, plants with showy flowers and broader leaves than the grasses, are frequently found in slight depressions or pans on the high marsh. They include sea lavender (*Limonium nashii*) (fig. 2.8), pink gerardia (*Gerardia maritima*), arrowgrass (*Triglochin maritima*) (fig. 2.7), seaside plantain (*Plantago maritima*), and salt-marsh aster *(Aster tenuifolius)*. Arrowgrass and seaside plantain are actually not grasses, but have long, grass-like leaves. These forbs vary widely in size and vigor depending upon environmental conditions. Sea lavender is a flowering herb with yellow- and lavender-colored flowers and blooms from July to October. Its leaves grow

Fig. 2.8. Seaside lavender in the fall. *Photo by P. Weis.*

up to a foot in length and remain until the middle of winter. Seaside gold-enrod (*Solidago sempervirens*) has bright yellow flowers in the fall.

Marsh elder (*Iva frutescens*) (fig. 2.3) is a shrub that can grow to be ten feet tall but is usually less than six feet. It is found at the highest margins of the upland border in a zone that is rarely flooded by spring tides. The plants have thick opposite leaves with serrated edges and tiny composite flowers. Marsh elder also grows on the locally elevated areas of the high marsh which are well-drained, especially along the banks of mosquito ditches. Groundsel tree (*Baccharis halimifolia*) (fig. 2.4), which looks su-perficially similar, is actually a shrub that grows from six to ten feet in height. It has thin alternate leaves without serrations and is also found at the upland border, as is switchgrass (*Panicum virgatum*), an attractive grass that can be three to six feet tall. Its clumps or tussocks sometimes form a distinctive belt of vegetation. Landward of the upper border, true upland soils and vegetation are present.

Common reed (*Phragmites australis*) (fig. 2.9) grows up to twelve feet tall and has a characteristic highly branched, feathery purple-brown tas-sel when it flowers. While the flowers produce seeds, more reproduction takes place with rhizomes that can go long distances underground. The rhizomes provide nourishment, enabling their stems to grow in otherwise unfavorable habitats. It can form dense, nearly pure stands, outcompeting other plants. Conditions such as disturbance, reduction in tidal flow, and

Fig. 2.9. Common reed. *Photo by P. Weis.*

freshwater runoff favor the establishment of this species. While previously a minor resident in the high marsh, a new genetic variant from Europe is taking over mid and lower sections of brackish marshes throughout the East Coast. We will discuss invasive species further in chapter 6.

Marshes have many plants that can spread using underground rhizomes. These plants are *clonal* since they are genetically identical. Individual stems, called *ramets,* are connected underground to their clone mates, and they can share resources and avoid environmental stresses. Stems are able to grow in areas that are unfavorable (e.g., too salty, too wet) because they are physically connected to clone mates that are in more favorable environments and can provide them with water and nutrients. Clonal plants can spread through marshes without needing sexual reproduction and can settle in places where seed germination and growth would be impossible. One reason cordgrass is so successful in anoxic soils of the low marsh is because the aeration of the soil by the larger plants allows seedlings and small ramets to survive and grow far better than they could otherwise. Common reeds are another example of plants that can grow in hostile, higher-salinity areas because they remain physically connected to clone mates living in lower salinity conditions.

Plants of the West Coast Marshes

There are comparatively few salt marshes on the West Coast. The major ones are in San Francisco Bay in California and Puget Sound in Washington, and other important ones are Tijuana Estuary, Elkhorn Slough, and Willapa Bay. They exhibit a zonation of plant species that is similar to the marshes on the East Coast. Cordgrass (*Spartina foliosa*) occurs in the low marsh in California but doesn't grow in the Pacific Northwest. Like *Spartina alterniflora,* the cordgrass species that dominates in the East, its stems are hollow, permitting oxygen to reach its roots, and it has salt glands to excrete excess salt. *S. foliosa* grows best in pure stands as it is a poor competitor with other plant species. It cannot survive where *S. alterniflora* has been introduced because *S. alterniflora* outcompetes it.

Further up the West Coast marsh, pickleweed (*Salicornia virginica*) the same species as on the East Coast, is common. These plants store salt in their tissues and continue to move water into the tissues even though they are rooted in saline soil. Growing with the pickleweeds are saltgrass (*Distichlis spicata*) and sea blite (*Suaeda californica*). On the high marsh, the prickly leaved succulent jaumea (*Jaumea carnosa*) is common, as are sea arrowgrass (*Triglochin maritime*), bushy shoregrass (*Monanthochloe littoralis*), and the endangered salt-marsh bird's beak (*Cordylanthus mar-*

itimus). The green saltgrass (*Distichlis spicata),* the same species as on the East Coast, is widespread in the middle to high marsh. Other plants in the high marsh include sea lavender (*Limonium californicum*), sea milkwort (*Glaux maritima*), sea plantain (*Plantago maritima*), gumplant (*Grindelia stricta*), salt bush (*Atriplex patula*), salt rush (*Juncus leseurii*), sand spurrey (*Spergularia macrotheca* and *S. canadensis*), and dodder (*Cuscuta salina*), as well as the rare Humboldt Bay owl's clover *(Castilleja ambigua).*

A brackish tidal marsh contains cattails (*Typha angustifolia* and *T. latifolia*), salt hay, Lyngbye's sedge (*Carex lingbyei*), and alkali bulrush in the lower tidal portions. Species found in the mid-marsh are spike rush, Baltic rush, three-cornered grass (*Scirpus olneyi*), and saltgrass. In the high marsh common pickleweed, saltgrass, gumplant, and alkali-heath are found.

Algae

Algae have no roots, no true leaves, and no tissues for transporting nutrients or wastes. They include microscopic forms that can be found floating in the water (called *phytoplankton*) or on the bottom and larger plants called macroalgae or seaweeds. Seaweeds are abundant in rocky shorelines, and some species can be found in salt marshes, where they have adapted to living part-time in the air. The most common species found in marshes is the brown alga rockweed (*Fucus*) (fig. 2.10). They can often be found growing around the bases of salt-marsh grasses or attached to ribbed mussels that protrude at the edge of the marsh. They attach to the shells or to other hard surfaces with a flattened disc-like structure called a *holdfast*. Rockweeds have air bladders for flotation, and when the tide is in, they float erect with their branches waving in the water. As the tide ebbs, they sag lower and lower and eventually become a collapsed mass.

Sea lettuce (*Ulva lactuca*) (figs. 2.10 and 3.9) is found in tidal creeks. It is a bright, fragile, flat green sheet that is initially attached to a substrate but is more often found drifting free, torn from its holdfast. *Ulva* grows especially well in areas that are rich in nutrients, and it may form huge detached sheets that can cover the muddy bottom surface, depriving mud-dwelling animals of oxygen. Another green algae, *Enteromorpha,* can be seen on creek banks. It is long and thin and flat and looks like Ulva that has been sliced into strips. Mud snails prefer to graze on macroalgae because they are they are softer and more appetizing than marsh grasses. Nevertheless, much of the production of macroalgae is utilized as detritus after they die and decay.

Microalgae can cover the surface of the mud with an inconspicuous

Fig. 2.10. Rockweed, *on right,* ribbed mussels, *on left,* sea lettuce, *below under water. Photo by P. Weis.*

community of microscopic plants which are mostly *diatoms.* Diatoms are better known as the dominant forms in phytoplankton, the chief primary producers of the ocean that float in the water. These microscopic single-celled photosynthetic organisms have a shell of silica that is composed of two valves like a pillbox. Diatoms reproduce by dividing in two halves, one half in the top valve and the other in the bottom valve. These valves generally have intricate patterns of notches and lines. The bottom-dwelling (*benthic*) forms tend to have well-developed longitudinal lines (*raphes*) that are used for locomotion. The diatoms living on the surface of the mud are a different group of species from the planktonic ones in the water column, and they have tougher shells because they have to cope with moving sediment particles. They migrate from the surface of the mud to just below the surface at high tide and at night, and then they come to the surface at low tide in the daylight. In recent years it has been shown that they are responsible for a considerable amount of the photosynthesis of the marsh. At certain times of year, they can trap most of the nutrients produced in the sediments and prevent them from getting to the phytoplankton.

These important primary producers, called benthic microalgae or *microphytobenthos* (from words of Greek derivation; *micro,* meaning "tiny";

phyto, meaning "plant"; and *benthos,* meaning "bottom dwelling") are invisible to the naked eye and therefore have been referred to as a "secret garden." Each zone has a particular species or group of species that prefers that habitat. The microalgae growing on the marsh surface provide food for a variety of small animals and make a significant contribution to the overall primary production of the marsh. Currents can move them up into the water column, where they can be consumed by other animals. Their photosynthetic activities are particularly important in the winter in northern areas when the grass production is non-existent.

Algal mats with many kinds of blue-green and green algae are found in the upper marsh. The mats help retain moisture for the microbial breakdown of plant material, and a variety of small invertebrates live in the mats. Blue-green algae, which are responsible for much of the nitrogen fixation in tidal marshes, may form ribbons and mounds on creek banks and can flourish underneath dense *Spartina* growth.

Floating single-celled phytoplankton, mainly diatoms and dinoflagellates, are present in the water that enters and leaves marshes with the tides. Diatoms, which may occur as chains of cells, are generally the most important groups at the base of the marine food chain and are consumed by filter feeders, animals with filtering structures to strain them out of the water. Dinoflagellates are second in abundance in the plankton and have two hair-like flagellae used for movement. Some of them have hard protective outer coverings referred to as *armor,* some are bioluminescent, and some can produce toxins responsible for so-called red tides.

Microbes

Microbes (bacteria and fungi) play major roles as decomposers of plants and animals in salt marshes by changing the chemicals in their bodies into forms that can be recycled. There are also some photosynthetic bacteria on the marsh, the most abundant being purple sulfur bacteria. They are limited to the zone below the surface of the mud, where there is no oxygen but light can still penetrate so that photosynthesis does occur.

While microbes are in the process of breaking down plant tissues, the carbon present in complicated molecules like carbohydrates and proteins gets returned to the environment as carbon dioxide that plants can re-use in photosynthesis. The nitrogen in proteins and nucleic acids gets converted back to inorganic nitrogen that can be re-used by plants. The protein present in the bacteria and fungi enriches the food value of the decaying plant material, so that detritus is a richer food than living plant material. In salt-marsh sediments, nitrogen and sulfur cycles that are powered by microbes are very important. Microbes are also involved in breaking down many pollutant chemicals that enter the marsh.

Microbial communities are different around the roots of marsh plants (the *rhizosphere*) than elsewhere in the marsh sediment. The rhizosphere is a particularly rich habitat because it contains materials exuded from plant roots and it is oxygenated due to the activity of the marsh plants. Some plants have specialized fungi associated with their roots, call *mycorrhizae*, that help the plant take up nutrients from the soil. Different species of marsh plants have different microbial communities associated with their roots, but they all carry out decomposition and provide additional nutrients to the plants. Sulfate reduction (turning sulfate into sulfide) by the microbes in the rhizosphere is highest during the plant's growing season, and it increases as the plant grows. Decomposition of wetland plant roots releases organic compounds into the sediments, where a different microbial community degrades the compounds. The typical smell of a salt marsh is due to the decay of plants and animals caused by the bacterial activity. Decomposing animals release nitrogen and phosphorus into the mud. The marsh mud releases hydrogen sulfide when disturbed, the source of a familiar smell to marsh visitors.

Primary Production

Photosynthesis is the main activity of the marsh grasses and of the macroalgae and microalgae in the marsh. Photosynthesis is called *primary production* because it is the foundation of most food webs on earth, the biological energy that sustains all other forms of life. Photosynthesis by green plants uses energy from the sun to produce food, and that food sustains small animals that are eaten by larger animals, which are eaten by even larger animals—so plants are the primary (original) producers. During the process of photosynthesis, inorganic carbon in the form of carbon dioxide is converted by energy from the sun into organic carbon in the form of carbohydrates which provide nourishment for the plants. The green pigment chlorophyll, contained in structures called chloroplasts in the plants' cells, enables the reactions to take place.

In tidal marshes, the power of the sun is supplemented by the power of the tides. Tides bring in nutrients needed by the plants and transport excess nutrients and wastes back to the estuary as they ebb and flow. They deliver oxygen-rich water to marsh soils as well as the suspended sediments necessary for the continued vertical growth of the marsh.

Primary productivity of marsh plants and other marine plants is generally limited by the amount of nutrients available. Marsh plants obtain most of their nutrients from the soil, and scarce nutrients reduce plant growth. The availability of nutrients in sediments depends on particle size and organic content and on the hydrologic characteristics of the marsh. Nitrogen and phosphorus are the two major nutrients that control plant growth in coastal marshes. Freshwater marshes tend to be limited by phosphorus because it is not abundant in the form of dissolved phosphate (PO_4^{3-}), which can be taken up by plants and incorporated into complicated biological molecules.

Salt-marsh plants are generally limited by nitrogen and respond with increased growth to additional nitrogen that comes into estuaries as a result of human activities such as the input of sewage or fertilizers. The forms of nitrogen that are usable by marsh plants are inorganic nitrate (NO_3^-), nitrite (NO_2^-), and ammonium (NH_4^+). These substances can be taken up by the plants and converted to amino acids and other biologically essential substances. Organic nitrogen consists of all the nitrogen bound up in living or dead animals and plants, including protein, DNA, RNA, and chlorophyll. These materials eventually get broken down into inorganic nitrogen by the activities of the microbial decomposers. The excess nitrogen enrichment (*eutrophication*) of estuaries (see chapter 5) can alter marsh zonation patterns and ecology.

As mentioned previously, the overall productivity of salt marshes is very high, comparable to tropical rain forests, which are among the most productive areas on earth. Salt marshes can produce up to ten tons of organic matter per acre in a year, which is higher than what is produced by many agricultural systems. Georgia's salt marshes are some of the most biologically productive natural systems on earth, four times more productive than the most carefully cultivated cornfields, according to the Georgia Department of Natural Resources. Unlike tropical rain forests, the diversity in salt marshes and estuaries is not high due to the harsh and variable environmental conditions.

Marshes are extremely productive for a variety of reasons: light is direct and bright, unlike in regions where water is deeper; nutrients are in abundant supply, which promotes plant growth; the tides mix the waters, diluting and removing waste products and making nutrients available to plankton and other producers. Abundant nutrients are brought in by the freshwater inflow from rivers and from the ocean, and some nutrients are produced in the marsh by nitrogen-fixing bacteria. Nutrients are recycled very quickly rather than being stored in organic materials (wood in trees, for example), where they remain for many years. The productivity of salt marshes in the southern parts of the United States is much higher than those in temperate areas because in the south the marsh plants remain alive and active all year, while in temperate areas they die back in the fall and grow again in the spring. In the north, only the algae remain active throughout the year.

In contrast to some terrestrial grassland areas, where large populations of grazing animals eat the plants, there are relatively few animals that consume living marsh grasses. These plants have a high salt content and their leaves consist of tough cellulose and silica. In the case of cordgrass, the leaves contain chemicals called *phenols,* which make them unappetizing to many herbivores. Grasshoppers, other insects, and some mud crabs do eat living cordgrass leaves, but most of the grass is not eaten directly when it is alive. About 90 percent of the primary productivity of salt-marsh grasses is utilized at the end of the growing season when the leaves and stems of the plants die and decompose.

The decay actually begins when the plants are dead but still standing, and it is carried out at that point primarily by fungi. Unlike animals, bacteria and fungi can utilize cellulose, which is the main structural component of cell walls of the plants. Later on, when the leaves fall off onto the marsh surface, bacteria in the mud and water continue the process of decomposition. The breakdown is helped by the chewing action of small invertebrates, such as amphipods and isopods, which break up large pieces into smaller pieces that are then more rapidly broken down by the microbes. The food value of the plant material increases during decomposition because as detritus particles decrease in size, they increase their protein content due to the presence of bacteria and fungi.

Salt marshes produce several tons of detritus per acre per year, of which much is washed into the estuary and is consumed by small invertebrates and fish, which are, in turn, consumed by larger animals. Detritus production varies by plant species, with the greatest production by the short form of cordgrass. Many commercial species of fish are ultimately dependent on this production by marsh grasses. While most of the detritus of cordgrass is washed away, most of the detritus from salt hay remains in place under the following year's growth, decomposing in place and providing food for small animals on the marsh surface. The detritus that stays within the marsh system combines with sediments to produce marsh peat, which is the substrate on which the marsh grows. The peat has dense roots and rhizomes intermingled, so it is both tough and permeable.

When plant tissues decompose, they may do so under aerobic (oxygenated) conditions on the marsh surface or they may become buried in sediment and decompose under anaerobic conditions. In the absence of oxygen, the decay bacteria use sulfate from seawater and reduce it to sulfide, which is precipitated as iron sulfide or pyrite. Anaerobic decomposition is incomplete, so plant material accumulates as peat. When plants are actively growing and oxidizing the sediment, much of the pyrite is oxidized and exported to the waters of the creeks, where it provides a substrate for the growth of sulfur bacteria.

3   Animals of the Salt Marsh
Consumers

Bubbling splashing sounds of crawling, swimming creatures hint at the vast abundance of life that dwells in the wetlands.

—Jack Rudloe, *The Wilderness Coast,* 1988

Animals of the salt marsh, like the plants, must be able to deal with periodic immersion in water and with major swings in salinity and temperature. Animals of the salt marsh include those that are basically aquatic and have adapted to periodic drying out and ones that are basically terrestrial and have adapted to periodic wetting. Aquatic animals tend to be found mostly in low marsh areas that are seldom exposed to the air, and terrestrial ones are found in higher areas that are seldom exposed to the water. Some animals burrow into the mud to escape drying out, while others climb up the marsh plants to escape the water. Some aquatic animals (fishes and crabs) move into the marsh with the tidal waters and move out as the tides ebb. Some terrestrial animals (insects and mammals) move in as the tide ebbs and out when it floods again.

An important distinction among animals in the marsh is whether they live on top of the sediment or inside it, or if they swim in the water. *Epifauna* are animals of marine origin that live on top of the mud, mainly species of crabs and snails. *Infauna* are animals that burrow into and live under the surface of the mud, primarily clams and worms. *Nekton* are animals that swim in the water, mostly fishes, but also some crabs and shrimp.

Animals that feed in the intertidal marsh have many different ways of obtaining food. Ebbing tides carry detritus into the estuary, where it is the food source for detritus feeders. Such feeders are primarily small invertebrates like amphipods, isopods, and worms. They are in turn eaten by predators such as crabs and small fish, which are eaten by larger fish, birds, and other animals. Detritus or deposit feeders ingest the substrate over which they move, which can include, in addition to detritus, sediment particles, microbes, small invertebrates, and microalgae. They are constantly reworking the sediments in order to acquire enough food, eating and swallowing large quantities of sediment and extracting the organic material from it, in the same way earthworms eat on land. Their processing of the sediment rearranges it, a process which is called *bioturbation*. Filter feeders, also called suspension feeders, filter small plankton and detritus out of the water column. They have filtering structures or mucus that catches these particles, which are then moved into their mouths. Some are dependent on water flow to bring them their food, while others are more active and create their own current flow to bring new water and plankton to their mouths.

Herbivores consume living plant material, grazing on large beds of seaweed or eating algal films. Most of the production of salt-marsh grasses is not eaten until the plants die, but there are some important animals that graze on the live plants. Aquatic snails graze using a rasping, tongue-like structure called a *radula*. Among terrestrial species, rabbits and deer feed on marsh grasses, and insects also eat living plant material. Grasshoppers and beetles are dominant herbivores that chew plant tissue, while leaf-hoppers and aphids are sap-sucking insects. Ducks and snow geese consume substantial amounts of living marsh plants along their routes of migration, and large flocks of geese are capable of destroying so much marsh area that the distribution and abundance of marsh grasses is affected. Livestock in Europe and North America have historically grazed in the high marsh, affecting species distribution. Cattle remove dominant plants and reduce the amount of vegetation, and feral horses in marshes of the eastern shore of Chesapeake Bay graze on cordgrass and salt hay and substantially reduce plant cover. Their trampling of the soft marsh sediments does major damage to the habitat.

The Role of the Tides

For animals that live on the marsh or in estuarine waters, tidal flow is critical for both nutrition and reproduction. Flooding tides allow fishes and crabs to move onto the marsh surface to find food. The tides also deliver water with plankton to stationary filter-feeding organisms like ribbed mussels and striped anemones. Stems of marsh grass, accessible only at high tide, provide protected places for killifish (*Fundulus heteroclitus*) to lay their eggs. Marsh areas serve as breeding grounds and nursery areas for many marine animals, including commercially important fishes which live in deeper water as adults. Marshes are extremely productive habitats for shrimp, crabs, killifish, pipefish, sticklebacks, and eels and for wading birds that eat the fishes.

The ability of a number of invertebrates and fishes to reproduce is also dependent on the spring tides that flood the high marsh every two weeks. The vast majority of invertebrates release eggs and sperm into the water, and fertilization and embryonic development into planktonic larvae takes place in deeper water. After a period of time they are returned from the ocean or larger estuary into the marsh by the tides. The tiny larvae are mostly at the mercy of the currents that may carry them long distances. They live near the surface of the water and spend their time consuming single-celled plants (phytoplankton) and each other. The vast majority of these animal plankton do not survive the larval period, but a relatively few lucky ones get carried in and deposited on the marsh by the tides, where some of them metamorphose into juveniles that resemble small adults.

Marsh plants provide habitat and shelter for many animals. Their roots stabilize the sediments and provide a surface onto which animals can attach. Ribbed mussels use elastic *byssus* threads to attach themselves to a hard substrate, and in a salt marsh the roots of the plants act as this substrate. The shells of the mussels provide a hard surface to which rockweed attaches, and barnacles settle on and cement themselves to the shells. Plants in the marsh also reduce wave action, providing a more stable environment for animal residents; and they provide shade, which reduces the temperature on the surface of the mud. Various small animals utilize the marsh plants as a refuge from predation, hiding in the grasses to avoid becoming a meal for some larger animal. However, predators that are carnivores have a variety of strategies for obtaining their food. Some ambush or chase and consume whole prey, while others have to drill through, open, or crush the shells of their prey before they can have a meal.

Activities of the animals in the marsh may in turn benefit the plants. The waste matter produced by ribbed mussels provides nutrients to the plants, and colonies of mussels, for example, can reduce erosion at the edge of the marsh. Some animals consume the algae (*epiphytes*) that grow on grass blades. These algae reduce the amount of light that reaches the grass, so removing them enhances the plants' ability to grow. The burrowing activities of fiddler crabs (genus *Uca*) aerate the soil, an action that fosters drainage, stimulates decomposition and recycling of underground debris, and increases nutrient availability. While this activity is generally good for plants and stimulates their growth, extensive burrowing activities may damage the roots of the plants.

Animals of Aquatic Origin

Arthropods

This is a large group of invertebrate animals that have jointed appendages and are covered with a protective cuticle. Examples are insects, crustaceans, arachnids, millipedes, and centipedes. Large crustaceans such as crabs and shrimp are important in marshes and estuaries, and small crustaceans make up the majority of small zooplankton in the marine environment. Crabs, lobsters, and shrimp have five pairs of legs, including a claw-bearing pair in front, followed by four pairs of walking legs. In some species, the last pair is modified into flat paddles for swimming.

Molting is a process that is universal among all arthropods, because they must shed their outer shell (exoskeleton) in order to grow. The shell of a crustacean is comprised of chitin, a proteinaceous material that is strengthened with calcium. When a crab is getting ready to molt, the calcium is reabsorbed into the body and stored near the stomach, and the inner layer of shell is dissolved, making the shell thinner and weaker. Meanwhile, the rudiments of a new shell are laid down underneath the old shell. At the time of molting, or *ecdysis,* the softened old shell cracks along a particularly weak seam along the back of the animal, and the crab must extricate itself from the old shell, taking along all of its mouthparts, legs, eyestalks, and so on. Imagine yourself in a suit of armor that cracks down the back, and you have to get out of it without using your hands. Some crabs cannot manage to molt successfully and they die in the process. If the animal molts successfully, the newly emerged crustacean has a very soft shell which it expands by taking in a lot of water, making room for future growth before the shell hardens. Hardening of the new shell involves redepositing the calcium that was stored internally by the stomach. A soft-shelled crab is extremely vulnerable and tends to hide.

The entire molt cycle is coordinated by a number of hormones. In order to grow rapidly, small crustaceans go through their molt cycles frequently, spending most of their lives either preparing for a molt, molting, or recovering from a molt. The growth rate is slower for large crabs and lobsters, and some molt only once a year. Some species reach a final maximum size and then do not molt again. While this type of growth seems very cumbersome and dangerous, arthropods are the most abundant group of animals on earth, so it obviously works for them.

Fig. 3.1. Sand fiddler crab. *Photo by P. Weis.*

Crabs. Fiddler crabs have squarish shells and prominent eyestalks, and they are found in large colonies. Their most obvious trait is that the males have one enlarged claw. There are three species of fiddler crabs in the middle Atlantic marshes. The sand fiddler (*Uca pugilator*) (fig. 3.1) has a marbled purple pattern on its upper shell (carapace) and is found mostly in sandy areas. The mud fiddler (*U. pugnax*) (fig. 3.2) is darker colored with a blue patch on its back and lives in the mud. The brackish water or red claw fiddler (*U. minax*) is the largest of the three species, up to one and one-half inches wide; it is found mostly in very low salinity areas in mud with high organic content. The joints of its claws have orange coloration.

Fiddlers burrow in intertidal marshes and flats, and unlike most intertidal animals they are active in the air at low tide and retreat into their burrows when the tide comes in. Fiddlers feed on detritus, bacteria, and algae from the marsh surface. Females can feed at a faster rate than males, who function with only one claw suitable for feeding themselves. Using their small claw, or claws, in the case of females, they scoop up mud and transfer it to their mouth, where their mouthparts separate edible material (algae and detritus) from sand, silt, and clay. Water floods the mouth during feeding, and the lighter edible material is separated from the sediment particles by flotation. Flat-tipped hairs in their mouthparts are used to sort the material. In the sand fiddler, these hairs are spoon-shaped, enabling them to feed efficiently in sand, where there is less food than in

Fig. 3.2. Mud fiddler crab. *Photo by P. Weis.*

mud. The inorganic sediment particles are returned to the marsh surface in the form of piles of balls of processed sediments.

Fiddlers can remain out of the water for long periods of time, utilizing the dampness of the marsh surface. They have a gill chamber with many blood vessels that acts like a lung, and this tissue only needs to be kept damp to obtain oxygen from the air. The tall stems and dense leaves of the grass provide the crabs with cover from predators when they are out of their burrows. At high tide, the crabs withdraw into their burrows under water and are able to manage with very little oxygen. In the cold winter months, they retreat to the deepest portion of the burrow and hibernate.

Males wave their large claw to attract wandering females for mating. This oversized appendage can comprise up to 50 percent of the crab's weight and is found only on mature males. They wave it around in territorial and courtship displays as if to say to females, "Come hither," and to other males, "Stay away—this is my territory!" The waving is probably the reason for calling these crabs "fiddlers." Males of different fiddler species each have a specific pattern of waving to attract females. The sand fiddler moves the large claw up and out while rising onto tiptoe, and then comes down smoothly. The mud fiddler raises the claw diagonally upward and then down with several jerks. The brackish water fiddler stands on its back legs and holds the claw halfway up and then suddenly raises it up and jerks it back down in several stages. Marsh visitors can observe them waving in synchrony, looking a bit like an aerobics class. The large claw is also used in fighting with other males that may intrude on the male's territory. Sand and mud fiddlers also use sound as a part of courtship. They can produce sound by rubbing the large claw against the first walking leg (*stridulation*) or by stamping their walking legs on the ground. Smithsonian scientist John Christy has spent his career looking at behaviors of different species in Panama. He has a study site near the Panama Canal, where he can sit in the middle of a mud flat in a beach chair and look around in different directions and watch many different species, each in their own part of the mudflat, each doing their own unique type of waving and other behavior.

Behavior of Fiddler Crabs

While doing research in Indonesia, we examined the behavior of four species of fiddler crabs that lived fairly near each other but had such different "personalities" that we gave them nicknames. One species is bright red and lives on very rich mud in mangrove areas. Being bright red, it would be dangerous to move around since they could easily attract the attention of a predator, and they tend to sit in one place quietly feeding. Being inactive, they could be mistaken for a leaf on the marsh surface. We called these crabs "couch potatoes." Because they live in rich mud, they can afford to stay pretty much in the same place and still be able to obtain enough nutrients.

Another species lives in sandy areas and is very active, feeding most of the time that the tide is out. Their sandy habitat has much less detritus available to eat than the muddy habitat of the first species, so they have to keep moving around to find new food sources. They form very large feeding aggregations. This species is easily frightened and will become aggressive, so we dubbed them "type-A personalities."

The third species lives in a pebbly environment near a jetty and feeds largely on algae that grow on the rocks. Their diet of algae is richer in nutrients than the detritus that the other crabs eat, so they can afford to spend less time feeding and they have more time for other activities, such as reproduction. They are the least aggressive of the four species, and we called them the "make love not war" crabs.

The fourth species lives in a muddier area and feeds slowly, but they manage to make multiple pinches of the mud, thus getting more into their mouths with each clawful of mud. We called these efficient feeders the "gourmands." The behavioral differences among the four species reflect their responses to the diverse resources available to them.

Mating may take place in the male's burrow or on the marsh surface, and after mating the female retains a batch of developing eggs (called a *sponge*) attached to the underside of her abdomen. When the eggs hatch, the female releases the larvae into the water of the estuary, where they molt several times during a two-week period. They then settle to the bottom in intertidal areas and molt and metamorphose into small juveniles. Nancy O'Connor of the University of Massachusetts has found that the presence of adult crabs somehow stimulates them and increases the likelihood that they will settle and metamorphose.

As is true of other crustaceans, fiddlers can break off (*autotomize*) claws and legs at a preset breaking plane in the second joint of the leg and, subsequently, a new claw or leg can be regenerated. Autotomy is a reflex, an automatic response that separates an injured limb from the body, providing an excellent way to escape from a predator that will be left holding only a leg. A special muscle bends the limb in such a way that it breaks along the line of weakness. By having a preset breakage plane with a thin membrane covering the exposed area, injury and bleeding are minimized. Regenerating limbs start out as small projections that grow in a folded position under a thin layer of shell, and they unfold only when the animal molts. A common but erroneous idea is that if the large claw of a male is lost, the claw on the other side will enlarge. The regenerated claw will not initially be as large as it was previously, but it will increase in size with each molt, so that after a few molts it will have regained its original size.

Fiddlers rapidly dart into their burrows if they are disturbed. Burrows protect the crabs from most predators, although blue crabs and some birds are able to fish them out of their holes. Their burrows are slanted, going down at an angle to a depth of up to two feet, but when root density is very high or sediments are dense peat, burrowing is difficult. Burrows of mud fiddlers in stiff cohesive mud remain open throughout the tidal cycle. The sand fiddlers (*U. pugilator*) burrow in sand, however, and their burrows collapse when the water floods them. As the tide rises, these crabs pull sand into the burrow using the legs on one side of their body, eventually plugging the opening once they are securely inside. When water reaches the burrow, the crab waits out the high tide inside in a pocket of air.

When crabs dig and re-dig their burrows, the upper layer of sediments is extensively reworked. Newly excavated burrows are surrounded by stacks of waste pellets that the crabs bring up to the surface attached to their legs. These activities increase soil drainage, the rate of decomposition of detritus, and the depth of oxygenated soil, all of which stimulates greater growth and productivity of cordgrass. Roots and rhizomes of the

Fig. 3.3. Marsh crab. *Photo from South Carolina Department of Natural Resources.*

grass stabilize the sediments and reduce the tendency of the crab burrows to collapse at high tide.

Salt marsh mud crabs, *Sesarma reticulatum* (fig. 3.3) and *Armases cinereum,* are larger than fiddlers, but like fiddlers they have squarish shells and dig burrows in the intertidal zone. Unlike fiddlers, they are active at high tide. *A. cinereum* often climb on grass stems, and *S. reticulatum* stay in the mud at both high and low tides. They are omnivorous feeders, with leaves of *Spartina,* algae, and detritus serving as the major portion of their diet, supplemented by the occasional fiddler crab or other animal. Smaller mud crabs, *Panopeus* and *Eurypanopeus,* are abundant in the low tidal zone and move up into the edge of the marsh. They are active at high tide, wandering around grass stems to find food. Mud crab activity is suspected of causing dieback (progressive death) of some New England marshes (more in chapter 4).

Blue crabs (*Callinectes sapidus*) (fig. 3.4) and green or shore crabs (*Carcinus maenas*) (fig. 3.5) are quite mobile and able to swim. They are often found in tidal creeks and ditches and in low salinity waters high up in the estuary. The blue crab's swimming ability is derived from its last pair of legs, which form flattened paddles. Using these powerhouse appendages, they are able to come up on the marsh surface at high tide to eat. They are important predators and can limit the distribution of many organisms by restricting the location of prey to higher elevations where they are less accessible. Blue crabs are large, highly mobile, voracious predators that eat fish, clams, and small crabs, including smaller blue crabs. Cannibalized blue crabs can make up over 10 percent of a crab's diet. They, in turn, are food for fish, gulls and other shorebirds, and raccoons and other terrestrial animals. These tasty, beautiful swimmers (*calli,* from the Greek word for "beautiful"; *nectes,* meaning "swimmer"; and *sapidus,* from the Latin word for "savory") are prized as food and are an important commercial species. Whoever thought up the term "crabby" must have been thinking of this species because they are quick and aggressive, and a pinch from even a small one can be painful; they must be handled with care.

Thomas and Donna Wolcott of North Carolina State University study blue crabs using a biotelemetry device that can be strapped to the crabs

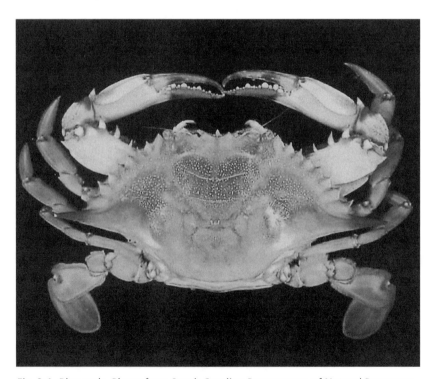

Fig. 3.4. Blue crab. *Photo from South Carolina Department of Natural Resources.*

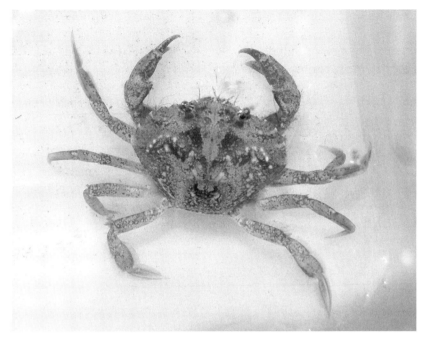

Fig. 3.5. Green crab. *Photo by P. Weis.*

with copper wires. The electronic devices transmit data pertaining to feeding frequencies and locations and depth in the water. They found that the crabs eat at any time, but most frequently at dawn and dusk. At times they migrate to another large feeding area which may be several miles away. A different transmitter also signals when the old exoskeleton splits. By tracking the crab, they can know what habitat the crab finally chooses for molting. Molting sites vary but generally are along creek banks away from their numerous predators.

An immature female blue crab will molt about eighteen to twenty-three times before reaching maturity. They reach maturity at approximately twelve to eighteen months of age, growing to approximately five inches wide. Female blue crabs become sexually mature immediately following a final, pubertal molt. They mate only once in their lifetime. When approaching this pubertal molt, they release a chemical substance called a *pheromone,* which attracts males, into the water. The male crabs may have to compete with each other, and then chosen male protects the female until she molts. When her shell is soft they will mate. She stores the sperm and will fertilize the eggs later. Once her shell has hardened, the male will release her and she will migrate down to higher salinity waters in lower estuaries or at the mouth of the bay. Viable sperm can live in the female's reproductive tract for over a year and can be used to fertilize two or more broods. Females spend the winter burrowing in the mud and release their eggs the following summer. Spawning occurs from May to September.

They extrude about two million fertilized eggs into a lemon-colored mass called a *sponge*. The sponge remains attached to the female's abdomen until the larvae emerge. As the embryonic crabs develop, the color of the egg mass darkens to orange, then brown, and finally black. Blue crabs release their larvae over a period of one or two weeks. The "zoea" larvae develop offshore, going through many molts until they reach the "megalopa" stage, at which time they return to the estuaries to settle and metamorphose into juveniles. The juveniles gradually migrate into shallower, less saline waters in the upper estuaries and rivers, where they grow and mature.

Blue crabs sometimes harbor a parasite called *Sacculina* (a relative of the barnacle, of all things) which prevents them from reproducing and is known as a *parasitic castrator*. An infestation of Sacculina appears as a mass on the underside of the crab. The mass functions as a reproductive organ system for the parasite, which itself consists essentially of a network of rootlets that penetrate through the entire body of the crab to absorb its nutrients.

Green crabs, *Carcinus maenas* (fig. 3.5), are not native to the United States, having been introduced to the East Coast from Europe well over one hundred years ago. They are especially hardy and eat shrimp, algae, detritus, small clams, mussels, annelids, fish, and living cordgrass. They can be found in rocky habitats as well as in marsh environments, and they are very effective feeders that can outcompete blue crabs for food. They are technically swimming crabs, but their last pair of legs is only slightly flattened, not paddle-shaped like that of blue crabs.

Horseshoe crabs, *Limulus polyphemus* (fig. 3.6), are not true crabs or even crustaceans, but are more closely related to spiders and other arachnids. They are living fossils, estimated to have evolved at least three hundred million years ago and having changed very little in all that time. A purified component of their blood is used in the pharmaceutical industry to detect bacterial contamination, and they are of considerable scientific interest. Fortunately, most of the crabs appear to survive the removal of blood for this biomedical purpose.

Horseshoe crabs spend most of their time on the bottom of bays and shallow coastal areas, feeding on clams and worms. Mark Botton of Fordham University has found that adults feed on a wide variety of infaunal and epifaunal invertebrates during their spring spawning migration in

Fig. 3.6. Horseshoe crab. *Photo by P. Weis.*

Delaware Bay, but they are picky eaters. The most abundant potential prey item, the clam *Gemma gemma,* was avoided, while a less abundant clam, *Mulinia lateralis,* was preferred.

While its long, pointed tail and spikes along its shell look danger-ous, the horseshoe crab is quite harmless. The dome-like shell protects its more vulnerable, thinner-shelled moving parts, and its shape causes it to be forced down by the current as it moves along the bottom in search of prey. It swims upside down and the shell provides lift in the water col-umn. The fact that the upper shell comes down quite low on the front and sides can be a problem if the crab is upside down, since its legs cannot be used to right it. This is a position in which the crab might land following an upside-down swim or if tossed ashore by waves. The long, hinged tail sometimes enables the crab to right itself when upside down, although this maneuver is not always successful. Sometimes the more the crab thrusts with its tail, the deeper the tail sinks into the sand.

The horseshoe crab's large compound eyes are located on the upper sides of its shell, and they detect light and help the crabs navigate during their migration to and from offshore wintering grounds. A smaller pair of simple eyes, located on either side of the midline of the upper shell, is extremely sensitive to ultraviolet light.

In May and June, when the water temperature reaches fifty degrees, horseshoe crab mating takes place, reaching its peak during the very high and low spring tides. On days and nights of the full and new moon, the female makes her way out of the water onto a sandy beach with smaller males following close behind, clinging to her shell with their claws. Near the high-tide line, she excavates a slight depression and deposits a few thousand gray-green eggs in sticky clumps below the surface of the sand; the male releases his sperm to fertilize them. Jane Brockmann of the University of Florida has studied horseshoe crab reproductive behavior in the field and noted that there are often additional males crowding around the female, trying to get in on the action by releasing sperm that might fertilize some of the eggs. Males in good condition arrive at the nesting beach and spawn while attached to females, whereas those in poorer condition come ashore unattached and crowd around the nesting couples. By doing genetic studies, the researchers have found that the unpaired "satellite males" are actually highly successful at fertilizing eggs. A satellite male's location around the female greatly affects his chances of success. But why do some females have multiple suitors and some have only one? They found that females that attract satellite males are larger and lay more eggs than females that do not. In addition, once a satellite joined a pair, it remained longer with pairs with eggs underneath, showing that satellite males use their sense of vision to choose the female, then chemical cues to decide whether to remain with a nesting female.

At the same time the horseshoe crabs are coming ashore to lay eggs, hundreds of thousands of shorebirds are migrating north from South America to summer breeding grounds. Many species stop along the way at the Delaware Bay and elsewhere to feast on the horseshoe crab eggs, which provide the energy these birds need to complete their migration up to the Arctic. The eggs that aren't consumed by shorebirds will hatch in two weeks into larvae resembling miniature horseshoe crabs without the tail, and they will swim out into the estuary with the next high tide. During their first year, they will molt five or six times, growing 20 percent with each molt. They may take a decade to reach maturity. Molting is accomplished by splitting the shell along the forward lower edge and crawling out. Empty horseshoe crab shells are commonly found along the beach.

Hermit crabs belong to a group of crustaceans called *Anomura;* and, like the horseshoes, they are not true crabs, although they are indeed Crustaceans. Their abdomen or tail section is not flat and tucked nicely underneath them like in true crabs; nor is it large and sticking straight back like in lobsters; rather it is relatively large and soft and bent only slightly. They have fewer pairs of walking legs than true crabs and the abdomen is not covered with a shell, so it is soft and vulnerable. This is a good reason to seek protection inside an empty snail shell, which is what hermit crabs do.

For both male and female hermits, one claw is larger than the other. The larger one is used for defense and food shredding, and the smaller claw for eating. The second and third pairs of legs are for walking, and the stubby last two pairs hold the crab into its shell. The abdomen is bent like a corkscrew so that it fits into the curvature of the snail shell. Hermit crabs can rapidly contract their abdominal muscles to withdraw quickly and as deeply as possible into the shell in case of danger; they then use the large claw to close off the entrance. Some species are terrestrial, but in water the shell weighs less, which gives the crab greater mobility than it has on land. Most hermit crabs are scavengers, feeding on dead plant or animal matter. In order to defecate, they must bend the abdomen around to the front of the shell to release their wastes into the water.

Hermit crabs depend upon a properly fitting shell for protection from predators. When the crab's body grows and no longer fits into its borrowed snail shell, it has to look for a bigger-sized shell. They can locate shells by the smell they exude when the original snail inhabitant dies and begins to decay. They can also detect calcium, the major component of snail shells. When a new shell is located, the crab investigates the shell's surface and internal size by rolling it over and exploring it. If it looks to the crab like a good fit, the crab quickly withdraws its abdomen from the old shell and inserts it into the new one in an action so rapid that it can be difficult to observe.

Although they will not kill a live snail for its shell, when empty snail shells are not readily available hermit crabs can get into major battles with one another over a desirable shell. This may sometimes result in the death of one of the combatants. A typical hermit crab would rather be torn limb from limb than be pulled out of its shell. The only times that it willingly leaves its shell is if it locates another, more suitable one, or if it is molting out of its old exoskeleton. Molting requires temporarily exiting its dwelling just long enough to wriggle out of its old shell.

The most common species in East Coast estuaries is the long-clawed hermit, *Pagurus longicarpus* (fig. 3.7), which grows to about one-half inch in length and is found in periwinkle and mud snail shells. The larger, flat-clawed hermit crab, *Pagurus pollicaris* (fig. 3.8), reaches an adult size of one and one-quarter inches long, and adults may be found in the larger shells of moon snails or whelks.

Shrimp. Grass shrimp (*Palaemonetes pugio*) (fig. 3.9) move up onto the marsh surface at high tide and may be consumed by killifish. They are small and transparent, less than two inches long, and are the most common shallow-water shrimps along the Atlantic coast. They consume detritus and smaller invertebrates but cannot survive on detritus alone. Since

Fig. 3.7. Long-clawed hermit crab. *Photo by P. Weis.*

Fig. 3.8. Flat-clawed hermit crab in whelk shell covered with algae. *Photo by P. Weis.*

Fig. 3.9. Grass shrimp. *Photo by P. Weis.*

they are eaten by many kinds of fishes and birds, they are a very important link in the marsh-estuary food web. After mating, gravid (egg-bearing) females carry their eggs on their abdomen until the larvae are ready to hatch into the water. Grass shrimp may sometimes have a large lump on their side; this is a parasite, another crustacean called an *isopod,* which prevents the shrimp host from becoming reproductively mature. This isopod is another example of a *parasitic castrator* species. This interaction between parasite and host ensures that the shrimp will be able to provide nutrition for the parasite instead of expending energy on its own reproduction.

Sand shrimp (*Crangon septemspinosa*) (fig. 3.10) are often numerous in the creeks and ditches. They grow up to three inches long and have large claws. Their body color varies from mottled brown to gray so that they blend in well with their background. The sand shrimp is a predator that feeds on amphipods, other small invertebrates, and small fish like young winter flounder. While grass shrimp can swim as well as walk on the bottom, sand shrimp are generally found walking on the marsh bottom.

Barnacles. Acorn barnacles (*Balanus* spp.) (fig. 3.11) are most abundant in rocky intertidal zones, but they may also be found in marshes. Barnacles are crustaceans, although they are unique in that they are attached and sedentary as adults. The animals inside their shells look like small shrimp with their heads down, and they are firmly cemented to the

Fig. 3.10. Sand shrimp. *Photo by P. Weis.*

bottom of the shell chamber that they have secreted. The shell consists of six solid plates that rise and surround four smaller horizontal plates that form a hinged structure that encloses the animal. When the tide is out, the shell closes up and the barnacles are inactive. When the tide returns, they resume filter feeding, sweeping their feathery appendages through the water to catch plankton. Barnacles attach their shells to ribbed mussels, stiff lower stems of *Spartina,* and other solid objects like boats and rocks. They attach themselves using cement produced by glands in their head.

Eggs develop inside the parent and hatch into the water as planktonic larvae. They undergo several molts, growing and changing slightly with each molt, and ultimately descend to the bottom, where they settle on a solid substrate, metamorphose, and cement themselves down. If the place where they initially settle is not appropriate (soft sediment, for example), they can move about by drifting on currents and tides for several days until they find a proper hard substrate.

Amphipods and Isopods. Less conspicuous, small salt-marsh residents include little crustaceans called amphipods, such as *Gammarus palustris,* which are found predominantly in the lower marsh where they are submerged at every high tide. This beach hopper is found associated with cordgrass, rocks, brown algae, and debris. Other hoppers or beach fleas in the genus *Orchestia* can found in higher intertidal areas. *Uhlorchestia spartinophila* is an amphipod that lives in close association with standing, dead leaves of smooth cordgrass in salt marshes along the Atlantic coast of North America. Another small crustacean, the salt-marsh isopod *Sphaeroma,* burrows into the edges of the marsh and can tolerate high levels of salinity. *Cyathura polita* is a widely distributed, burrowing isopod that is found in both the low and high marsh and tolerates a wide range of salinities. Other isopods, such as *Porcellio, Philoscia,* and *Armadillium,* are semi-terrestrial to terrestrial in habitat and are important detritivores. Amphipods, which are flattened side to side so that their features are visible only in profile (fig. 3.12), and isopods, which resemble flat insects (fig. 3.13), play important roles in the degradation of leaves of marsh plants into detritus. These crustaceans break up larger pieces into smaller ones, providing additional surface area for the marsh bacteria.

The high marsh is a terrestrial environment most of the time, but it is flooded by some spring tides. Marine-derived invertebrates in the high marsh include species of isopods and amphipods that eat partly decomposed marsh grasses, algae, and other material. Most female isopods and

Fig. 3.11. Acorn barnacles from San Francisco Bay. *Photo by Patrick S. Lee.*

Fig. 3.12. Amphipod from Virginia. *Photo from Virginia Coastal Reserve, Long Term Ecological Research program, by Diane Barnes.*

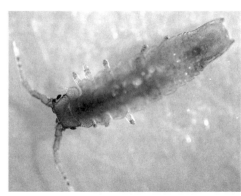

Fig. 3.13. Isopod from Canadian marshes. *Photo from Division of Fisheries and Oceans, Canada.*

amphipods retain eggs in a brood pouch on the abdomen, and they release their larvae into the water column. In an adaptation to their terrestrial environment, some species hatch out of the brood pouch in their adult form instead of going through an aquatic larval phase.

Mollusks

Mollusks are a group of animals that are generally covered with a hard, calcium-rich shell that is not molted. Typically seen in salt marshes are snails with one shell (*Gastropods* or *univalves*) and clams and their relatives that have two shells (*Pelecypods* or *bivalves*).

Snails. Three species of periwinkle snails can be found in salt marshes. They have a hard *operculum*, which is like a door that fits tightly within the shell. It is used to close the opening of the shell so the snail can withdraw its body inside and seal itself off during low tide. These snails feed by using a file-like structure called a *radula* to scrape the surface of the mud, rocks, or plant leaves. They reproduce by producing eggs that hatch as planktonic larvae. The common periwinkle, *Littorina littorea* (an introduced species) (fig. 3.14), is commonly found on rocky shores, but it is also found in salt marshes. The northern rough periwinkle, *L. saxatilis,* also known as the marsh periwinkle, has a rough shell and gives birth to live young rather than depositing eggs on rocks in the water like other snails. It also can breathe air, another adaptation to terrestrial life, and so these snails tend to climb out of the water at high tide.

The southern or Gulf periwinkle, *Littoraria irrorata,* is abundant in marshes south of Chesapeake Bay. They can be very numerous on cordgrass stems, and they migrate up the stems as the tides come in. This may offer them some protection from predators such as blue crabs and terrapins (turtles). This species was previously believed to consume mostly detritus, epiphytes (plants that grow attached to other plants), and bacteria from the stems, but it has recently been shown by Brian Silliman that they also damage healthy plant tissue. They injure the leaves of the plant, which makes the leaves vulnerable to attack by fungi, and then eat the damaged leaves that have begun to decay.

The snails are themselves preyed on by blue crabs. In a simple and elegant experiment performed by Brian Silliman, blue crabs were kept out of an area of the marsh by caging it off. In that area the snails became so abundant that they destroyed much of the cordgrass. This is an example

Fig. 3.14. Marsh periwinkles climbing on marsh grass. *Photo by National Oceanic Atmospheric Administration (NOAA).*

Fig. 3.15. Marsh mud
snail. *Photo from Bill
Frank, Jacksonville
Shell Club.*

of how carnivores can have a major impact on their prey, which is known
as a "top-down" effect in the food web. When a carnivore (the blue crab)
significantly affects an herbivore (the periwinkle) and this interaction
alters the plants (cordgrass) two trophic levels down the food web, this
three-level interaction is referred to as a "trophic cascade" (from the Greek
trophe, meaning "food").

Below the edge of the marsh is an area of smooth, dark, fine-grained
mud that may be covered with mud snails that congregate in large numbers. Mud snails (*Ilyanassa obsoleta*) (fig. 3.15), also called dog whelks,
have thick dark shells with an elevated spire. They actively forage on the
mud surface, eating microscopic algae, dead plants, and seaweeds such as
sea lettuce. When they are numerous, their feeding reduces the density of
the microalgae. They also feed on dead animals, which they detect with
their acute sense of smell. A dead animal can be quickly covered with
hungry mud snails.

The salt marsh snail *Melampus* (fig. 3.16) is an important detritus feeder
in the upper marsh, where it may occur at high density. It has a fragile,
light brown shell and climbs up the grasses. It is adapted for breathing
air and has a lung rather than gills. While its existence is largely terrestrial, it is still dependent on the water for reproduction because it has an
aquatic larval stage. Egg-laying, hatching of the larvae in the water, and
subsequent settling of the larvae onto the marsh occur during spring tides
when portions of the high marsh are flooded. The snails congregate in
masses on stems and deposit eggs in the high marsh where spring tides
wash over them, keeping the eggs moist. The eggs develop in the air and
are timed to hatch in about two weeks with the arrival of the next high

spring tide, at which time the larvae are washed into the water. The larvae spend about two weeks in the estuary eating phytoplankton and then are again washed up into the high marsh by the spring tide, and they settle out and metamorphose. As air-breathing adults, they spend much of their time avoiding water by moving up grass stems as the flood tide moves in. Because they cannot tolerate low salinity, they are scarce in low-salinity and freshwater marshes.

The slipper shell or boat shell snail, *Crepidula fornicata* (fig. 3.17), lives in sheltered creeks. This snail's shell is atypical since it is not coiled but has a shelf, resembling a slipper or a rowboat with a seat. They feed on plankton with their enlarged gills and tend to live in groups with one animal settling on top of another until there are up to about ten forming a pile or chain. These animals change sex as they grow. The lowest, oldest ones are females, the middle ones are of intermediate sex, and the upper, young ones are males. All are found mating with individuals above and below them, giving them their species name (*fornicata*).

Bivalves. Some *bivalves* (clams) are filter feeders that use siphons to filter plankton from the water, and others are deposit feeders with siphons that suck up detritus from the mud. The soft shell (or steamer) clam (*Mya arenaria*) and the quohog (*Mercenaria mercenaria*) dig in soft mud and sand and cannot tolerate exposure to air. They are found in marsh pools or mud flats below the marsh proper. Their siphons circulate water through their shelled body, and food particles are extracted from the water.

An important filter feeder in the low marsh is the ribbed mussel, *Geukensia demissa* (seen in fig. 2.7). They live half buried in the peat or mud

Fig. 3.16. Salt-marsh snails from a Massachusetts marsh on a quarter. *Photo by David Samuel Johnson* (Manayunkia .wordpress.com/ photos).

Fig. 3.17. Boat shells (slipper shells) stacked up, plus two empty shells. *Photo by P. Weis.*

among the roots of the marsh grasses with only one end protruding from the marsh surface. They are anchored by *byssus* threads to rhizomes, stems, and other solid objects such as shells of other ribbed mussels. These tough elastic threads, which extend out in all directions to anchor the mussel, are produced by a gland in its foot which releases a secretion that solidifies on contact with water. The threads are applied to the hard substrate by a groove in the foot, and each thread has a rounded disk where it meets and attaches to the substrate.

Ribbed mussels may occur at very high densities. They are densest near or at the edge of creeks and ditches and can tolerate a wide range of salinity. Juveniles can move freely over the marsh surface using their foot, and they are stimulated to produce byssus threads and settle down when they come in contact with a clump of mussels. They can open slightly and gape for air at low tide, and they can survive long periods in the air provided they do not dry out. When the environment is not suitable, they can close up for long periods of time.

They actively pump water over their gills, removing food in the form of phytoplankton, bacteria, small zooplankton, and detritus. When they occur in dense beds, there may be so many animals that they may actually be able to process all the water entering the marsh during every tidal cycle. Small edible particles are eaten, while larger particles, inedible materials, and wastes are deposited on the marsh surface in a ribbon of mucus and mud, called *pseudofeces,* which enriches the sediment for detritus feeders. Their production of feces and pseudofeces provides nitrogen to the marsh plants, enhancing their growth. Unlike blue mussels (*Mytilus edulis*), they are not generally eaten by people, but they would be edible if they were kept in a bucket of clean seawater for a day or two to give them time to purge the grit they have ingested.

Intertidal oysters (*Crassostrea virginica*) were once common in the Northeast but are now only abundant in southern marshes. They form dense aggregations or beds, and their planktonic larvae are attracted to the adults for settling and metamorphosis, guaranteeing that they will have a suitable place to live. Unlike ribbed mussels, when these larvae settle they cement themselves down permanently. Like ribbed mussels, they are active filter feeders that pump water over their gills. In the North, they have been subject to overharvesting and their numbers have been further reduced by infectious diseases and pollution. Oyster fishing was once a major part of the economy and culture of the Chesapeake Bay and Delaware Bay regions, but it is sadly in severe decline. At one time, oysters, being abundant filter feeders, were able to filter the water of Chesapeake Bay and control phytoplankton populations. But now their scarcity contributes to undesirable plankton blooms that reduce the light available for submerged plants and the visibility in the water.

There have been many attempts to create new oyster habitat with transplants of cultured oysters. These attempts have had limited success, since the transplants are vulnerable to the same diseases as the oysters they are replacing. There is a controversial plan under consideration to stock Chesapeake Bay with a species of oyster native to the Pacific (*Crassostrea ariakensis*), one that is more resistant to the diseases. This controversy will be discussed in chapter 6 when the broad subject of exotic, non-indigenous, and invasive species is taken up.

Infauna. Infauna are aquatic animals that live under the surface of the mud. Most of them are segmented worms, or Annelids, which have a body that is subdivided into segments. Each segment has its own set of internal and external organs that are all under the control of the head region. The common segmented worms in the marine environment are Polychaetes, which tend to be small and to live near the surface. They have outgrowths with bristles on each segment, in contrast to earthworms that lack these bristles. Many of them burrow in the mud or sand of tidal flats or on the marsh surface, and although they are somewhat sheltered from environmental extremes, they still have to cope with tides and changing salinity and temperature.

Annelids that are burrow dwellers slow down their activities when water fills their burrows because they have to adjust to the very low oxygen levels in the water. Capitellids are common types of reddish worms that resemble earthworms and burrow in soft, nutrient-rich, oxygen-poor mud. Some worms construct tubes out of sediment particles that they cement together with mucus, while others secrete the tubes. Most tube-dwelling worms are oriented vertically, some head up, and some head down. The head-up worms may be suspension feeders, feeding on plankton from the water, or they may be deposit feeders, feeding on benthic microalgae and detritus from the mud's surface. The head-down species feed on detritus buried below the mud surface and deposit their fecal pellets on the surface. This can contribute to *bioturbation* (the stirring up of sediment) and the formation of a loose layer that is removed by the tides. The carnivorous polychaetes *Nereis* (clam worm) (fig. 3.18) and *Glycera* (blood worm) burrow through the marshes. Predation on small benthic invertebrates near the surface of the mud is so intense that the distribution of the benthic invertebrates can become restricted to higher marsh areas or densely vegetated areas that the predators cannot easily reach.

Fig. 3.18. Nereis, polychaete worm. *Photo from South Carolina Department of Natural Resources.*

Meiofauna. An inconspicuous group in the salt-marsh mud is a community of very small animals known as *meiofauna* or *interstitial* fauna. They are small enough to crawl through the spaces between grains of sand. Most of them are found near the sediment surface, where there is more oxygen, and a few species are found in deeper sediments. A dissecting microscope or at least a strong magnifying glass is necessary to see these animals. When particles are small (such as in mud flats or marshes, as contrasted with sandy beaches) the spaces are small and the meiofauna are very small. Sediments made up of smaller particles are likely to contain more organic matter than sandy soil, and therefore they tend to contain more meiofauna.

The interstitial community is dominated by *nematodes* (roundworms) and *harpacticoid copepods.* Copepods are very abundant tiny crustaceans, most of which are zooplankton in the water column. However, harpacticoids are a group of copepods that are especially adapted for a benthic burrowing existence. All meiofauna are elongated or wormlike in shape, which allows them to crawl around in between the sediment particles. They may consume benthic microalgae, bacteria and fungi, or detritus, and some are carnivorous and consume other meiofauna. Meiofauna are, in turn, eaten by larger marsh animals. In intertidal areas including salt marshes, meiofaunal communities exhibit zonation with some species preferring the low marsh and others the higher marsh.

Swimming Animals: The Nekton

Some species of estuarine fishes swim up onto the salt marshes with the incoming tide and retreat back to the creeks when the tide ebbs. Fish in this changing environment must have a wide tolerance for salinity fluctuations. In fresh water, they tend to absorb water and then excrete a large amount of dilute urine in order to maintain the balance of salt in their bodies. In salt water, where they tend to lose water from their tissues, they drink seawater, excrete little urine, and get rid of excess salts through specialized cells in their gills.

Tidal creeks and mosquito ditches serve as nursery areas that provide food and refuge for fish, some of which are permanent residents and some of which are there only as juveniles. The most abundant permanent residents of the creeks and ditches are the common killifish or mummichog, the striped killifish, the sheepshead minnow, and the Atlantic silversides. Juvenile winter flounder may also be found in these creeks. Eels may spend part of their life cycle in the marshes, eating mummichogs and grass shrimp.

The common killifish or mummichog, *Fundulus heteroclitus* (fig. 3.19),

Fig. 3.19. Common killifish or mummichog (female). *Courtesy of NOAA.*

is generally the most abundant fish in Atlantic coast salt marshes from Canada to northern Florida, including highly polluted estuaries where they may be the only fish that can tolerate the conditions. They grow to almost five inches in length, do not migrate, and have a very restricted home range during the warm months, although they can tolerate a wide range of temperatures and salinities from fresh water to full-strength seawater. As Stephen Weisburg, at that time a graduate student at University of Delaware, showed, they do much of their feeding up on the marsh surface during the incoming tides.

Weisburg put killifish in two types of cages that were placed in the marsh creeks. One cage kept them in the tidal creek, giving them access to the mud and all food resources. The other type of cage had an extension that allowed them to get up onto the marsh surface as well. The ones that were restricted to the tidal creeks did not grow anywhere near as well as those that could feed up on the marsh surface at high tide. Their diet includes detritus, grass shrimp, algae, amphipods, isopods, copepods, and insects, including mosquito larvae. We have seen them engage in feeding frenzies that, pound for pound, would put sharks to shame.

On a falling tide, killifish sometimes get trapped in small pools of water where, until the next incoming tide several hours later, they may have to endure low levels of oxygen and rising water temperatures and salinities as the sun heats and evaporates the tide pool. Even if the water completely drains, they can survive by burrowing into the mud. During spring tides, they can feed in the high marsh on snails, isopods, and amphipods. Killifish predation can have a major impact on the abundance and size distribution of populations of salt-marsh snails and amphipods. Killifish consume detritus, but it is not nutritious for them, and why they eat it is a mystery.

Common killifish also use the marsh for reproduction. In the breeding season in the late spring and summer, males develop a yellow coloration and spawn every two weeks on a lunar cycle, using the spring tides to access the high marsh. Fertilized eggs are deposited on the inner surface of *Spartina* leaves, in algal mats, or in the open shells of dead ribbed mussels. The eggs may have sticky filaments on the outer membrane (*chorion*) to help them adhere. These sites keep the embryos well aerated, generally in the air rather than water, and tend to protect them from predators. The eggs are resistant to drying, and once they are fully developed, they hatch when submerged by the next series of spring tides two weeks later. The larvae reside in shallow pools on the marsh for over a month. By remaining on the marsh surface at low tide, they are protected from predators in the creeks. By the time they reach about one inch in length, most of them have entered the ditches and tidal creeks.

The diet of the striped killifish (*F. majalis*) (fig. 3.20) is similar to what was described above, but this species is not as well adapted to foraging in the upper marsh and is found in greater numbers in the tidal creeks, ditches, and shallow bays where the salinity is higher. Unlike most fish that migrate offshore into deep water to overwinter, these two killifish species remain close to shore and hibernate in winter, burrowing into the sediments of ditches and creeks.

Sheepshead minnows (*Cyprinodon variegatus*) (fig. 3.21) are primarily herbivores that typically ingest living plant material and detritus, but they also eat mosquito larvae. These are chubby fish, and the males acquire bright orange coloration during the breeding season. *Gambusia affinis*, also called mosquito fish, are more common in southern estuaries and marshes. They bear live young and, as their common name implies, eat lots of mosquito larvae.

Fig. 3.20. Striped killifish (male). *Courtesy of NOAA.*

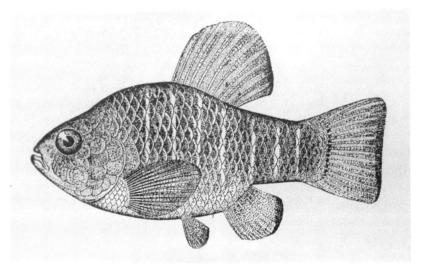

Fig. 3.21. Sheepshead minnow. *Courtesy of NOAA.*

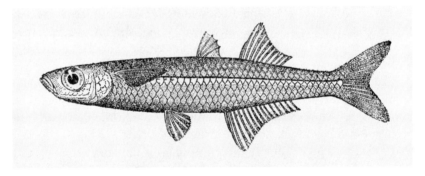

Fig. 3.22. Tidewater silverside. *Picture courtesy of NOAA.*

Atlantic silversides (*Menidia menidia*) and tidewater silversides (*Menidia beryllina*) (fig. 3.22) feed mostly on copepods and other plankton, but they have been found with a great variety of foods in their stomachs, including horseshoe crab eggs, amphipods, isopods, and small shrimp-like mysids. Great schools of adults congregate in the upper reaches of bays and harbors to spawn. Their small spherical eggs adhere to one another in large masses. The young feed primarily on zooplankton, and as adults they will follow an incoming tide into the salt-marsh grasses to feed. They are a very abundant estuarine fish in the Atlantic estuaries, but, unlike killifish, they are fragile and susceptible to pollution. Silversides are, in turn, consumed by terns, herons, cormorants, flounders, and bluefish, to name just a few of their predators. Silversides are a key link between the productive salt marsh and the deeper, offshore areas of the estuary, including the ocean itself. They migrate during the fall to deeper waters offshore, where they become food for offshore predators. Consequently, these fish may be important in bringing energy and nutrients from shallow salt-marsh systems to open-water offshore areas.

Young winter flounder (*Pseudopleuronectes americanus*) (fig. 3.23) consume annelids, amphipods, flat worms, detritus, algae, and shrimp. Flounders go through a remarkable transformation after hatching as rather normal-looking fish larvae. One of the eyes migrates to the opposite side of the head and the mouth twists to one side as well, which enhances its ability to pick prey off the bottom. This metamorphosis requires a major internal rearrangement of nerves, blood vessels, bones, and muscles and results in one gill being located on the underside of the fish, which makes it quite useless when the fish is lying on one side, flat on the bottom, as it tends to do most of the time. While many bottom dwellers can change their coloration to match their background, few can match the speed and accuracy with which the flounder changes the pattern of its pigment cells. Flounders placed in an aquarium with a checkerboard pattern on the bottom took on this pattern quite effectively.

Sticklebacks such as the three-spined *Gasterosteus aculeatus* (fig. 3.24) live in brackish water. Different species each have a particular number of spines along their back. They have elaborate reproductive behavior whereby the male constructs a nest by binding together seaweed with

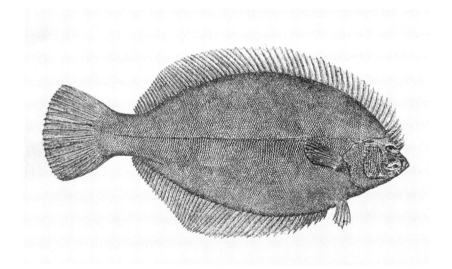

Fig. 3.23. Winter flounder. *Picture courtesy of NOAA.*

threads secreted by his kidneys. After attracting a female to the nest to lay her eggs, he fertilizes them and guards them until they hatch. This habit of protecting the eggs is relatively rare among marine and estuarine fishes. But the next species is even more unusual.

The northern pipefish (*Syngnathus fuscus*) (fig. 3.25) lives among seaweed and eelgrasses in estuaries, salt marshes, and coastal areas. These fish are more slender relatives of the sea horse and, like the seahorse, have armor made up of bony rings. They have a tube-like snout that is used to vacuum up zooplankton prey. They use a sit-and-wait strategy, and when a planktonic organism comes within range, they slurp it up by taking water rapidly into their mouths. They grow to about six inches long and have a waving dorsal fin on their back and a fan-shaped tail fin. They share with the sea horse the unique reproductive trait of the male getting pregnant. Females deposit eggs into the male's brood pouch (which is made from folds of skin that meet to enclose the eggs), where he fertilizes them, carries them, and then gives birth to live young. From the time the young

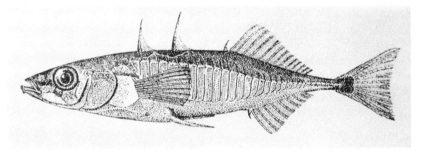

Fig. 3.24. Three-spine stickleback. *Picture courtesy of NOAA.*

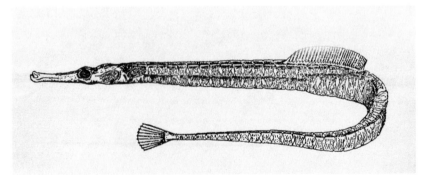

Fig. 3.25. Northern pipefish. *Picture courtesy of NOAA.*

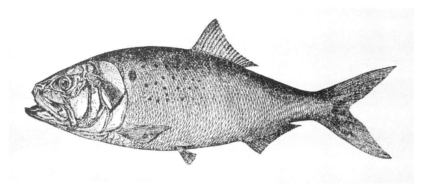

Fig. 3.26. Menhaden or mossbunker. *Picture courtesy of NOAA.*

emerge from the father's brood pouch, they resemble miniature adults and live independently.

Other fishes that may appear in tidal marshes are menhaden and anchovy, which are both filter feeders that use their closely set gill rakers to collect zooplankton. Menhaden (*Brevoortia tyrannus*) (fig. 3.26) are a type of herring that travel in large schools. In the 1800s and early 1900s they were harvested for an oil that was used in cosmetics and paints. They are an important ecological link between plankton and upper-level predators. Because of their filter feeding abilities, they consume and redistribute a large amount of energy from plankton. They are, in turn, an important prey fish, like striped bass, bluefish, mackerel, and flounder. They are also eaten by birds such as egrets, ospreys, seagulls, northern gannets, pelicans, and herons. They are still harvested commercially for bait, for omega-3 oils for human consumption, and for animal feeds; there is concern that their overharvesting is damaging the ecology of Chesapeake Bay. Alewives are a type of herring that are *anadromous,* which means that they migrate like salmon from salt water to fresh water when they are ready to spawn. Their migration occurs early in the spring, and after spawning they return to the sea, although less than half of them survive the journey.

The small fish of the tidal creeks and ditches are eaten in turn by larger predatory fishes such as bluefish (*Pomatomus saltatrix*) (fig. 3.27), fluke or summer flounder (*Paralichthys dentatus*), and striped bass (*Morone saxatilis*) (fig. 3.28) that forage in shallow water. Bluefish spawn in the ocean, but the juveniles move into estuaries at the beginning of the summer, where they eat menhaden, silversides, killifish, and other small fish over the summer. In the early fall, when they are called *snappers* and are large enough to catch with a hook and line, they migrate back out of the estuaries, having fattened up on estuarine and marsh production which will sustain them through the cold winter in the ocean. The bigger they are and the greater their energy stores at the time of migration to the ocean, the better are their chances of surviving the winter.

Striped bass are also anadromous and move from the ocean to fresh water to spawn, consuming marsh fish along the way. Other predators of marsh fishes include crabs and birds such as terns, snowy egrets, and great blue herons. While most species of fishes leave the marshes during the winter for offshore waters, mummichogs bury themselves in the mud for the winter. They can survive subfreezing temperatures by producing a kind of antifreeze that prevents their tissues from freezing.

The American eel (*Anguilla rostrata*) (fig. 3.29) has a *catadromous* life

Fig. 3.27. Bluefish. *Picture courtesy of NOAA.*

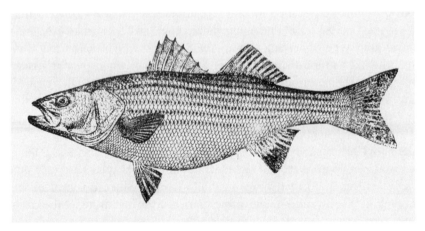

Fig. 3.28. Striped bass. *Picture courtesy of NOAA.*

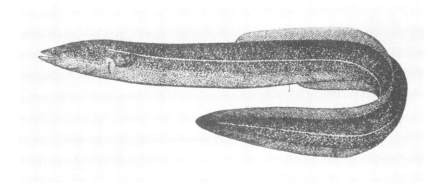

Fig. 3.29. American eel. *Picture courtesy of NOAA.*

cycle, which means that it lives most of the time in freshwater and upper brackish areas and then migrates out to the ocean to spawn in the Sargasso Sea of the Atlantic Ocean. Its larvae, which don't look at all like adult eels and were once thought to be a different species of fish, drift north with the Gulf Stream and later metamorphose and move into coastal estuaries. Eels have very small scales embedded in their skin, which makes them slippery and difficult to hold. They are omnivores, can grow to several feet in length, and their shape makes them very well adapted for burrowing. If they are not large enough to migrate to the ocean during the winter, they burrow into the estuarine mud, and fishermen can catch them by spearing through holes chopped in the ice.

Other fishes reside in marsh creeks during part of the year. These include spot (*Leiostomus xanthurus*) and white perch (*Morone americana*), which may spend a considerable amount of time in this habitat and benefit from the productivity of the salt marshes without actually moving onto the surface of the marsh. On the Pacific coast, juvenile chinook salmon (*Oncorhynchus tshawytscha*) use estuaries and marshes extensively when they migrate between freshwater streams and the open ocean.

Animals of Terrestrial Origin

The people hereabouts are said to be troubled in summer with immense swarms of gnats or mosquitoes, which sting them and their cattle. This was ascribed to the low, swampy meadows, on which these insects lay their eggs, which are afterwards hatched by the heat.

—Peter Kalm, *Travels in North America*, 1751.

A basic environmental challenge for terrestrial animals adapting to a salt marsh is the ability to either tolerate salty water or find alternative water sources. Salt-marsh soils differ from terrestrial or freshwater marshes in that they have a greater abundance and diversity of soil animals (benthos) and a low abundance and diversity of seeds. They also have anaerobic conditions and high levels of sulfur in the substrate.

Insects

The marsh, especially the high marsh, is home to animals of terrestrial origin such as insects and arachnids (spiders and mites). Most insect adults avoid the incoming tides by crawling up the stems of plants to escape the water. Among the hundreds of species found in the marsh, common marsh insects include meadow grasshoppers, ground crickets, planthoppers, leafhoppers, aphids, plant bugs, beetles, greenhead flies (*Tabanus*), and salt-marsh mosquitoes (*Aedes sollicitans*). Predatory, insect-eating spiders such as the highly mobile wolf spider (*Pardosa* sp.) are abundant on the marsh, where some species weave webs.

Many insects deposit their eggs in the mud or within cordgrass stems. Plant bugs are most abundant in the tall form of *Spartina* in the low marsh. Grasshoppers and crickets graze directly on the grasses of the high marsh meadows, and certain species tend to be associated with particular species of plants. The grasshopper *Orchelium fidicinium* lives on cordgrass and is one of a few large insects that live in the salt marsh for their entire life cycle. Leafhoppers, planthoppers, aphids, and plant bugs suck juices from the plants in a process that does not severely harm the host plant. Although these insects may be abundant, they consume relatively little plant material.

Certain species of beetles are associated with particular types of marshes. Some beetles are plant or detritus feeders, and some prey on other insects. Many beetles live in burrows or cracks in the mud. Parasitic wasps live as larvae within an insect host, eating the host from the inside until the adult wasp emerges from the body of the host (as in the movie *Alien*). Greenhead flies (*Tabanus* sp.) are voracious predators. They are found throughout the marsh in both low and high areas, to the dismay of field biologists and other marsh visitors. Because they bite during daylight, occur in large numbers, have a long flight range, and attack persistently, they can spoil the enjoyment of coastal areas during much of the summer. On the other hand, they are fairly slow and easy to swat. Someone we knew came to our favorite beach armed with a fly swatter along with the sunscreen. Female greenheads deposit clusters of eggs on vegetation near moist substrate, and their larvae (maggots) are found in the mud near cordgrass and salt hay. The larvae, which undergo several molts in the upper layers of marsh soil, are predators that feed on animals in the mud, including other insect larvae and amphipods. Up to seventy larvae may be found in one square yard of marsh soil.

Other unpleasant insects one may encounter on the marsh are horse-flies and deerflies (*Chrysops*) that breed in the wetlands. They feed on visi-tors to the marsh and provide food for birds. They require a blood meal in order for their eggs to develop, and their painful bite can make the blood flow. They are found primarily just below the mean high-water level on sloping banks associated with cordgrass. Additional nuisances are "no-see-ums" (*Culicoides* spp.), which are gnats or midges. Their larvae eat small invertebrates, and the adult females require a blood meal for egg production. They are most active after sunset, to the distress of those go-ing on sunset cruises or having a beach barbeque.

The salt-marsh mosquito (*Aedes sollicitans*) breeds on the high marsh in shallow depressions where there is damp soil, and it provides another source of discomfort to marsh visitors. Its eggs must stay wet, and under proper conditions they hatch into larvae that live in pools and eat organic matter in the water. They pupate in the water and adults emerge. They can tolerate large changes in salinity and are fairly resistant to desiccation. Adults feed mostly on plant nectar, but after mating females seek a blood meal. This mosquito is a vector in the spread of Eastern equine encepha-litis. Tidal inundation is a critical factor limiting their distribution, and areas that are infrequently flooded with tides, such as the salt hay zone, are sites in which they can breed and their larvae can survive. Much ef-fort has been devoted to the control of salt-marsh mosquitoes, including ditching of marshes and spraying of insecticides, which will be discussed in chapter 4. Juvenile mummichogs (killifishes) consume mosquito larvae while foraging on the marsh surface during high tide.

Reptiles

Diamond-backed terrapins (*Malaclemys terrapin*) (fig. 3.30) are the only reptiles in mid-Atlantic salt marshes that live exclusively in the estuary. They have several adaptations that enable them to survive long periods in seawater, including skin that has a very low permeability to salt and water and salt glands near their eyes that excrete excess sodium chloride. They are commonly found in salt marshes and tidal flats, and in the winter they hibernate in muddy burrows along tidal creeks and ponds. They have a gray, light brown, or black top shell (*carapace*) that is broad and diamond-patterned. The under shell (*plastron*) can range from yellowish to greenish gray, with or without bold, dark markings. Their large feet are webbed,

Fig. 3.30. Diamond-backed terrapin. Mud snail in foreground. *Photo by Amanda Jordan.*

and the head and limbs may be spotted. They occur from Cape Cod to Cape Hatteras and also on the Gulf Coast; they eat snails, ribbed mussels, and fiddler crabs. At high tide, they may go up on the marsh surface to feed.

These terrapins always mate in the water, and in June and July the heavy, egg-laden females leave the salt marsh and trek toward the sandy ocean dunes, where they each dig a hole with their hind feet and deposit up to a dozen leathery eggs. They lay their eggs at high tide, ensuring that the eggs will be above the high-water level. Like other turtles, they have temperature-dependent sex determination. Low temperatures produce males, while higher temperatures produce females. Their eggs may be eaten by laughing gulls and crows as well as mammals such as raccoons. Eggs that are not consumed by predators hatch in August and September. The hatchlings can be eaten by the same predators that eat the eggs and also by black crowned night herons. The hatchlings emerge during the daytime and head for the nearest vegetation. Their first years of life are spent foraging for small invertebrates beneath mats of *Spartina* grasses that form the wrack line (floating dead plant debris) in the marsh. Feeding on a largely carnivorous diet of crabs, snails, mussels and worms, males reach maturity within three years, while females, which are considerably larger, take eight years to mature.

From the 1880s through the 1920s, terrapin meat became such a popular gourmet food item that many local populations were nearly exterminated. Marsh loss and development further reduced their populations. They were ultimately saved by the economic impact of the Great Depression, when people could no longer afford to buy terrapin meat. Additional hazards they face include motorboat propellers and crab and lobster pots that can trap and drown them. During the nesting season, many females are killed as they attempt to cross roads in search of nesting areas. Studies have shown that protecting adults from human impact due to, for example, roadkills and habitat loss is the best long-term conservation strategy for these turtles.

Another turtle that may be found in brackish marsh areas is the snapping turtle (*Chelydra serpentina*). These are large, primarily freshwater turtles with a long tail and neck and three rows of points on their carapace. They prefer water with a soft bottom and aquatic vegetation and will eat almost anything, including aquatic plants, algae, arthropods, insects, fish, amphibians, reptiles, birds, and mammals. The female digs a bowl-shaped nest cavity in loose sand, loam, or plant debris. About twenty to forty eggs are laid, some or all of which may be eaten by raccoons and other mammals. Hatchlings and juveniles are eaten by herons and egrets as well as by predatory fish. When approached by humans, they sometimes lunge and bite viciously.

Birds

Over 250 bird species frequent tidal wetlands, including 44 species of waterfowl, 35 species of rails and shorebirds, 23 birds of prey, and 15 species of waders. Many birds rest and feed on the marshes in the winter and during migration. Neotropical migrants such as red-winged blackbirds (*Agelaius phoeniceus*) and other birds that travel to wintering grounds in Central and South America utilize brackish marshes. Brackish marshes also have swamp sparrow (*Melospiza georgiana*), belted kingfisher (*Megaceryle alcyon*), and the wood duck (*Aix sponsa*). Even the highly developed and polluted marshes around New York City are home to many species of herons, egrets, and ibis, which seem to be successful living near industrial sites and oil refineries.

The distribution of marsh birds reflects their responses to vegetation, tidal flooding, and salinity, all of which affect their feeding and reproductive cycles. Birds that utilize salt marshes deal with the salt either by reduced drinking or by drinking salt water and excreting the salt using special glands in their noses that concentrate and remove the salt. Brine is blown out with expired air or droplets drip down the beak. Some bird species, like the swamp sparrow, have no ability to ingest seawater and are restricted to low-salinity marshes. Many species that breed in salt marshes as well as in other habitats tend to have smaller clutches of eggs in the salt-marsh habitat. The reduced level and seasonality of resources or the high levels of nest failure in coastal marshes may be responsible for the smaller clutches. Part of the reason for high levels of nest failure is flooding, which is unpredictable and depends on the amount of rain, the winds, and the tides. Tidal marsh birds typically build nests on elevated platforms, and the simplicity of the marsh vegetation can make the elevated nest more vulnerable to predators. The salt-marsh sharp-tailed sparrow (*Ammodramus caudacutus*) is a species that is found only in coastal marshes of the eastern United States. It spends most of its time on the ground in search of insects and seeds. They are secretive and breed in dense marsh vegetation, placing the nest above the ground in shrubs or grasses.

Waterfowl. Waterfowl often feed in shallow water at the edge of the marsh and may also nest in the marsh. Mute swans (*Cygnus olor*) (fig. 3.31) were introduced from Europe because of their dramatic appearance and are sometimes found in the marsh, along with Canada geese (fig. 3.32) and snow geese (*Branta canadensis* and *Chen caerulescens,* respectively). There are also many species of ducks, such as wood ducks (*Aix sponsa*), black ducks (*Anas rubripes*), mallards (*Anas platyrhynchos*) (fig. 3.33), teals (*Anas crecca*), pintails (*Anas acuta*), canvasbacks (*Aythya valisineria*), and ruddy ducks (*Oxyura jamaicensis*).

Every autumn and spring, thousands of ducks and geese find tempo-

Fig. 3.31. Mute swans. *Photo by P. Weis.*

Fig. 3.32. Canada goose. *Photo courtesy of U.S. Army Corps of Engineers.*

Fig. 3.33. Mallard ducks in a row. *Photo by P. Weis.*

rary stopping places in salt marshes. Canada geese are found largely along tidal creeks, while pintails, blue-winged teal, and American widgeon (*Anas americana*) are found in open ponds with poor drainage or in impounded areas. Black ducks are found mostly in higher-salinity areas amid *Spartina alterniflora, Spartina patens,* and *Juncus roemerianus,* particularly in areas where there are ponds. While black ducks feed extensively in the tidal marshes, they nest on drier land, mostly woodlands.

Grazing by geese can reduce the amount of plant biomass in the marsh. Some species pull up the entire plant in order to graze on the leaves, producing a long-lasting impact. Some species (Canada geese and snow geese) feed on underground rhizomes of marsh plants, discarding the top and roots of the plants. When goose populations are dense, marsh vegetation can be removed from an area to such an extent that it lowers the marsh surface and creates a pond. Geese have very large appetites, and a flock of five thousand snow geese was reported to denude three hundred acres of *Spartina alterniflora* in six weeks near Pea Island in the area of Cape Hatteras, North Carolina.

Long-Legged Waders. Herons and egrets are long-legged, long-necked wading birds with long, tapering bills. The great blue heron (*Ardea herodias*) (fig. 3.34), the green-backed heron (*Butorides striatus*) (fig. 3.35), black-crowned night heron (*Nycticorax nycticorax*), American bittern (*Botaurus lentiginosus*) (fig. 3.36), glossy ibis (*Plegadis falcinellus*) (fig. 3.37),

Fig. 3.34. Great blue heron. *Photo by Michael Horn.*

Fig. 3.35. Green-backed heron. *Photo by Bernard Klempner.*

Fig. 3.36. American bittern. *Courtesy of U.S. Fish and Wildlife Service.*

and snowy egret (*Egretta thula*) (fig. 3.38) are common species. The great blue, a graceful and elegant bird with a dark gray body with bluish highlights, is four feet tall with a wingspan of up to six feet. Herons and egrets feed on small fish, crabs, and other animals in the marsh creeks. They have also been known to eat frogs and snakes in other habitats but not in salt

Fig. 3.37. Glossy ibis. *Courtesy of Wikimedia.*

Fig. 3.38. Snowy egret, fishing. *Photo from P. Weis.*

marshes. They may either wait motionless and strike at prey that comes within range or stealthily stalk prey by slowly walking and hardly disturbing the water.

Great blue herons form colonies (*rookeries*) in which they build stick nests in the tops of trees. In the Northeast they do not migrate south in the winter, even though the bulk of their prey (small fish and crustaceans) are out of reach because they are buried in the mud or overwintering in the deep water of the bays and oceans. Great blue and green-backed herons are usually solitary feeders, while snowy egrets and black-crowned night herons may feed in flocks. Black-crowned night herons are nocturnal foragers except during the breeding season, when they hunt for food both day and night to feed their young. They stand at the water's edge hunched over like little old men, waiting for a meal (generally a fish) to come by. Bitterns eat shrimp, fish, and small rodents.

Rallids. This group includes rails, common moorhens, and American coots. The clapper rail (*Rallus longirostris*) is restricted to salt-marsh habitat within dense *Spartina alterniflora*. Its diet includes marsh crabs, snails, fiddler crabs, and fish. It usually nests on slightly elevated areas such as hummocks of grass along creek banks. Though elevated above the marsh surface, nests can be subject to flooding; but the eggs will still hatch, and the young birds are able to swim in the water of the incoming tides. The king rail (*R. elegans*) and Virginia rail (*R. limicola*) (fig. 3.39) are more common in lower-salinity (less than 5 ppt) and freshwater tidal marshes. Virginia rails eat crustaceans and insects, while king rails ingest plant material as well. Nests are placed in uniform stands of vegetation. The sora rail (*Porzana carolina*), common in freshwater marshes, consumes mostly plant seeds and insects and also vegetation. All rails are secretive and hard to find and forage in areas near their nesting territory.

Shorebirds. Willets (*Catoptrophorus semipalmatus*) (fig. 3.40) are large flocking birds related to sandpipers. They are found close to marshes, often nesting in the salt hay zone. Like clapper rails, they consume insects, marine worms, small crabs and mollusks, and small fish from creeks and

Fig. 3.39. Virginia rail. *Photo courtesy of U.S. Fish and Wildlife Service.*

Fig. 3.40. Willet. *Photo courtesy of National Park Service.*

mud flats using their long, straight bills. Their courtship behavior occurs in open areas of the marsh, and they are territorial during the breeding season. They are well known for their piercing calls and black-and-white flashing wings. The various species of birds that feed on invertebrates in mud or sand flats have long beaks that differ in length and/or shape, each being suited to catching the types of infauna that are their preferred food.

Gulls and Terns. Laughing gulls (*Larus atricilla*) may nest in tall cordgrass marshes in areas vulnerable to flooding by spring tides and storms because their eggs can withstand some submergence. They more commonly nest in coastal sand dunes. They are frequently preyed upon by herring gulls (*L. argentatus*) (fig. 3.41) and other birds such as crows and owls. Terns (*Sterna* spp.) sometimes breed in marsh habitats because of human disturbances on the beaches that are their natural breeding sites. When breeding in marshes they usually use the high marsh in areas with dead vegetation, though some choose sites in short-form cordgrass. Least terns (*Sternula antillarum*) (fig. 3.42) are smaller than other terns and hunt primarily in shallow estuaries and lagoons where smaller fishes are abundant. They hover until spotting their prey and then plunge into the water to get their dinner. Breeding colonies are not dense and tend to appear in areas free from humans or predators along marine or estuarine

Fig. 3.41. Herring gull with crab. *Photo by Bernard Klempner.*

Fig. 3.42. Least tern. *Photo courtesy of U.S. Fish and Wildlife Service.*

Fig. 3.43. Ospreys tending their nest. *Photo by Michael Horn.*

shores or on sandbar islands in large rivers. Nests are built on barren or sparsely vegetated places near the water.

Birds of Prey (Raptors). Various piscivorous birds (birds that feed on fishes) have different hunting techniques that focus on fishes of different sizes, at different depths, and in different parts of the estuary. This specialization reduces competition for the diverse resources.

The osprey or fish hawk (*Pandion haliaetus*) (fig. 3.43) hunts in flight and dives into the water to capture prey with its claws. They are about two feet long with a wingspan of four to five feet. They circle high overhead, hover, and then tuck their wings in as they plunge head first toward the water, adjusting at the last moment to hit the water feet first. Their talons are adept at catching and holding onto slippery fish. Their dives are fairly shallow, to about three feet below the surface of the water. Herring (*Alosa aestivalis*), menhaden (*Brevoortia tyrannus*), and flounder are taken in substantial quantities by these birds.

Ospreys nest near the water on the tops of solitary trees, utility poles, nesting platforms erected for them in the marsh, and other similar structures. They have a distinctive call, consisting of a series of high-pitched whistles. They fly south to Florida, the Caribbean, and South America for the winter.

Ospreys are a symbol of the fragility of the natural world as evidenced by the crash in their population following the introduction of DDT into estuarine food chains. After DDT was banned in the United States in 1972 their population eventually began to recover, but osprey numbers continued to plummet for a decade after the ban went into effect, and the population has yet to rebound to pre-DDT levels. Their population recovery has been assisted by people erecting nesting poles near the water. These artificial structures replace the large snags (dead trees) that are their normal nesting sites but which have become scarce due to development.

Marsh hawks or harriers (*Circus cyaneus*) nest on hillocks projecting out of the marsh and, unlike most other marsh birds that eat fish or other marine life, prey on rodents and small birds in the marsh.

Other Birds. Other marsh specialists include marsh wrens (*Telmatodytes palustris*), (fig. 3.44) and seaside sparrows (*Ammodramus maritimus*). Wrens live near creeks, where they are hidden in the tall *Spartina* grass, and breed in coastal marshes in loosely spaced colonies. Sparrows breed in coastal marshes, where they place nests in tussocks of grass or on other elevated areas in the short-form cordgrass or salt hay zone. If water rises during spring tides and floods the nest, the eggs or young will die. The amount of flooding determines habitat selection for the sparrows, which are generally found at higher marsh elevations. They are territorial and are largely carnivorous.

Fig. 3.44. Marsh wren. *Photo by Bernard Klempner.*

Fig. 3.45. Red-winged blackbird. *Photo courtesy of U.S. Fish and Wildlife Service.*

Fig. 3.46. Black skimmer. *Photo courtesy of U.S. Fish and Wildlife Service.*

The red-winged blackbird (*Agelaius phoeniceus*) (fig. 3.45) eats marsh plants and insects and is common in low-salinity marshes. In their breeding colonies, the males are territorial. Nests are placed among the marsh plants above the mud or in bushes near the water, where they are fastened to stems.

Skimmers (*Rynchops niger*) (fig. 3.46) fly at the surface of the water, obtaining food by immersing their flattened red lower mandible into the water and skimming along the surface for small fish. The lower half of the bill is longer than the upper and it is very thin, well-adapted to provide minimal drag as it slices through the water. Unlike in other birds, the lower mandible is fixed to the skull and rigid, which prevents it from being wrenched off as it skims. The upper mandible is movable, enabling it to snap shut and trap a fish. To compensate for the wear and tear of skimming, the lower mandible grows at roughly twice the rate of the upper. Fish, mostly silversides and killifish, are the skimmer's predominant food item. Since they hunt by feel and not sight, skimmers are not limited to fishing during daylight hours. They can take advantage of the daily vertical movements of fish and of the greater numbers found near the surface at night. They have quite specific hunting areas within the estuary, focusing on zones where the water is four to eight inches deep, including tide pools and salt-marsh creeks. The back of the bird is black and its ventral side is white. They are colonial and may nest with other species, especially terns, whose aggressive territorial behavior protects not only their own nests but those of the skimmers as well. Breeding occurs in estuaries, with nests built on open spaces in beaches, salt marshes, and dredge spoil islands.

Cormorants, including the double-crested cormorant (*Phalacrocorax auritus*) (fig. 3.47), are about two feet long with a wingspan of about four feet. These large, gangly birds are abundant in estuarine and freshwater habitats on lakes, rivers, swamps, bays, and salt marshes. They have dark brown to black feathers, a long, hooked bill, a long tail, and webbed black feet. They dive from the water's surface for fish and invertebrates. They nest in colonies, building nests of sticks and vegetation in trees and shrubs and on the surface of rocky cliffs and islands. Unlike other diving birds, cormorants do not have well-developed oil glands and are not waterproof. They dry their feathers by perching in the air and stretching out their wings.

Fig. 3.47. Double-crested cormorants drying their wings, sharing a sandbar with common terns. *Photo by P. Weis.*

Fig. 3.48. American oystercatcher. *Photo courtesy of Wikimedia.*

Oyster catchers, *Haematopus palliatus* (fig. 3.48), are large, unusual-looking shorebirds with strong white or black-and-white markings. They have powerful, bright red, bladelike bills that are triangular in cross section, and they use their bills to open the shells of bivalves or to consume crabs and sandworms. Their habitat includes both seacoasts and inland waterways, and they nest in shallow cavities in the sand.

Many marsh-dependent birds have declined across North America. Among them are the pied-billed grebe, American bittern, least bittern, northern harrier, Virginia rail, sora, American coot, common snipe, black tern, and even the red-winged blackbird. Only a few species show minor increases (marsh wren and swamp sparrow). Marsh birds appear to be declining more seriously than other groups of birds because marshes are still under considerable pressure. In addition to wetland loss, the birds have to cope with water pollution and invasive, non-native species that are degrading many marshes.

Since the loss of coastal wetlands has been extensive, there have also been declines in populations of birds that are dependent on them. Many migratory birds stop in Delaware Bay on their way north, where they feed on horseshoe crab (*Limulus polyphemus*) (fig. 3.6) eggs deposited in the sand. There is great concern that declining horseshoe crab populations may affect shorebirds because the horseshoe crab eggs are the migratory shorebirds' primary food resource in Delaware Bay. Researchers have documented the arrival and departure of 500,000 to 1,500,000 migrating shorebirds within a span of three to four weeks in Delaware Bay, their timing corresponding to the breeding cycle of horseshoe crabs. Sanderlings (*Calidris alba*), red knots (*Calidris canutus*), and ruddy turnstones (*Arenaria interpres*) consume as many as nine thousand eggs per bird per day during this stopover, doubling their body weight over a two-week period. It has been calculated that the six most abundant shorebird species can consume approximately 539 metric tons of horseshoe crab eggs as they refuel during their long, strenuous migration. This requires at least 1,800,000 female horseshoe crabs to spawn on the shores of Delaware Bay.

There is great concern about decreases in the numbers of migratory birds, particularly endangered red knots that migrate from the tip of South America up to the Arctic every spring. Red knots in the Delaware Bay have declined from over one hundred thousand in the 1980s to only fifteen thousand in 2005. Other migrating shorebirds are also being affected, and steps have been taken to limit the number of horseshoe crabs people are permitted to catch to use as bait for catching eels and whelks.

Mammals

Mammals can live in salt marshes and cope with salt water using a number of mechanisms. Unlike humans, some can drink seawater and produce highly concentrated urine; others drink dew or rainwater rather than the seawater.

Muskrats (*Ondatra zibethica*) are conspicuous, two-to-four-pound semi-aquatic rodents that historically have been hunted and trapped for their thick and dense fur. They are named after their musk gland, which is under the tail and secretes chemicals that mark territory and warn others muskrats to keep their distance. They construct houses on the marsh surface using vegetation that is heaped into a pile in order to provide their young with a dry nest at an even temperature. With webbed hind feet acting as paddles, they are good swimmers, capable of swimming three miles per hour. They prefer low-salinity brackish marshes with slow-moving creeks and are uncommon in more saline and freshwater marshes. Most active at night, they are largely herbivores that consume plant rhizomes and destroy large amounts of vegetation with their feeding and digging. They also feed on shellfish such as clams and mussels. One muskrat can eat one-third of its body weight per day, and when populations are dense, they can turn marshes into open water and mudflats. Their home construction and tunnel excavation can also have a major impact on the marsh because their feeding shelters and lodges accumulate debris, and piles of dead vegetation can smother living plants. However, on the plus side, their burrows and lodges may make the wetland more attractive for other animals like turtles and waterfowl.

Shrews (*Sorex* spp.) are also found in the upper reaches of brackish marshes. The meadow vole (*Microtus pennsylvanicus*) is a high-marsh resident during the warmer months, feeding on stems of cordgrass, spike-grass, and grass seeds. Voles construct nests of matted grasses and breed throughout the year. The white-footed mouse (*Peromyscus leucopus*) also utilizes the high marsh. Other rodents include the rice rat (*Oryzomys palustris*) and the harvest mouse (*Reithrodontomys* spp.) in southern marshes. Rice rats are found in the higher, drier parts of marshes. Harvest mice make compact nests off the ground using shredded leaves of marsh grasses. Marsh rabbit (*Sylvailagus palustris*) and swamp rabbit (*S. aquaticus*) live in the brackish marshes of the Southeast. Raccoons and otters also can be found in salt marshes, foraging for food among the tall grasses. Raccoons (*Procyon lotor*) feed on mussels and crabs in tidal marshes; and they, along with red foxes, may also eat the eggs of beach-nesting birds such as plovers and oystercatchers. Otters (*Lutra canadensis*) may be seen swimming in the creeks, and mink (*Mustela vison*) may visit the marsh to feed on mussels, clams, and crabs. Larger mammals such as deer (*Odocoileus virginianus*) and moose (*Alces alces*) may sometimes graze in the marsh as well.

II Human Alterations
to Salt Marshes

4 Physical Alterations

The draining of the swamp lands is not a new idea. Such lands are not only unproductive of anything which can subserve any important purpose, but they are productive of numerous evils. Teeming with miasma, the home of mischievous and annoying insects they are blotches upon the otherwise fair face of nature. To tender them fruitful and productive of good rather than evil, is a problem for which a solution has been anxiously sought, but heretofore only partially obtained.

—*Scientific American,* 1868

In past centuries, marshes were generally considered useless land which needed to be eliminated or transformed to become useful to people, as the above quote indicates. The term that has been used is "reclamation," which suggests taking something back, yet what people were actually doing was just "claiming" the wetlands for their own purposes. Wetlands have been recklessly filled to expand land for agricultural use or urban development throughout most of this country's history. This reflects the prevailing value on human dominion over nature; taming the land for human purposes was considered righteous behavior until recently.

In 1997, the U.S. Fish and Wildlife Service estimated that 104 million acres remain of the 220 million acres of salt marshes that were here when the country was first settled by Europeans. Losses vary in different regions. In the Chesapeake and Delaware bays, 28 to 55 percent of the original salt marsh remains, in New England about 50 to 65 percent remains, in San Francisco Bay and other parts of California only around 20 percent remain, and in the Columbia River in the Pacific Northwest about 30 percent of the tidal wetlands remain. Losses in the Gulf of Mexico are even more severe than in other regions of the country. Similar dramatic losses of mangroves, the tropical cousins of salt marshes, have also occurred.

The history of how salt marshes have been used tells us the extent of the loss and degradation of wetland areas and demonstrates the prevailing point of view of typical wetland conservation initiatives. Contemporary sentiments are generally positive, recognizing that "the loss and degradation of wetlands reduce their ability to provide goods and services to humankind and to support biodiversity, and are therefore associated with economic costs" (Ramsar Convention on Wetlands meeting, 1996).

Historical Uses of Salt Marshes

In North America, so-called land reclamation was practiced as early as 1675 along the Delaware Bay. When Dutch settlers arrived in the United States, they installed systems of dikes in salt-marsh areas, similar to the widespread practice used in the Netherlands to increase their land area and to protect farmland from flooding. The dikes consisted of raised trackways that protected the land from saltwater inflow; the protected areas could then be used for development or farming.

Among the attributes that made marshes targets for destruction was the association of wetlands with pestilence and disease. Projects with dikes and sluice gates that restricted the flow of tidal water into the marshes were widespread along the Atlantic seaboard and became even more common after the Civil War. These projects were considered a useful way to decrease crowding in cities and to increase the amount of fertile farmland, while at the same time ridding the world of mosquito-infested wetlands. Most of the city of Boston was built on salt marshes and tidal flats, as was much of Queens, significant parts of the Bronx and Brooklyn in New York City, and many of the towns in northern New Jersey near the Hackensack Meadowlands.

Salt Hay Farming

Marshes were traditionally used for grazing, and in some areas of the world they are still used as pastures for sheep or cattle. Early settlers of North America from Holland and England recognized that salt hay was a valuable crop with a myriad of uses. They harvested salt hay as bedding for horses and cattle, fodder for cattle, thatch for barn roofs, mulch for strawberry plants, packing for glassware and pottery, insulation for icehouses, and traction on roads (fig. 4.1). Harvesting salt hay in the northern New Jersey Hackensack Meadowlands for shipment to southern New Jersey glass manufacturers was a substantial industry until the early twentieth century. Salt hay has also been used for protecting newly poured concrete and pavement roads and in constructing airport runways.

Engineering the landscape for producing salt hay involved a considerable amount of alteration of the marshes. Mud banks and dikes were

Fig. 4.1. Farming salt hay in southern New Jersey. *Photo courtesy of National Park Service.*

built along Delaware Bay so that farmers could easily access the salt hay meadows. They opened sluice gates during the spring to allow the tidal flow to bring salt and nutrients into the meadows. Even marshes not engineered for harvest could be productive sources of salt hay. Along the Atlantic Coast where marshes had not been reclaimed, farmers would wait for extremely low tides or for the meadows to freeze over before they would attempt to cut the hay. Horses wore special mud boots strapped to their hooves to keep them from sinking in the marsh mud. Prior to mechanization, farmers stacked portions of the crop onto stattles—circles of posts driven into the peat about one or two feet high—in the meadow. Stattles kept the hay above the flooding tide, allowing it to dry. Farmers then waited for the marsh to freeze before bringing the horses and sleds or wagons onto the meadow to retrieve the hay.

In some farms, the harvested hay was loaded onto barges for transport during spring tides. In Accabonac Harbor on Long Island, we have personally located remnants of cedar log tracks laid down in the nineteenth century for farm wagons to access the salt hay harvest (fig. 4.2). Hay-filled wagons were taken to the meadow banks and loaded onto oyster barges in the creeks for transport. The scows were either pushed by two men on

Fig. 4.2. Planks from old road from salt hay farming become visible as marsh bank erodes. *Photo by P. Weis.*

board, using cedar poles, or they were towed up the creek by one man walking along the bank and the other following with a pole to keep the craft from running ashore.

The invention of new machinery for digging ditches and building banks brought changes to the salt hay industry. Increasing the number of ditches within a meadow made the meadow drier and more capable of supporting heavy machinery. Roads were constructed through the meadows to support cranes, and farmers used the cranes to keep the ditches cleared and the banks reinforced. By the 1930s, hay was collected by mechanical stackers. By the late 1940s, tractors had replaced horses except where the ground was extremely soft.

Salt hay farming is still going on in some areas, such as Plum Island Sound in Massachusetts. Today, most salt hay is used by plant nurseries, in road construction, and in making rope. Despite new technology, muskrats and fiddler crabs can interfere with salt hay farming by burrowing into the protective banks that keep the tidewaters away from the meadow. They can create breaches and widen creeks, making functioning in the marsh environment more difficult for people and equipment. Salt hay is a natural resource, and it is important to find a way to continue to harvest it, while preserving the habitat of muskrats, fiddler crabs, and other animals. Another environmental concern is that harvesting salt hay removes a significant portion of organic matter that would otherwise accumulate at the soil surface to increase the elevation of the marsh. Another problem is created by contemporary farmers who often use regular, heavy farm equipment which is not designed for the soft, compressible salt-marsh soils and can leave permanent ruts on the marsh surface in which mosquitoes breed.

It is interesting that now, in the twenty-first century, many of these salt hay farms are being restored as functional salt marshes, as we shall see in a later chapter.

Filling Marshes for Urban Development

Salt hay farming—whether industrialized or traditional—exploits the natural resources of the salt marsh. Filling in marshes changes the ecosystem in a more profound way, and large areas of marsh have been filled to create highways, railroad beds, and airports. The airports in New York and Boston, for example, were built on filled tidal wetlands. John F. Kennedy Airport and Floyd Bennett Field were constructed on marshes surrounding Jamaica Bay, causing a great deal of disturbance due to the extensive dredging to create navigation channels and to provide fill. Between 1974 and 1994, 526 acres of marsh islands were lost at an average rate of 26 acres per year. Between 1994 and 1999, 220 acres were lost at an average rate of 44 acres per year. At present, just 11,000 acres of salt-marsh habitat remain within the Jamaica Bay ecosystem. The loss of part of Jamaica Bay for the construction of Kennedy Airport affected the flora and fauna of the immediate area, but that wasn't all. Being part of a larger, interconnected water system, the altered patterns of water flow adversely affected wetlands beyond the marsh area itself. Other examples of marshes being filled for urban expansion include Back Bay in Boston, the New Orleans delta, and San Francisco Bay. Filling in salt marshes started long ago in Europe and in other parts of the world, so this practice is certainly not limited to the United States.

Even when the marsh is not totally eliminated, filling can lead to changes in elevation and the isolation of parts of the marsh, cutting those parts off from the action of the tides and having a drastic effect on drainage. Even small changes in elevation inhibit the growth of marsh plants, allow the growth of invasive plants such as the common reed, and can disrupt habitat and migratory corridors for some birds.

Shoreline Development

Consider what happens when construction for shoreline condominiums begins in the vicinity of the marshlands. Removing woody vegetation on the border of marshes degrades the marshes and destroys habitat for fishes. Beside the conversion of wetland to solid earth, other ecological, hydrological, and chemical effects occur. Water flow shifts; soils become less saline and more nutrient-enriched with nitrogen. This results in reduced levels of oxygen in the water, creating favorable conditions for the invasive growth of the common reed. The reed is a tall plant that, other factors being equal, can outcompete other species for light.

Pristine salt marshes without developed shorelines have far less of this invasive plant than marshes with developed borders. The nutrient enrichment associated with shoreline development can give the reed an even greater competitive advantage, and its spread displaces many other species of marsh plants and causes reduced biodiversity. The reed grows very tall and blocks people's view of the estuary, so it also reduces the value of the marshes as a natural amenity.

Another feature of development is the creation of what are called "impervious surfaces." Along with every house or building come paved sidewalks, roads, and parking lots that form a network for getting from here to there. More impervious surfaces mean more runoff, and increased runoff means more pollutants in the water. Water can't filter into the soil if paved surfaces stand in the way, and when it rains, large quantities of pollutants are picked up from the paved surfaces as the water runs off the impermeable pavement into creeks or storm sewers. When a watershed has 10 to 30 percent impervious cover, these negative effects on the ecology begin to appear.

As neighborhoods develop, it is generally considered a good thing to have clustered housing developments rather than sprawl. This allows greater amounts of open space to remain unpaved and generally helps to decrease damage to the surrounding environment. But *where* the houses are located is a crucial question, because high-density development right at the edge of a marsh degrades the habitat and defeats the environmental purpose of green cluster development.

Shoreline Hardening

Shoreline hardening structures are artificial vertical barriers that are usually built by homeowners or developers in order block the water so they can have a lawn that is flat rather than sloping, and also to allow their property to be as close to the water's edge as possible without having to be concerned that wave action will cause their land to recede. While this is a serious concern for property along the ocean, homes along protected bays with proper setbacks are not really at serious risk of being undermined by the water.

There are several types of shoreline hardening structures made of vari-

Chicago's Alleys

Chicago has approximately two thousand miles of alleys bisecting its blocks, adding up to a paved surface area equivalent to five midsized airports. The alleys mostly contain garbage bins and garages, giving the main streets a cleaner appearance but creating a large area prone to flooding and dumping polluted runoff into the city's sewer system.

In Chicago's recent Green Alley initiative, the paving in the alleys is being replaced with permeable concrete or porous asphalt, which will reduce polluted runoff. Water penetrates to the soil through this porous pavement, filtered by stone beds under the surface layer. In this way the underground water table is renewed, instead of the polluted runoff ending up contaminating rivers and streams. Some of the filtered water may flow into Lake Michigan, replenishing the major source of Chicago's domestic water supply. By the end of 2007, the city was expected to have completed forty-six green alleys, and every alley it refurbishes in the future will be done in this environmentally conscious manner.

---

ous materials. A *seawall* is generally a massive concrete structure, whereas a *bulkhead* is a vertical retaining wall generally made of wood, and a *revetment* is a sloping structure composed of rocks of various sizes (*rip-rap*). These hardening structures form the border between a homeowner's property and the shoreline, effectively eliminating the intertidal marshes (fig. 4.3). An unintended drawback of the hard structures is that sediment at the base of the structure is lifted and carried away whenever the high tide washes against it. This results in the loss of beach or wetland in front of the structure. Furthermore, building a bulkhead or placing rip-rap along the upland edge of a marsh eliminates the possibility of marsh migration landward in the face of rising sea levels.

The normally sloping intertidal zone provides habitat for a variety of plants and animals, many of which use the shallow water as a refuge against larger predators. Replacing the slope with vertical hard structures removes this habitat and leads to the loss of wetlands both at the site of the installation and in adjacent areas due to the changed *hydrology* or water flow. These hard structures also cause increased erosion of neighboring property.

Bulkheads are generally made with chemically treated wood, which leaches out chemicals that can be toxic to nearby organisms in the sediments. Natural marshes have a higher abundance and diversity of benthic (bottom-dwelling) animals and fishes than are found in habitats adjacent

Fig. 4.3. Bulkheads turn intertidal marsh into a vertical wall and lawns. *Photo by P. Weis.*

to hardened shorelines, suggesting that this altered habitat is less suitable for them. Extensive bulkheads are found in marinas, which usually include numerous docks which are also made from treated wood. Between the leaching from the treated wood in the bulkheads and docks, leaching of antifouling paints from boats, possible sewage released from the boats, and hydrocarbons from the boats' motors, the water quality in marinas is far from ideal.

Even worse than marinas are residential developments in which marshes have been carved into networks of canals, each lined with treated-wood bulkheads, providing each homeowner with a dock in the backyard. These canals, common in Florida, are poorly flushed by tides and have very poor water quality, adding low oxygen to the list of problems. As an aside, when too many docks are built over wetlands, the productivity of marsh grass decreases because it doesn't get sufficient sunlight, and erosion increases as a result of pilings placed at the edge of the water. Floating docks may rest on the bottom during low tides and can damage vegetation and suffocate benthic communities. Boating in these areas can cause accelerated erosion of marsh edges when waves from the boats' wakes reach the marsh. Boaters are told to drive slowly in marshy areas to prevent this, but they do not always understand or follow this advice.

A new approach to erosion control is the concept of *living shorelines* that use native plants, stone, and sand to deflect wave action, conserve soil, and provide shoreline habitat. The creation of a fringe marsh, for example, provides for better habitat than a vertical wall. Living shorelines stand up reasonably well to wave energy, and they are used mostly in areas with low to medium levels of wave activity, where they generally cost less than bulkheads or revetments.

Dikes and Impoundments

Impounding a marsh is a way of creating an enclosed lagoon and artificially maintaining a high water level by putting in a dike to prevent tidal water from coming in and out. Impoundments use earthen dikes to section off an area of the marsh, and in many instances these dikes enclose an entire marsh-creek system in which water control structures, called *trunks,* regulate water exchange, water levels, and salinity. The water level and salinity inside the impoundment can also be controlled through the use of embankments or levees, *weirs* (low dams), and tide gates which are opened and closed to regulate the water's flow. In general, impoundments disconnect areas above them from the estuary below. The disconnect is physical, which leads to biological changes. A typical impoundment contains a shallow mudflat area that occupies 30 to 60 percent of the total surface area, and a ditch produced when soil was excavated to build the dikes generally borders the impoundment on three sides. Some of the first impounded salt marshes were originally constructed in the Pacific Northwest in order to provide land for cattle grazing, and impoundments elsewhere were for salt hay production, for the evaporation of water for the commercial production of salt, or to attract waterfowl for hunting. Because the fluctuation of the water level is minimized, they have also been used to prevent the breeding of salt-marsh mosquitoes and for brine shrimp aquaculture in mangrove swamps in many tropical countries. Impoundments were made in marshes in San Francisco Bay in the nineteenth century in order to turn natural pans and ponds (*salinas*) into artificial salt ponds for evaporating water and harvesting the salt for local use and regional trade. The artificial salt ponds were relatively small, ranging in size from twenty to one thousand acres, and they had a range of ecological and economic benefits. In the twentieth century, salt production became a large-scale industrial operation. The ponds were expanded and subdivided so that the original landscape of marsh with scattered ponds became mostly open water ponds fringed with a bit of marsh.

Impoundments can encourage the growth of vegetation favorable for breeding sites of certain birds, and in New England they have generally been built for waterfowl management. While duck populations and other waterfowl may increase in impounded areas, other birds, such as clapper

rails, willets, and various sparrows, are likely to disappear because their
nesting sites and food no longer exist. Organisms are separated from the
food supply provided by salt-marsh vegetation and from the associated
animal species.

Streams that previously entered marshes and provided nutrients and
sediments are often diverted around diked marshes, and their materials
are deposited directly downstream, which results in reduced water quality. The amount of dissolved oxygen varies greatly and may be quite low
at times. Tidal marshes that have been diked for decades often undergo
compaction and *subsidence* of the sediments (a downward shift of the land
relative to sea level), and an attempt to recreate the marsh by breaching
the dikes to introduce tidal flushing will result in the area becoming open
water rather than a marsh. Lowering the water level is a better strategy
because it can increase mudflat area that will attract migratory shorebirds
and may restore some vitality to the marsh. Although the population of
salt-marsh mosquitoes diminishes when a marsh is impounded, other
mosquito species tend to breed more under the new conditions (thus
trading one nuisance for another). Impoundments can also reduce habitat
for the biting greenhead (tabanid) flies.

Fish communities are harmed by impoundments, since reducing tidal
flow results in lower production of species that rely on the natural tidal
cycle to maintain their population, including juvenile finfish and shellfish.
Fishes, such as killifish, breed with the tidal cycle, timing their spawning
activity to coincide with the highest spring tides and depositing eggs high
in the marsh. When natural tidal cycles are interrupted or reduced, spawning success is diminished. Isolating the lagoon prevents juvenile fish and
shellfish from coming into the marsh and using it as a refuge and nursery
area, and there is less habitat available for estuarine-dependent fishes that
travel up into tidal creeks and onto the marsh surface in search of food.

The dependence of estuarine species on natural tidal cycles became
clear in the "Biosphere 2" experiment of the 1990s in which many habitats, including a rain forest, coral reef, and estuary, were created inside a
large facility built near Tucson, Arizona. The populations of fish stocked in
the created estuary habitat gradually declined because the designers and
builders neglected to incorporate tides into their artificial estuary as a way
of saving money. Although the water quality was maintained at a reason-
able level, in the absence of tides many of the species did not reproduce,
resulting in a gradual decline of their populations.

Similar tidal restrictions can be produced by dikes, roads, or railroad
crossings with inadequately sized drainage pipes (culverts). The expansion of roads and railroads required that bridges and culverts were built

over creeks, and water was often forced to flow through a very small space. When flow is restricted the ecology is altered, and areas that had been frequently flooded with salt water became brackish or fresh since seawater could no longer reach them. Lowered salinity, caused by the reduction of tidal input, results in major changes in salt-marsh vegetation and wetland chemistry. A common result of these changes is the invasion of the common reed and other freshwater species, such as cattail, widgeon grass, purple loosestrife, and switchgrass, as well as the leaching of acid sulfides into the estuarine water.

Dredging

Dredging, the opposite of filling, removes large amounts of sediment from the bottom of the estuary in order to deepen it, usually to accommodate boat access. Dredging is an ongoing process that tries to be one step ahead of the continual deposition of new sediments on the bottom of estuaries as river water laden with sediments enters. If dredging were to be stopped, ships could not come into many ports because the harbors would continually get shallower as sediments come down the rivers and settle out. To make the problem worse, ships keep getting bigger and bigger, so the channels must be dredged ever deeper to accommodate them. Dredging causes significant changes in the vegetation and in the invertebrate population of the marsh surface. Large amounts of sediments are temporarily suspended in the water, and the rapid sedimentation during the dredging period buries benthic animals. Hydrology is also altered as a result of dredging—tidal water moves in and out to a greater degree and faster, moving the salt wedge further upriver where brackish and freshwater wetlands can be lost. The more rapid water movement can also erode edges of marshes.

Where to put the dredged material, known as spoil, has always been a problem. In the past it was dumped into the ocean, but that is no longer legal. Marshes were once a prime choice for dredge spoil disposal, with the notion that one estuary's dredge spoil is another marsh's fill. A lot of tidal marsh loss has been a result of dumping dredge spoil into the marsh, resulting in the marshes being smothered and losing their biological value. If dredged material was regarded as a resource, it might be put to good use, for example, to raise the height of marshes in areas such as the Louisiana delta around New Orleans, or Jamaica Bay in New York, where the marshes are getting submerged. Dredged material can also be used to create new intertidal wetlands by placing the spoil on shallow bay bottoms, although care should be taken not to place dredged material on top of valuable sea grasses that are growing in the area.

But what happens when the dredged material is contaminated? Many estuaries in urban areas have received metals, organic pollutants, and other contaminants in industrial waste, and the contaminants tend to bind to the sediments. Disposal of *contaminated* dredge spoil is a particularly thorny issue, since the sediments contain harmful materials that can be toxic to marine life and to humans. While various laws exist which establish responsibility for the disposal of contaminated sediments, in practice it is often a very contentious matter to ensure proper disposal. For example, a dredging crisis occurred in the New York–New Jersey Harbor because of amended federal regulations that changed the testing requirements for toxic contaminants in sediments. Dredged material with levels of contamination that had previously been tested and considered suitable for dumping into the ocean was now found unsuitable for ocean disposal. This required different management and disposal facilities and substantially increased the costs of dredging.

Upland disposal of sediment runs into the justified opposition of communities that don't want highly contaminated mud drying out in their back yards and blowing with the wind onto residential property. This raises issues of environmental justice, where industrial waste products and commercial zones meet residential areas. There are railroad cars full of sediments dredged from Newark Bay that are sitting in various locations nearby, awaiting the development of technology to clean them up so some suitable use for them can be found.

Let's consider a famous and controversial case in New Jersey. In an August 2005 decision, a federal court judge ruled that a massive dredging project by the U.S. Army Corps of Engineers violated the National Environmental Policy Act by ignoring the impact of dredging in the middle of a dioxin-contaminated site beneath the ports of New York and New Jersey. The area in question is the Diamond Alkali Site in the lower Passaic River, which contains high levels of dioxin and other toxic chemicals from industrial facilities on the Passaic River, including a now-closed plant that made Agent Orange during the Vietnam War. Parts of Newark Bay are contaminated from these chemicals, as are portions of the adjacent Kill van Kull and Arthur Kill, which border on Staten Island. The site is a Superfund site, one of the most highly contaminated areas on the list for cleanup. But how to clean it up without causing more problems?

Without proper protections, dredging would spread the dioxin contamination from the site into surrounding waterways. The decision to halt the project until a thorough environmental impact statement was produced resulted from a lawsuit filed by environmental groups. They sued to ensure that the project, part of a ten-year multibillion-dollar project by the Corps and the Port Authority of New York and New Jersey to deepen the harbor to accommodate larger container ships, does not interfere with the effort of the Environmental Protection Administration (EPA) to study and clean up the pollution.

A similar controversy began in 1999 in California over dredging the Port of Oakland and using the highly contaminated dredge spoil to create additional wetlands adjacent to Suisan Marsh, the largest marsh in Northern California. The Suisan Bay wetlands are used by many plant species and by almost one hundred species of birds, including some rare ones. Fifteen percent of the dredged material was so contaminated that it had been declared unsuitable for aquatic disposal, so government officials were inclined to dispose of the dredged material on land rather than dumping it in the bay or in the ocean. They argued that if wetlands could be expanded in the process, it would be the best solution (a win-win situation). If marshes are in need of additional sediments, and they are available from dredging projects, the "waste" from one project becomes the "resource" for another. Many local people, however, were concerned that dumping the contaminated sediments would ruin the sensitive wildlife habitat of Suisan Marsh, and they felt that that the project was merely an expedient solution to the problem of finding a dump site for the contaminated dredge materials.

According to a May 2007 report, approximately six million cubic yards of material have been dredged and placed into Suisan Marsh. This "beneficial reuse" project will restore over eighteen hundred acres of wetlands using approximately twenty million cubic yards of dredged sediment. The managers of the project state that through restoration of the wetland and upland ecosystem with intertidal brackish marsh and seasonal wetlands, freshwater drainages, and an upland buffer, the restoration project will provide for protection and recovery of numerous wetland-dependent fishes, wildlife, and plant species. Suisan Marsh is the first privately sponsored wetland restoration in the nation. It is not compensatory mitigation (see chapter 7) since its funding is derived solely from dredge disposal. Future contracts are planned for monitoring and adaptive management at the site.

Mosquito Ditching

In colonial times, ditches were dug in some salt marshes to increase salt hay production, and this continued to be a recommended practice as late as the early twentieth century. But if you notice straight ditches in a salt marsh today, it is very likely that they have been dug for the purpose of mosquito control (fig. 4.4). Parallel grid ditching for mosquito control

Fig. 4.4. Straight, right-angled mosquito ditches. *Photo by P. Weis.*

began before the early 1900s, and in the 1930s during the New Deal many salt marshes were ditched by the Civilian Conservation Corps.

Saltwater mosquitoes develop from egg to adult in the small tidal pools and puddles left behind on the marsh surface when the tide ebbs. Because of their role in spreading disease and their general nuisance value, a lot of effort has been devoted to mosquito control over the years. Mosquito ditching drains the tidal pools by digging channels, and often, particularly early on, the excavated material was piled right beside each ditch to form a dike. The ditches eliminate standing water in the upper marsh by accelerating drainage directly into open tidal waterways. This accelerated draining in the ditches also results in greater and faster nitrogen flow into shallow water (see chapter 5). In addition, the *spoil piles* of excavated material placed along the sides of the ditches impede the flow of water over the surface of the marsh. This permits the invasion of high-marsh plants such as marsh elder, and the changes in the plant community reduce its value for marsh wildlife.

In actuality, the ditching eliminates pools of water that support killifish; and since the killifish eat the mosquito larvae, the result, contrary to the intention, is sometimes an increase in the mosquito population. Creating new drainage patterns in this way alters normal wetland hydrology by draining the peat and lowering the standing water level, and this has negative consequences for the marsh. When the marsh soil is oxidized as a result of lowering the water table, invertebrate populations are reduced. When soils dry out, the sulfides are oxidized and some sulfuric acid is produced, reducing the pH level needed by mollusks and crustaceans for shell building. On the other hand, because it dries out areas of the marsh, ditching appears to be beneficial to rushes and can provide habitat for birds such as willets and herring gulls that normally breed in higher marsh environments. The ditches themselves can provide additional aquatic habitat for local fishes, crabs, and other animals. But because the steep sides of the ditches are not a favorable habitat for cordgrass or invertebrates, the result is frequently a greatly reduced invertebrate population. This is ecologically important since invertebrates account for much of the diet of fishes and birds. Fewer fishes are found in sites adjacent to deeper, steeper-sloped creek banks compared to shallow-sloped creek banks, possibly because of the relatively reduced availability of invertebrate prey.

Ditched areas tend to have fewer individuals of many fish species, smaller bird populations, and reduced bird use compared to unditched marshes. Ditching disrupts waterfowl, songbird, and wading bird habitats because of the absence of pools. Birds such as rails that require low, wet marshes diminish along with the food supply. Ditching also leads to a reduction in muskrat houses.

A newer and better approach to mosquito control is to deepen the pools on the marsh or add elevated dams in the tidal creeks so that water levels are high enough to enable fishes to stay on the marsh throughout the whole tidal cycle and to eat mosquito larvae full-time. The deeper pools also create an enhanced habitat for many species of water birds, crabs, and muskrats as well as for submerged aquatic vegetation and benthic microalgae, which provide food for the fishes, shrimp, and other invertebrates.

This approach is called open marsh water management (OMWM). It greatly reduces the need for insecticide spraying of mosquitoes, and it reverses some of the changes that were made in marshes when they were originally ditched. OMWM was developed in New Jersey in the late 1960s and early 1970s, and since then it has been used in other parts of the eastern seaboard (fig. 4.5). OMWM ponds are usually less than one-tenth of an acre in size and average six to eighteen inches in depth, with a deeper area to harbor fishes. Mosquito breeding areas with wet-dry cycles are eliminated, and the newly created permanent pools are both unattractive for mosquito egg deposition and attractive to mosquito-eating fishes, particularly killifish that arrive with the incoming tides. Depending upon the design and circumstances, successful OMWM systems may need periodic

Fig. 4.5. Barriers keep pools of water on marsh as tide ebbs, part of Open Marsh Water Management (OMWM). *Photo by P. Weis.*

water renewal by opening sluice gates in order to maintain water quality, since without healthy fish populations OMWM ponds and ditches can become mosquito-breeding habitats.

Dams and OMWM ponds can produce additional environmental benefits beyond mosquito control. In Accabonac Harbor and Northwest Creek, a rural area in the town of East Hampton, Long Island, New York, fecal coliform levels in the water were high. This caused bacterial contamination in shellfish beds, which then had to be closed to fishing, causing great concern. From 1991 to 1994 the clams, oysters, and scallops for which Long Island is famous were declared unfit for human consumption, leading the State Environmental Conservation Department to close the waterways for harvesting shellfish.

Accabonac Harbor comprises one of the major undeveloped coastal wetland ecosystems on Long Island. Portions of the habitat are preserved by the Nature Conservancy, and others have been designated as part of the national Coastal Barrier Resources System, one of only sixty-seven such areas on Long Island, and much of the land adjacent to the marshes has been preserved. This diverse area is important to a variety of fishes and wildlife, and finding elevated coliforms in this relatively pristine place was particularly troubling.

The culprit turned out not to be human waste but instead waste from raccoons, deer, and other wildlife. The waste reached the shellfish because the mosquito ditches acted as a direct conduit, flushing the fecal material right into the harbor waters. The economical solution supported by a local citizen's group, the Accabonac Protection Committee, was to dam the ditches near their openings with plywood planks and sandbags, which slowed the draining and retained more water behind the dams. The deeper waters provided an environment in which the fecal coliform bacteria began to settle and die off, lessening the flow from the ditches into the harbor. As a result, the coliform levels became low enough to reopen some areas to shellfish harvesting for the first time in ten years. As reported in the July 14, 1996, *New York Times,* Jorie Latham, a spokeswoman for the Accabonac Protection Committee, said, "O.M.W.M. has solved a lot of problems for those of us who live around Accabonac and Northwest Creek. The baymen are returning, and locals are starting to go clamming again. But O.M.W.M. has given us something more important, peace of mind just knowing the marshlands are not only beautiful, but, more importantly, they're safe."

Other Physical Changes in Salt Marshes

Next we will discuss some physical changes that can take place in a marsh that are not directly caused by humans. They may be the indirect result of human activity, or they may simply be due to natural changes.

Subsidence

Subsidence, or sinking, refers to the downward shift of the land relative to sea level. In Louisiana alone, over a million acres of wetlands have disappeared under water since 1930, with dire consequences seen clearly in the aftermath of Hurricane Katrina. In addition to losses attributed to sea-level rise and the normal settling of the land, channels have been dredged through the wetlands, disrupting the flow of the water, and the removal of subsurface oil and gas has resulted in subsidence of vast areas of the Louisiana coastal marshes.

New Orleans is located in southeastern Louisiana along the Mississippi River, some fifty miles from the Gulf of Mexico. Dams constructed on the Mississippi River and its tributaries hold back sediments, and levees along the edges of the river built to control flooding funnel the fresh water and sediments directly into the gulf instead of into the wetlands on the sides of the river. Had the sediments been flowing normally into the Mississippi delta, the marshes would have been higher and more extensive and could have absorbed some of the storm's impact, offering more protection from the flooding. One end result of the extensive subsidence of the Louisiana marshes was the devastation caused by Hurricane Katrina. Most scientists agree with Louisiana State University ecologist John Day that extensive coastal marsh restoration should be a major component of the city's rebuilding plans.

The marshes of Jamaica Bay in New York also have been shrinking and sinking. A study released by New York State in 2001 reported that approximately eighteen acres of tidal wetlands are being lost each year from the salt marsh islands of Jamaica Bay. By using satellite imagery and more sophisticated investigational techniques, an updated report released in August 2007 found that the rate of loss is even worse; more like thirty-three acres are lost each year. The reasons for this loss are not as clear as in Louisiana.

The interior portions of marsh islands in Jamaica Bay appear to be at a lower elevation than normal and seem waterlogged, soft, and compressed rather than spongy like healthy marshes. Some of the marsh islands have deteriorated extensively, having lost almost 80 percent of their vegetation cover, so that these formerly intertidal areas are becoming bare underwater habitats. The reasons for this are not understood, but a lack of sediments may be a significant factor.

Sea-level rise may also be partly responsible for the marshland loss at Jamaica Bay, but since not all coastal marshes have been disappearing at the same rate, sea-level rise does not completely explain the problem. Huge areas of dead mussels have been seen that might be smothering the marshes in some areas and creating mussel dams. Nutrient-loaded water from wastewater treatment plants could be causing the mussels' explosive growth, since thirty-five thousand pounds of nitrogen are released into the bay every day from the treated outflow from four New York City sewage treatment plants. At the present time, the city has no plans to equip the Jamaica Bay sewage plants to reduce this pollution, and the city's position, according to an article in the *New York Times* on August 2, 2007, is that "the link with nitrogen is very weak." Restoration efforts are trying to stabilize these marshes by placing additional sediments on the marsh surface.

Erosion of marsh edges has been noticed in many areas, due in large part to wave energy. An eroding marsh edge does not slope gently downward but appears undercut by the water, so that pieces of marsh can then fall off into the water. Sandy marsh sediments are more likely to erode than are denser, more cohesive muddy sediments and peats containing more organic matter. Beds of ribbed mussels might be able to help stabilize edges that are subject to erosion. Erosion is a frequent problem in restored marshes, since they are on new soil with little detritus, and many restored marshes fail because they simply wash away. Placing marsh fences (made sometimes from recycled Christmas trees) at the edge of the restored marsh to trap sediments and reduce erosion can be a very effective technique for reducing deterioration and increasing the chances of a restored marsh being successfully established.

Flooding and Storms

Television news programs regularly show townspeople paddling boats along the streets and dealing with flooded basements. Some of the low-lying towns built in areas that were once part of the Hackensack Meadowlands find themselves under water almost every spring when there is a heavy rainfall. The conversion of wetlands to urban uses increases the economic and environmental cost of floods because wetlands provide natural water storage and slow the release of floodwater. Increasing the amount of impervious surface accelerates the runoff of the water and increases the amount of flooding. Storm damage has become more severe in recent years and is expected to continue to worsen as a result of increased building near the shore and the effects of climate change. Global warming is expected by many experts to intensify the strength of hurricanes.

It has been estimated by economists (for example, Costanza and Farley 2007) that the loss of 2.5 acres of marsh leads to a thirty-three thousand dollar increase in the cost of storm damage. Using these calculations, coastal wetlands provide over twenty-three billion dollars a year in storm protection, confirming that they are well worth preserving.

The Threat of Sea-Level Rise

One of the greatest future threats to salt marshes is sea-level rise as a result of global warming. An average temperature rise of three degrees Celsius causes a one-meter rise in sea level. This is predicted to cause a loss of 65 percent of the coastal marshes in the mainland United States over the next century, assuming that marshes will be unable to increase sediment deposits and root and rhizome growth at a rate equal to that of sea-level rise. Already some coastal states have reported subsidence resulting in the drowning of their tidal wetlands, as in the Louisiana story discussed above.

As sea level rises, marsh systems will have to raise their elevation (accrete) to stay in place, and they will have to migrate landward as seaward edges erode. Landward migration can occur only so far as there is available land. In some areas, sea-level rise is altering the zonation of plant communities because plants in high-marsh habitats are very sensitive to how often waters flow in, known as the inundation frequency.

Sea-level rise is a result of warming temperatures, caused by increasing levels of greenhouse gases. These factors affect salt marshes directly. Some marsh vegetation can adapt to warmer temperatures by accumulating organic matter and sediments, but the rate of accumulation must keep up with sea-level rise. *Spartina patens* grows faster under warmer conditions, and it can moderate temperature changes on the marsh surface and act as a buffer for hypersalinity and storms. Elevated carbon dioxide, which is one of the main causes of climate change and sea-level rise, increases the productivity of salt hay, which can help the soil elevation keep up with sea-level rise. *Spartina alterniflora* can also increase its production to enable the marsh to build up more and keep up with sea-level rise. But the danger is that when the rate of sea-level rise is too high, the marsh will not be able to maintain a suitable elevation and will simply drown.

An increase in elevation in response to sea-level rise also causes a landward migration of the marsh, but not all species will be able to migrate inland, or they will not migrate fast enough, and species diversity will decline. Further, as mentioned before, landward migration can occur only so far as there is available land. High-marsh habitats are lost when migrating marshes come upon human-dominated shorelines. Developed and paved areas are common just landward of a salt marsh, and they prevent the marsh from moving onto the main roads of coastal towns. The marsh cannot compete for territory with Route 1. Landward movement is also prevented where seawalls, lawns, and other structures exist at the edge of the wetland. Hardened shorelines with rip-rap (rocks) or seawalls protect urban or residential development from flooding, but they damage coastal marshes by directing the energy of waves downward, eroding away plants, animals, sediments, and seed banks, and reducing the possibility of recovery.

As sea levels rise, salt marshes may disappear completely from some coastal areas. The extent of this problem will inevitably increase unless action is taken. In order for marshes to survive, a broad buffer of undeveloped land should be preserved to allow them to migrate inland.

Marsh Dieback

Although some marshes haven't changed at all, many acres of *Spartina alterniflora* are dying off in marshes in Long Island and lower New York State, New Jersey, Georgia, Louisiana, Delaware, and New England. Since 1974, Long Island marshes, for example, have lost fourteen hundred acres or 8 percent of the estimated seventeen thousand acres of marsh, without significant areas growing back. In New England, the high marsh as well as the low marsh has suffered from dieback.

The loss of one acre of marsh results in the loss of tons of algae, fishes, shellfish, and birds because they are deprived of food. This phenomenon has been called *sudden wetland dieback,* and the causes of this dieback are unknown and are being actively investigated. Actually, sudden wetland dieback has been going on unnoticed for at least two decades, and some affected areas recover and some do not. In a healthy marsh, cordgrass holds the sediment together with its roots, but along the edges of dying marshes, stretches of bare mud are pockmarked with holes, cavities left behind by dying cordgrass. Possible factors that are contributing to the dieback include sea-level rise, drought, pathogens, and overgrazing.

Sea-Level Rise. It has been suggested that global warming and rising sea levels are playing a role in the dieback, creating a situation where marshes may be unable to keep up with the sudden sea rise, as discussed in the previous section. Long-term tidal cycles (an 18.6-year lunar cycle called a tidal epoch) have caused dieback in the past and the grasses grew back, and this cycle may be playing a role in the present loss. *Spartina patens* (salt-marsh hay) cannot stand prolonged submergence in water because it only absorbs oxygen though its roots. In theory, it could keep up with sea rise by trapping sediment and building peat banks as plants die off and are replaced by new ones, with dead plant matter eventually adding to the height of the marsh. That works only if the rise isn't too rapid, but if the marsh cannot keep up with the rate of sea-level rise, large areas of high-marsh grass could be in a severely stressed state that could make them susceptible to other maladies.

Drought. A marsh dieback in Georgia and Louisiana in 2001 and 2002 was triggered in large part by a drought, with 390,000 acres affected in Louisiana, according to Karen McKee and her colleagues at the U.S. Geological Survey. They and other investigators in the Louisiana marshes are researching how drought caused changes to soil chemistry that weakened and started killing off plants. Insufficient soil moisture during the drought led to soil oxidation, acidification, and metal toxicity. The areas of dieback were found to have fewer fiddler crabs and snails than in vegetated areas of the marsh, so severe effects were seen on marsh fauna as well as on plants. There were also noticeable changes in the tiny meiofauna. Some of the affected areas are recovering, and in Louisiana the recovery has been aided by adding new sediments to increase the marsh elevation.

Pathogens. Pathogens have been implicated in the dieback of some New England marshes as well as in some other regions including Louisiana. Stressful conditions like drought can increase a plant's susceptibility to pathogens. Suspects are a fungus (*Fusarium*) that attacks *Spartina* and a tiny worm called a root knot nematode. Taking samples back to his lab, Louisiana State University researcher Raymond Schneider discovered that a fungus that attacks *Spartina* can cause the inner stem of the grass to rot and vulnerable plants to die. Healthy plants may be able to fight the infection—as people with healthy immune systems are able to fight off a cold. Nematodes are parasitic, microscopic animals that weaken plants and make them susceptible to disease and to other pathogens. It is thought that the nematodes may pre-dispose plants to being attacked by the fungus.

Where would this fungus have come from? In Louisiana, the fungus apparently drifted over with dust from Africa as part of the huge dust storms that are stirred up by ongoing drought in northern Africa. Scientists estimate that hundreds of millions of tons of dust from Africa reach the southeastern United States, the Caribbean, and the Amazon basin each year. It is possible that recent increases in droughts and desertification in Africa have increased the amount of dust heading to the Northeast. The dust can carry bacteria and other pathogens—including *Fusarium*—across the ocean, and it has been tied to respiratory problems, declining health of coral reefs, and harmful algal blooms. It is also possible that the fungus has always been present without causing problems, but that now there is something stressing the plants, allowing the fungus to become aggressive and actually cause disease. The presence of the pathogens also inhibits subsequent recolonization of plants in the dieback areas.

Overgrazing. Grazing by geese, snails, crabs, and other herbivores can weaken or kill plants. In New England, the activities of native nocturnal marsh crabs (*Sesarma reticulatum*) appear to be involved in the local dieback, according to Brown University scientist Mark Bertness (http://www.nhpr.org/node/11451). Scientists have photographed the crabs grazing on the grass in the middle of the night. The dieback leaves a pockmarked landscape in the marsh because the plants and their roots are killed, leaving the peat full of holes like Swiss cheese. This is evident in both the low and the high marsh, in which *Distichlis* and *Spartina patens* are lost.

Marsh crab populations are at a high level in the deteriorating Cape Cod marshes, while a major crab predator, the black-crowned night heron, has been disappearing. When Bertness set up cages around low-marsh grass to keep crabs out, the caged grass flourished, while unprotected plants were shredded (a sign of crab grazing) and died. Plants that had been previously grazed on recovered and grew back once they were protected by a cage.

Similar wetland diebacks caused by burrowing crabs have occurred in Brazil and Argentina. The burrowing crab's predators were overfished, causing the crab population to increase, and the large numbers of crabs devoured the marsh grass.

Dieback has been caused by snow geese in the Canadian Arctic, where large flocks of the geese consume the marsh grass at their summer breeding grounds around Hudson Bay. As long as there were not too many geese, the grasses were not harmed, but starting in the 1960s, high-yield crops and nitrogen-based fertilizers used in American agriculture provided an enriched food supply for the birds when they were wintering in the coastal marshes of Texas and Louisiana, and their population exploded from about six hundred thousand to three million or more. In one summer in Canada, the enlarged population of geese consumed over 247,000 acres or about a third of the Hudson Bay coastal marsh vegetation.

Summary, Statistics, Conservation

The total wetland acreage in the lower forty-eight states is estimated to have declined from more than 220 million acres three centuries ago to 104 million acres in 1997. Only in the past thirty years have there been serious efforts on the part of government to curtail the net annual wetland loss rate. Recent studies indicate that the rate of loss of wetlands has been dropping, and we are currently losing less than one hundred thousand acres annually. This is a significant improvement from the results of a survey of the period from the mid-1950s to the mid-1970s when the rate of loss averaged nearly five hundred thousand acres per year, according to the U.S. Geological Survey's "National Water Summary on Wetland Resources" (see http://water.usgs.gov/nwsum/WPS2425/history.html). During the late 1980s, the federal government adopted a policy of no net loss of wetlands, and this policy has reduced the rate of loss because it requires any project that proposes the destruction of marsh areas to compensate for their loss. The compensation can be done by creating new marshes elsewhere or by restoring other degraded marshes (see chapter 7).

A U.S. Fish and Wildlife Service (FWS) survey has confirmed that coastal wetland losses have been much smaller than those that occurred inland, although coastal wetlands comprise only 5 percent of the nation's total (see http://www.fws.gov/nwi/Pubs_Reports/sewet/execsum.html). Because coastal wetlands were not tracked as a distinct category in previous reports, the National Oceanic and Atmospheric Administration (NOAA) partnered with the FWS to assess the status and trends of coastal wetlands in the watersheds of the Great Lakes, Atlantic Ocean, and Gulf of Mexico for the period 1998 through 2004 (see http://www.nmfs.noaa .gov/habitat/habitatprotection/wetlands/index2c.htm).   Indications   are that coastal watersheds are still losing a substantial amount of wetlands due to population pressures along the coast. Coastal populations have increased steadily since 1970, and currently over half of the population of the United States lives in coastal counties, at densities about five times greater than those of non-coastal counties. The good news is that the rate of coastal wetland loss has declined over the past decades, particularly for salt marshes. In the 1950s, the rate of tidal coastal wetland loss was about forty-six thousand acres a year, but now it is around twenty thousand to twenty-five thousand acres a year. The bad news is that coastal wetland loss continues, and the economic pressures for development in coastal areas are unlikely to decrease.

Although coastal wetlands in saline environments have been lost to urban development and to the encroachment of coastal waters as a result of dredging projects, impoundments, and the rise in sea level, they are not well suited for conversion to agricultural use. This probably explains why they are disappearing less rapidly than freshwater wetlands, which have been extensively converted for agriculture. Also, wetland protection efforts in this country initially focused on coastal areas, so a relatively extensive array of federal and state initiatives already exists in these areas.

On the positive side, the environmental value of the wetlands has been recognized in many quarters, and laws have been enacted to try to save the remaining areas. All of the laws require permits in order to initiate a project that could cause damage or loss to a wetland. For example, under Section 404 of the Clean Water Act, permits are required from the Army Corps of Engineers before anyone can discharge dredge or fill material into wetlands. Also under Section 404, a landowner must obtain a permit to dig up or fill wetlands. While the lead regulatory agency is the Army Corps of Engineers, oversight is provided by the EPA and the U.S. Fish and Wildlife Service, and the National Marine Fisheries Service is expected to weigh in as well. Local estuary programs, such as the Narragansett Bay Estuary Program, foster cooperation among different conservation and restoration groups.

Because wetlands are protected in different ways by multiple laws and initiatives, the complexity of the protection effort can lead to confusing and overlapping jurisdictions. As a practical matter, the Army Corps of Engineers is frequently sympathetic to the interests of developers and routinely approves projects. The role of the oversight agencies is advisory and can be ignored by the Corps. Furthermore, tideland protection varies from state to state in terms of the numbers of permits issued involving potential damage to the wetlands.

Arlington Marsh

In September 2007, about 55 acres of a New York City–owned natural salt marsh on Staten Island's northwest shore was offered to the city's Department of Parks, whose goal will be to restore it and keep it wild. The approximately 90-acre Arlington Marsh, the last major unprotected tidal wetland in the region, is adjacent to the 111-acre Mariners Marsh, which has already been preserved. Together they were part of what was once a vast wetland in New York Harbor, including the other two great marshes in Jamaica Bay and the New Jersey Meadowlands.

The decision to preserve the Arlington Marsh follows the recommendation of the city's Wetlands Transfer Task Force, established in 2005 to determine which city-owned wetlands should be transferred to the Department of Parks. The task force recommended that a total of eighty-two properties be transferred to the Department of Parks, but the department cautioned that it would only accept a limited number of properties that it would be able to successfully manage. An important attraction of Arlington Marsh is that, although the site will require years of cleanup, about 15 acres consist of native *Spartina* grass, which indicates that the marsh is relatively healthy.

The northwestern shore of Staten Island was once a maritime and manufacturing center, but in the mid-twentieth century industry moved out of the area and only a shipping-container terminal remains. Wetland plants and animals have been returning to the abandoned area, including herons, ibises, and egrets that began nesting again in the harbor's wetlands in the 1970s. A recent article by Anne Schwartz reporting on the city's Wetlands Transfer Task Force stated, "More than one hundred species of birds feed or nest here. The mudflats and salt marshes are nurseries for fish, shellfish and other marine organisms. Plants and animals at the northern end of their range, including a number of rare and endangered species, flourish in the wetlands and uplands."

At the international level, the Ramsar Convention is an international treaty for the conservation and sustainable utilization of wetlands. The goal of the treaty is to stem the loss of wetlands and to recognize their important ecological functions and their economic, cultural, scientific, and recreational value. It is the world's oldest international conservation treaty, the only environmental treaty for a particular ecosystem, and the first global intergovernmental treaty to combine conservation and sustainable use of natural resources. The official title is "The Convention on Wetlands of International Importance, Especially as Waterfowl Habitat." While the initial focus was on protecting birds, its basic tenets have broadened over the years to recognize wetlands, including salt marshes, mangroves, and sea-grass beds, as ecosystems that are extremely important for both biodiversity conservation and the well-being of human communities. The convention was developed and adopted by participating nations at a meeting in Ramsar, Iran, on February 2, 1971, and came into force on December 21, 1975. The Ramsar List of Wetlands of International Importance now includes 1,755 sites (known as Ramsar Sites), up from 1,021 sites in 2000. The 153 Ramsar member nations have together designated an impressive 11 percent of the world's wetlands—covering about 350 million acres—for inclusion in the convention's List of Wetlands of International Importance (as of December 2006).

Wetlands have a wide variety of physical forms, and their wildlife habitat and water purification functions are quite variable. A controversy exists about whether *all* wetlands should be protected in the same fashion, which is the way in which federal laws are currently written. But despite conflicting opinions, wetland loss is slowing as restoration efforts have expanded, and some regions reportedly are approaching the national policy goal of no net loss. However, the value of restored marshes may not equal that of natural marshes, as will be discussed in chapter 7.

5 Pollution

It is a curious situation that the sea, from which life first arose, should now be threatened by the activities of one form of that life. But the sea, though changed in a sinister way, will continue to exist; the threat is rather to life itself.

—Rachel Carson, *The Sea Around Us,* 1951

Marine pollution is most severe in estuaries, marshes, and tidal creeks because they are closest to the land, and the land is the major source of pollution. Discharge pipes from factories or sewage plants, called "point sources" in this context, can release pollutants directly into the water. Point sources are easy to identify, and regulatory agencies have ways to measure and control their impact.

Some diffuse runoff into marshes comes from non-point sources such as lawns and farms when they become flooded beyond their capacity to absorb water. Particles or chemicals from the atmosphere that come down in rainwater are also non-point pollution, as is runoff from impervious surfaces such as paved streets, sidewalks, and parking lots; and these sources can deposit significant amounts of harmful substances into bodies of water during heavy rains. Storm water runoff into Puget Sound was recently declared the most severe pollution problem in the region because it carries oil and grease from paved surfaces, fertilizers and pesticides from lawns, heavy metals from wear and tear on brakes and tires, and animal waste. Because the sources of the pollutants are so varied, this type of pollution is extremely difficult to regulate.

Sewage and Nutrients

For many years, marshes were places for dumping sewage that often contained fecal coliform bacteria. When raw sewage enters the water it begins to undergo decay due to of the action of bacteria, and this process uses up oxygen from the water. A way to measure the amount of sewage in the water is by measuring the biological oxygen demand or BOD, which is the rate at which oxygen disappears from the water.

Raw sewage is no longer normally released into estuaries, but there are exceptions. Most states require marinas to provide pump-out facilities for boat toilets, but raw sewage is still discharged from some boats with toilets that flush their contents directly into the water. In older cities, *sanitary sewage,* the sewage that emanates from homes and businesses, is collected by a single sewage system with partially separated channels that also collect storm water runoff from paved and planted (vegetated) areas. These combined sewers normally feed all the waste into sewage treatment plants, where liquids and solids are separated in what is called primary treatment, followed by secondary or biological treatment, in which microbes decompose the organic material before it is released.

However, when there is a major rainstorm and the sewage system becomes overwhelmed with too much water for the treatment plant to deal with, the combined sewer overflow (CSO) containing all the untreated human and industrial waste is released directly into the water through a relief sewer in order to prevent backup into the streets or into people's homes. The relief sewer may contain a screen, but floatables like condoms, tampons, and cigarette butts are often part of this waste, and a recent publication reported that biology students from the New York City College of Technology detected gonorrhea in a drop of water from the Gowanus Canal. Some of this waste eventually washes up on beaches with the result that beaches are often closed for several days after a severe storm.

When they were first built, combined sewers seemed like a good way to carry away storm water along with garbage, animal waste, and other refuse that collected on city streets. Sewage plants were designed to handle twice the average flow of wastewater, but because of population increases, what was considered excess capacity is no longer enough after a storm. The result is that CSOs have become a major source of pollution, and bacterial contamination from the sewage can become concentrated in shellfish, rendering them unfit for consumption. Holding tanks and additional treatment plants have been built to cope with the overflow, but permanently correcting the CSO problem will take a sustained policy and many millions of dollars.

No one has the right to use America's rivers and America's Waterways, that belong to all the people, as a sewer. The banks of a river may belong to one man or one industry or one State, but the waters which flow between the banks should belong to all the people. (Lyndon B. Johnson, signing the Clean Water Act of 1965 [see http://www.siue .edu/OSME/river/RiverQuotes/RiverQuotes.htm.])

Small amounts of sewage can act as fertilizer and may have a positive effect on the marsh and estuary. For example, Ulrika Candolin of Finland and her colleagues found that increased macroalgae cover or increased turbidity caused by phytoplankton growth actually improved the parenting ability of male sticklebacks and enhanced their reproductive output. The increased algae and turbidity reduced aggressive interactions between males, probably due to the reduced visibility, and this increased the reproductive lifespan of the males and enabled them to complete more breeding cycles.

Excess nutrients (nutrient enrichment) from large amounts of sewage can have harmful effects. In coastal regions, nutrient enrichment is due to population growth and the clearing of large areas of land for urban, agricultural, and industrial development. Nutrients, primarily nitrogen and phosphorus, are carried in sewage as well as in runoff from farms and lawns; and human activities have more than doubled the amount of nitrogen globally from 1960 to 1990, mostly due to the use of synthetic fertilizers. As the excess nutrients are cycled through the marsh, they change the structure and function of aquatic communities; and about 20 percent of the nitrogen in the fertilizers seeps into groundwater, rivers, and streams, gradually making its way into the marsh-estuary systems. Other sources of nitrogen, besides fertilizers and waste-water treatment plants, include animal wastes and the combustion of fossil fuels. When these fuels burn, nitrogen compounds are released into the atmosphere and later come down in acid rain.

Waste from septic tanks also enters the marsh through seepage into groundwater. Boston University marine biologist Ivan Valiela has spent years examining the input of nitrogen from groundwater into areas of Waquoit Bay in Cape Cod that have different levels of residential development. He and colleagues found that where there was more residential development there were more septic tanks in the neighborhood and more nitrogen seeping into the nearby marsh. The nutrients from all these sources stimulate excessive growth of single-celled phytoplankton and seaweeds (macroalgae), a phenomenon known as eutrophication, which means too much of a good thing—as we will explain.

A number of phytoplankton species produce toxins that can harm other marine organisms and lead to environmental problems such as algal blooms. Some blooms, such as red tides, are harmful because they can cause toxic effects. Red tides, now referred to as harmful algal blooms or HABs, have occurred periodically along the coast of southwest Florida for over a century, resulting in the death of many species, including turtles, manatees, dolphins, and crabs. Decreased abundance of shrimp and several species of fishes has also been noted, and shellfish farms have been forced to shut down. Mass mortality of birds after having eating fishes that had consumed toxic algae has been reported. Red tide can also cause skin irritation and burning eyes among swimmers, and people who are not even in the water may cough and sneeze when winds blow its toxic aerosol onshore. The microscopic organism responsible for these blooms (*Karenia brevis*) produces a powerful toxin, *brevetoxin,* which kills by paralyzing the animals that ingest it.

The HABs along the west coast of Florida are spurred when seasonal changes in wind patterns move nutrients east from the Mississippi River. Normally, water from the Mississippi travels west, but wind changes in late summer and fall shift the water flow eastward toward Florida. The river water, rich in nitrogen and other nutrients, encourages the growth of the harmful algae. Winds push the algae toward the Florida shore, concentrating them into larger blooms.

The varieties of toxic algae include many different species, and harmful algal blooms have been popping up more frequently around the world, due some of the time to nutrient input from human activities. This increase includes more frequent blooms of familiar species as well as blooms of new species not previously known to be harmful or not known at all. In New England, a dinoflagellate species called *Alexandrium* causes a HAB that can poison humans. Marine mussels and clams that consume the phytoplankton tend to accumulate the toxins (*saxitoxins*), and humans who eat them can become seriously ill with paralytic shellfish poisoning (PSP), which has happened in eastern Canada and New England. Toxins from algae can transfer through the marine food web as well, sometimes with a lethal impact. This occurred with whales in New England that died due to saxitoxin in the mackerel that they had consumed. Toxic algae can be eaten by zooplankton, which are then eaten by larval and juvenile fishes, sometimes with disastrous consequences to the fishes or to their predators. Jennifer Samson, working in the Weis Lab at Rutgers, fed toxic *Alexandrium* to copepods, and then fed the copepods to fish larvae, which died after eating as few as six copepods (a pretty small meal). Fish larvae that ate fewer than six copepods showed altered activity and behavior that could make them more vulnerable to predators. If this happened in the wild, the predators could then be affected by the toxins.

In the late 1990s a very bizarre HAB organism, a dinoflagellate called *Pfiesteria* (nicknamed the "cell from hell"), showed up in the waters of North Carolina and Chesapeake Bay, producing open sores and killing billions of fishes and, frighteningly, causing neurological symptoms in the investigators that were studying it. Researchers in the North Carolina State University lab of JoAnn Burkholder found that its toxins cause neurological symptoms including memory loss, disorientation, and speech impediments. One researcher had to be hospitalized before adequate laboratory precautions were worked out. Burkholder published numerous papers on the high toxicity of *Pfiesteria* and its complicated variety of forms.

Pfiesteria spends much of its life as harmless-looking, microscopic cysts in the sediment. But when large numbers of fishes are introduced under the right conditions, it undergoes a transformation worthy of a horror movie. In minutes, the cysts turn into toxic flagellated vegetative cells and move toward the fishes as found by Burkholder. They stun the fishes by releasing a powerful toxin and then, after the fishes die, transform themselves into large amoebae that eat the carcasses. When the feeding frenzy is over, they revert to their cyst form and return to the sediment. Other stages of this organism are able to photosynthesize using chloroplasts "stolen" from algae they have eaten previously. *Pfiesteria* became a big problem in waters that had low oxygen levels and high nutrient loads caused by sewage discharges and agricultural runoff. The public looked at pictures of fishes covered in bloody lesions and wondered what the "cell from hell" would do to swimmers and fishers. *Pfiesteria* made the headlines and caused considerable concern and controversy in the scientific community for many years. Part of the controversy was due to an inability to isolate any toxin from the cells. The toxin has recently been identified chemically, and it was found to be a very unstable chemical that disappears from the water in a very brief time, which accounts for the previous difficulty in finding it. For some reason, *Pfiesteria* hasn't been heard from lately.

In the 1980s a brown tide of tiny organisms in eastern Long Island, although not toxic, was responsible for the loss of the commercially valuable scallop population, which has not recovered after many years during which there have been only occasional reoccurrences of moderate brown tides.

Other algal blooms are not toxic, but they are harmful anyway because of their sheer abundance and concentration. When the phytoplankton cells die, they sink to the bottom, where bacteria decompose them, using up large amounts of oxygen in the process. This causes the deeper water to become depleted of oxygen (hypoxic), which is necessary for the survival of benthic (bottom-dwelling) animals. Sea lettuce and other seaweeds can also bloom and form mats that cover the bottom and deplete oxygen. Normally oxygenated seawater can have up to ten parts per million (ppm) of oxygen. As the level drops to two ppm it is considered hypoxic and animals become stressed.

Zones of low oxygen reduce the abundance and diversity of adult finfish and reduce the growth rate of newly settled lobsters, crabs, and juvenile flounder. Species that cannot move or move slowly can die in these low-oxygen zones, disease resistance can be compromised, and reproduction and embryonic development can be impaired. Fish embryos that do survive and hatch may exhibit delayed effects. The fish larvae may be poor swimmers, more vulnerable to predation. In general, animals attempt to cope with low oxygen levels by reducing their rate of activity in order to consume less oxygen. This often means feeding for shorter periods of time and eating less food, sometimes creating an advantage for another species. For example, when bottom water is hypoxic, clams move up closer to the surface of the sediments and are more easily eaten by blue crabs that are more tolerant to the low oxygen and can make brief feeding forays into the hypoxic zone.

The infamous dead zone in the Gulf of Mexico, an area about the size of New Jersey, is a body of water with an extremely low level of oxygen. This is the receiving area for water from the Mississippi River, bringing with it all the runoff containing fertilizer and animal wastes from the agricultural center of the country as far north as Minnesota. This watershed encompasses 41 percent of the contiguous United States and contains a large portion of the nation's agricultural land. Only about 18 percent of the nitrogen in fertilizer goes into the produce; the rest is absorbed in the soil, runs off into the water, or enters the atmosphere. The amount of manure produced by huge herds of livestock may exceed the ability of the croplands to absorb it, so the remainder runs off into the streams that lead eventually to coastal estuaries.

As documented by Nancy Rabalais and her colleagues from Louisiana Universities Marine Consortium, every summer the oxygen level in this dead zone drops to less than 0.5 ppm, a condition under which hardly anything other than microbes can live. The high level of nutrients from the runoff leads to an overgrowth of phytoplankton that causes the yearly formation of the hypoxic water mass which lasts from spring through late summer.

Hypoxic conditions have become more severe since the 1950s as the nitrate input from the Mississippi River into the Gulf of Mexico has tripled. While increased nutrients enhance the production of some organisms, others are eliminated because they either leave the area or die when the oxygen level falls below 2 ppm for a prolonged period. When the benthic community is stressed to this degree, only short-lived, small, surface deposit-feeding polychaetes remain; crustaceans, bivalves, and gastropods can no longer survive. Similar but smaller dead zones occur regularly in Chesapeake Bay, western Long Island Sound, and other locations.

Because of their periodic exposure to air at low tide, these harmful effects of hypoxia due to eutrophication are not seen in salt marshes proper. A marsh can absorb nitrogen and other nutrients from runoff and reduce their input to the estuary. In salt marshes, additional nutrients act as fertilizers and can stimulate the growth of marsh grasses. Cordgrass becomes taller and more robust, and there may be shifts in the composition of salt-marsh plant communities so that the zonation changes. The abundance of nitrogen makes cordgrass a better competitor; it can outcompete some of the other species and move higher in the marsh, as shown by Brown University ecologist Mark Bertness. With increased nutrients, cordgrass can outcompete salt hay, which in turn can displace *Juncus*—a reversal of the usual competitive interactions. At the same time increased nitrogen supports the invasion of the common reed from the high marsh into lower parts of brackish marshes, displacing cordgrass, salt hay, and other species and reducing the diversity of marsh plants.

There are more deposit feeders and ribbed mussels in marshes containing elevated levels of nitrogen. Some snails, geese, crabs, and other grazers eat large quantities of the nitrogen-enriched grasses with disastrous consequences to the marsh. Nitrogen-enriched grass is also very palatable to insects. Experiments by Mark Bertness and others in which the chemical was deliberately added to marshes resulted initially in increased plant productivity, but eventually plant biomass was reduced due to greater insect consumption of the grass. Overall productivity decreased by over 50 percent.

In the estuary proper, submerged aquatic vegetation such as sea grass declines because the dense phytoplankton blooms cloud the water, and the growth of small algae attached to sea grass blades (*epiphytes*) further reduces the amount of light that can reach the sea grass leaves for photosynthesis. The decline of sea grasses generally involves sudden decreases in abundance rather than gradual changes, and high salinity and temperature and low light exacerbate the effects of the nutrients. Bottom-dwelling sea grasses also suffer from blooms of sea lettuce (*Ulva*). Shoot density, seedling density, leaf growth, and carbon content of sea grasses all decrease when there is increased sea lettuce. The sea grass and the detritus it generates provide food and shelter for a variety of animals, and when its growth is reduced, the associated animal community declines. Sadly, there are few known cases of sea grass recovery following the reduction of nutrient inputs.

A lot of effort and a huge amount of money have been expended over the years in attempts to improve water clarity, sea grass populations, and oxygen levels in Chesapeake Bay, but the results have been disappointing. In order for significant progress to be made, considerable cooperation from the area's farmers and substantial financial assistance will be necessary. Major changes in land-use practices are required in states that are hundreds of miles away from the affected estuaries and marshes. We do not yet understand how much reduction in nutrient inputs will be necessary in order to produce the needed improvement in environmental quality, and what the time lag is likely to be before results are evident. Voluntary efforts to monitor and control non-point runoff have been encouraged for the past two decades, but they don't seem to be able to deal with the magnitude of the problem.

There are various farming techniques that have been developed to reduce runoff, and incentive programs have been set up to encourage farmers to adopt them. Some groups are working to find new uses for manure, which might be used in energy production or sold as fertilizer. Some creative approaches include farmers who have anaerobic digesters that convert the urine and manure from their cows into electricity that runs their farms and produces extra electricity that they sell to the local power company to provide electricity for nearby homes. This approach not only reduces methane emissions and turns a waste into a resource, but it also eliminates runoff.

The state of Pennsylvania is trying to get farmers to reduce damaging runoff by letting them apply for pollution credits that can be sold to developers who want to build sewage treatment plants. Buffer strips of native vegetation can be placed along waterways to filter out pollutants, and Pennsylvania has asked farmers to build barriers to contain runoff into Chesapeake Bay. They have also been urged, with monetary incentives, to plant crops year-round so that the roots of the plants will prevent the soil from washing away in big storms. The state will then estimate how much pollution has been eliminated, using a complex equation that combines the impact of the improvement and the distance of the farm from the bay.

It is important to reduce the nitrogen coming in from agricultural land as well as from urban and suburban areas. The federal government should set clear guidelines for the maximum allowable amounts of nutrients that are released in waterways, and they should also take the lead on issues that span multiple jurisdictions. A great deal needs to be done to help state and local authorities address eutrophication problems, and the federal government should provide information and technical assistance to state and local coastal authorities. A systematic, nationwide plan is necessary for the government to make real progress on reducing the damage to coastal areas, to make sure that no other healthy areas become affected, and to repair and protect our waterways and coasts.

Holistic policy approaches may not be enough. A historical approach reveals that rainfall and runoff was high in the 1970s and 1980s, exacerbating the effects of increasing fertilizer use and nutrient input and leading to greater hypoxia. It is important to understand that increased rainfall and runoff due to climate change can have a major impact on the system beyond what we can control. Goals for the future need to incorporate this factor—it is not realistic to expect environmental improvement if wetter conditions persist due to climate change, even if nutrient inputs are reduced. It may be that improvement will not be possible and that the best we can hope for is for the problems not to get any worse.

Toxic Chemicals

Pesticides

Because salt marshes are well known as breeding areas for mosquitoes and other nuisance insects, they are frequently targets of chemical pesticide applications. On the West Coast, where burrowing shrimp are considered pests in oyster-growing estuarine areas, the pesticide *carbaryl* is used to kill the shrimp. Estuarine and marsh organisms can also be exposed to herbicides used on the marsh to kill unwanted plants like common reeds on the East Coast and cordgrass on the West Coast. In addition to the pesticides used directly in salt marshes or estuaries, other insecticides and herbicides wash into estuaries and marshes from farms, lawns, and golf courses. Here, however, we focus on insecticides used directly on marshes for mosquito control.

The types of chemicals that are of greatest environmental concern are those that are toxic, persistent (do not readily break down in the environment), and taken up by living things. After World War II, organic chemical pesticides were developed that consisted primarily of carbon and hydrogen, sometimes in combination with other elements. The post–World War II organic pesticides that included chlorine are called chlorinated hydrocarbons or organochlorines, and they are relatively insoluble in water and very persistent in soils. They bind to sediment particles and bioaccumulate in fat and in high concentrations can be quite toxic to humans.

DDT is an example of an organochlorine pesticide that was used on farms and was sprayed extensively in salt marshes to control biting flies and mosquitoes. It was considered a panacea in the 1940s and 1950s because it could be applied as a powder on the water in relatively small amounts, and it would keep killing mosquito larvae for months after just a single application. It could be used to kill all kinds of insects, but it was not considered particularly toxic to humans, and it enjoyed great success until the development of resistance by mosquitoes and the public. Resistance develops in insect populations because not all of the insects are killed when they are sprayed by the chemical. The few remaining resistant individuals breed, and their offspring are also more resistant to the chemical. An example of evolution at work, the insects eventually become so resistant that a different chemical has to be used.

Public resistance to DDT developed because the chemical caused severe environmental problems. It was not specific in targeting insects, and it killed crabs and other crustaceans and accumulated in the fatty tissues of all marsh animals, acting on their nervous systems and causing hyperactivity. It also altered hormones that affect calcium metabolism, resulting in reproductive failure among some birds because their eggshells lacked sufficient calcium and were extremely thin and broke when the birds sat on them. Many fish-eating birds were poisoned, and carnivorous birds such as bald eagles, ospreys, and pelicans were on the brink of extinction until DDT and other similar pesticides were finally banned.

The risks involved with pesticide use were not widely questioned until 1962, when Rachel Carson, a biologist working for the Fish and Wildlife Service and an eloquent science writer, published *Silent Spring*, which became one of the most influential books of the last half of the twentieth century. The book showed how modern society was poisoning the earth. Violently attacked by the agricultural chemical industry, *Silent Spring* was officially endorsed by President Kennedy's Science Advisory Committee and has been given credit for initiating the modern environmental movement. Her work increased public awareness of the impact of the use of pesticides on wildlife and on humans, the persistence of pesticides in the environment (originally considered a great benefit), and the inadvertent transport of pesticides outside of target areas that results in unintended environmental damage.

We stand now where two roads diverge. But unlike the roads in Robert Frost's familiar poem, they are not equally fair. The road we have long been traveling is deceptively easy, a smooth superhighway on which we progress with great speed, but at its end lies disaster. The other fork of the road—the one 'less traveled by'—offers our last, our only chance to reach a destination that assures the preservation of our earth. (Carson 1962, 277)

If man were to follow the teachings of Miss Carson, we would return to the Dark Ages, and the insects and diseases and vermin would once again inherit the earth. (A representative of the chemical industry)

DDT was the focus of considerable controversy following the publication of *Silent Spring* and the new realization among the general public that spraying chemicals could cause environmental damage. This awareness led to the formation of activist organizations such as the Environmental Defense Fund (EDF) and the Natural Resources Defense Council (NRDC), and it drastically increased public concern about the environment. An early victory for the young environmental movement was the banning of DDT in 1970. Sadly, Rachel Carson died of cancer two years after her groundbreaking book was published, so she did not live long enough to experience this victory.

Less ecologically damaging insecticides are presently being used to control mosquitoes in U.S. salt marshes, but organochlorines continue to be used for agricultural and mosquito control in developing countries. The recent arrival in North America of the West Nile virus has led to increased spraying for mosquitoes that might be carrying the disease. Currently used pesticides are not as persistent and do not bioaccumulate as much as chlorinated hydrocarbons, but they are not environmentally benign.

The next class of chemicals developed as insecticides were organophosphates. Unlike the chlorinated hydrocarbon insecticides that are still present in the environment more than thirty years after their use was banned, organophosphates break down in the environment in a matter of weeks. They were developed from chemical compounds similar to nerve gas and, not surprisingly, affect a chemical in the body that is important for the transmission of nerve impulses. At high doses, organophosphates can overstimulate the nervous system, causing nausea, dizziness, or confusion. Severe poisoning with organophosphates can cause convulsions and respiratory paralysis and has caused death in fishes and birds.

One organophosphate commonly used in salt marshes is temephos (Abate®), which is considered hazardous to fishes, birds, insects (the beneficial species as well as the pests), shrimp, and crabs. Reductions in fiddler crabs and zooplankton have been seen after temephos was used for mosquito control, and temephos was found to have accumulated in salt-marsh organisms, including sheepshead minnows, mussels, and fiddler crabs.

The liquid chemical Malathion can be applied as a blanket of fog from a moving vehicle and will permeate and penetrate through vegetation, killing adult mosquitoes. It is considered one of the safest organophosphate insecticides and has been used in large pest eradication programs. However, honeybees are quite sensitive to Malathion, and colonies are sometimes affected downwind from an application. It degrades rapidly in the environment, especially in moist soil, and has relatively low toxicity to estuarine organisms, birds and mammals. It is usually broken down within a few weeks by water and sunlight and by the bacteria in soil and water, but it can affect non-target estuarine organisms before it is completely broken down.

Dibrom (naled), another organophosphate, is used to kill adult mosquitoes. It is applied as an ultra-low volume (ULV) spray. ULV sprayers dispense very fine aerosol droplets that stay aloft and kill mosquitoes on contact. The exposure and risks to humans posed by ULV aerial and ground applications of naled are considered low because of the small amounts of the chemical being used. It degrades rapidly in the environment and is minimally toxic to birds and mammals. There is some concern about potential genetic and cancer effects, however, due to dichlorvos, an ingredient in Dibrom. Not much is known about its toxicity to fishes and invertebrates, but recent studies suggest it may be a problem.

Another insecticide used for salt-marsh mosquitoes is Scourge, which is not an organophosphate. Its label warns: "THIS PRODUCT IS TOXIC TO FISH AND BIRDS. DO NOT APPLY TO LAKES, STREAMS OR PONDS." Nevertheless, on Long Island, the Suffolk County Vector Control agency has been using it recently in salt marshes. According to the EPA, one thimbleful of Scourge is enough to kill all the trout in an average one-acre shallow pond, and Scourge is being applied at about three times this rate. The active ingredients in Scourge are resmethrin and piperonyl butoxide, which act together to kill mosquitoes. Piperonyl butoxide does not kill insects but increases the ability of resmethrin to do so. Resmethrin is similar to a natural group of pesticides called pyrethrins, which come from plants. Pyrethrins are broad-spectrum pesticides that have very low toxicity to birds and mammals but are quite toxic to fishes and other aquatic organisms. About one-fourth of the Scourge formula consists of "inert ingredients," including petroleum byproducts. These are of concern since they may be contaminated with benzene, a potent carcinogen. What is classified by the pesticide industry as "inert" is not necessarily inert to living things.

Larvicides are chemicals that target the larval stages of mosquitoes. They are less harmful to non-target organisms and generally more effective and specific than chemicals that focus on adults. Larvicides target the limited breeding habitat before adult populations have had a chance to disperse widely. One of the larvicides currently in use is methoprene, considered an insect growth regulator. It is a chemical mimic of the insect's juvenile hormone (JH), which normally prevents the larvae from metamorphosing prematurely into the adult stage. When the insect stops secreting JH during the pupal stage, it is then ready to develop into an adult. If methoprene is in the insect's system when it begins the pupal stage, the triggering of adult development is prevented and it dies as a pupa. While few toxic impacts have been observed in non-target aquatic organisms, there is some concern that the chemicals might have harmful effects on crustaceans since that group is closely related to the insects.

Another larvicide is *Dimilin*® (diflubenzuron), a chitin synthesis inhibitor. Chitin is a major constituent of the outer exoskeleton of arthropods (the phylum that contains both insects and crustaceans). A chitin synthesis inhibitor prevents the larvae from molting, resulting in their death. Unfortunately, crustaceans have the same chitin in their exoskeletons and also need to molt, so they can be severely harmed when diflubenzuron is sprayed near salt marshes. The majority of small animals in the zooplankton are crustaceans, and reduced numbers of zooplankton means less food for small fishes.

Bacteria that cause insect diseases can be used as pesticides. The principal one used on salt marshes is *Bacillus thuringiensis israelensis* (Bti), which produces protein crystals that are selectively toxic to mosquito larvae. When eaten, they rupture the digestive tract of the host, causing rapid death. When specific diseases of insects are used as pesticides there is less likelihood of harm to non-target organisms, but honeybees, butterflies, dragonflies, and other useful insects are also at risk.

Mosquito control in the United States has evolved from a reliance on insecticides to "integrated pest management" that includes surveillance of pest populations, source reduction, larvicides, and biological control. Surveillance programs track adults, larvae, and larval habitats, and only when populations exceed some predetermined level are control activities initiated. Source reduction involves elimination of larval habitats and includes open marsh water management and rotational impoundment management where the marsh is minimally flooded during the summer by temporary impoundments. Biological control includes the use of predators such as aquatic invertebrates, mosquito fish, and killifish.

Chemical problems in marshes and estuaries are not restricted to pesticides that are purposely sprayed there, but include a wide variety of industrial chemicals released accidentally or as waste products.

Polychlorinated Biphenyls (PCBs)

PCBs are chemically related to organochlorine pesticides. Each PCB molecule consists of chlorine atoms attached to a double carbon-hydrogen ring (a biphenyl ring). There are 209 different PCB molecules that differ in the number and location of the chlorine atoms on the rings. In general, PCBs with more chlorine atoms are more toxic than PCBs with less chlorine. Like chlorinated hydrocarbon pesticides, they remain in the environment for a long time, have low water solubility, and accumulate in fat. PCBs are suspected of causing cancer and have been linked to male sterility and birth defects. In birds and fishes they produce decreased egg hatchability, altered behavior, and decreased immune response.

Unlike pesticides, PCBs were never intentionally sprayed in the environment. They were used in industry, mostly as lubricants and heat dissipaters in electrical transformers and capacitors, and they got into the environment through carelessness. General Electric plants in upstate New York dumped over five hundred thousand pounds of these chemicals into the upper Hudson River over a thirty-year period until they were ordered to stop in 1977. Since that time, the spread of PCBs throughout the river has created a widespread toxic waste problem. The contaminated sediments have dispersed to cover a much more considerable stretch of the river than they did originally, making the cleanup more extensive and more expensive. An approximately two-hundred-mile stretch of the river is designated a Superfund site. Superfund is the federal law that identifies the most highly contaminated sites in the country and eventually impels their cleanup (see chapter 8 for a thorough discussion of this law in relation to the Hackensack Meadowlands). Though required by the Superfund law to clean up the PCBs, General Electric battled the EPA in the court system for decades until an agreement was finally reached in 2005.

The New York State Department of Environmental Conservation initiated intensive monitoring of PCB levels in fishes, and commercial fishing for striped bass in the region was prohibited in 1976 following the discovery of high PCB levels in this species. Since then, the PCB levels in the fishes around New York Harbor have dropped and then stabilized at an acceptable level. PCB levels in fishes in the upper Hudson, however, still exceed what is considered safe. Most of the PCBs in the lower Hudson originate from the upper Hudson, but around 40 percent of the elevated levels of PCBs in the New York–New Jersey Harbor are from local sources. Levels of PCBs in white perch are strongly related to the percentage of suburban and urban development in the local watershed. When development of the land in the watershed reaches about 20 percent of the total area, which is not particularly dense for our coastal states, PCB levels in the fish begin to exceed the recommended levels for food consumption.

PCBs have been banned in the United States since the 1970s, but they continue to be redistributed and dispersed. About thirty years after their prohibition, they are still accumulating in fish tissue to such an extent that state agencies recommend that people do not eat striped bass or blue crabs from the Newark Bay area and eat no more than one meal a week of seafood from other areas in the New York Harbor estuary.

Another PCB-contaminated site is an eighteen-thousand-acre tidal estuary in New Bedford, Massachusetts, where manufacturers of electric devices used PCBs and discharged wastes directly into the harbor and indirectly through the city's sewage system. PCB levels in fishes and lobsters at the site exceed the Food and Drug Administration's limit for PCBs in edible seafood. There is an increased risk of cancer and other diseases for people who regularly eat seafood from that area, and while some species have disappeared, killifish at the site have evolved to become tolerant to the PCBs. EPA scientist Diane Nacci and her colleagues found that the killifish were able to adapt to the high levels of pollution through genetic changes by developing an abnormal biochemical pathway.

Chlorinated Dioxins

Dioxins are, like PCBs, organic molecules with varying numbers and arrangements of chlorine atoms. They are an accidental byproduct from the manufacture of some herbicides, from paper mills when chlorine is added to bleach paper, and in incinerators when plastics are burned. They are considered among the most toxic substances known, and they are harmful even at extremely low concentrations. They are particularly toxic to the immune system and to developing embryos in which effects may be seen immediately or may be delayed for a long period of time, perhaps impairing reproduction when the individual is mature. They are known to alter hormones and to cause reproductive problems, liver damage, wasting syndrome, and cancer.

There is an estuarine-marsh dioxin site in Newark, New Jersey, in the lower Passaic River, located just before it enters Newark Bay. A chemical company manufactured the herbicide Agent Orange there during the Vietnam War and released dioxins as a byproduct. Newark Bay and the lower Passaic have layers of polluted sediment contributing to dangerous dioxin levels in blue crabs, fishes, and fish-eating birds. The dioxin levels recorded in Passaic River and Newark Bay blue crabs are among the highest ever measured in aquatic animals, and the New Jersey Department of Environmental Protection has banned crabbing in and around Newark Bay because the contamination poses a high cancer risk.

The presence of dioxins in the sediments of Newark Bay has also made the disposal of dredged materials from deepening the channel for the Port of Newark a highly controversial issue. In February 2004, the EPA determined that pollution in the bay posed an "imminent and substantial" risk to human health and to the environment, and it ordered the company that was responsible for the pollution to carry out a comprehensive study under EPA supervision and to design a cleanup plan. At this site and at many others in need of remediation, there is concern that when the bottom is dredged as part of the cleanup process, sediments will be stirred up and contaminants that are presently tightly bound to the sediments will be mobilized, causing additional exposure and risk of toxicity to animals and plants in the area.

Oil Pollution

While most coastal pollution comes from the land, oil pollution is generally a result of spills from ships. Smaller amounts of hydrocarbons are also discharged by two-cycle outboard motor engines, which release a lot of unburned fuel-oil mixture into the water, and there are some places where oil naturally seeps into deeper ocean water. Oil is a complex combination of various hydrocarbons that generally floats on the surface of the water, although some lighter-weight components (the water-soluble fraction) dissolve. The floating oil has the greatest effect on animals at the sea surface such as birds and sea otters. When the oil comes into shallow water and marshes it can coat and smother the resident communities. On rocky shores, lighter components of the oil evaporate, leaving behind the heaviest components and turning the oil into tar that erodes away from the wave action. Under those circumstances, biological communities will return rather rapidly since the oil is removed relatively quickly.

In marshes, however, oil can sink below the surface and remain there for many years. Oil accumulated in marsh sediments undergoes some microbial breakdown, but the process is very slow, and marshes have the slowest rates of recovery from oil spills. The major effects of a rather small oil spill in Falmouth, Massachusetts, in the late 1960s lasted for over a decade, according to a team of scientists from the nearby Woods Hole Oceanographic Institute, led by Howard Sanders, a distinguished benthic ecologist. It is rare that a spill occurs right in an area that has been intensively studied prior to the spill, so their information was particularly useful, though hotly contested by the oil companies.

The fiddler crabs on Cape Cod were particularly sensitive to the oil. It affected their burrow construction with the result that the burrows did not go straight down, but rather leveled off on a horizontal plane. Charles Krebs found that when winter came the crabs could not retreat below the freezing zone and froze to death. Benthic communities took about a decade to return to normal.

The site of the spill was revisited recently by another generation of Woods Hole scientists. Over thirty years after the barge *Florida* spilled approximately 190,000 gallons of number-two fuel oil, there is still substantial un-degraded residue at a depth of ten to fourteen centimeters within the salt-marsh sediments. Many years after the spill, Jennifer Culbertson and colleagues noted that fiddler crab burrows in oiled areas were shorter in length, often turned laterally at depths greater than ten centimeters, and sometimes even turned upwards. They found that crabs exposed to the oil avoided burrowing into oiled layers and suffered delayed escape responses, lowered feeding rates, and reduced population density. Cordgrass in low marshes with some oil remaining still grows less densely than in clean areas, and the loss of marsh grass (especially reduced roots) results in sediments that are more unconsolidated and more likely to erode away. Culbertson noted that ribbed mussels are still experiencing the effects of the remaining oil on these marshes. In an experiment, mussels were transplanted from a control site into the oiled site for short-term exposure, and others that had been exposed to the oil were transplanted from the oiled site to the control site. Both the short- and long-term exposure transplants had slower growth, shorter shell lengths, and decreased filtration rates. These results add new knowledge about the long-term, multigenerational consequences of spilled oil in salt marshes.

Marshes and sediments in Prince William Sound in Alaska retained oil for many years from the massive oil spill of the *Exxon Valdez* in 1989. This was the biggest oil spill in history, in which eleven million gallons of crude oil were spilled from a tanker with a drunken captain. The oil eventually spread over ten thousand square miles. Millions of birds, otters, and other organisms died as a result of the acute effects, but what remains controversial is how long the effects persisted. In a cold environment like Alaska, oil degrades much more slowly than in warmer regions; and, as demonstrated by Charles Peterson of the University of North Carolina and his colleagues, salmon embryos developing in the sediments a decade later did not develop properly. After over a decade, pockets of oil remained in these marshes; and mussels, clams, harlequin ducks, and other birds that feed on sediment-dwelling invertebrates showed evidence of harm in some localized areas. Sub-lethal effects of the persistent oil on growth, reproduction, and lifespan could be detected in a variety of organisms, and indirect effects cascaded through the food web.

The lifespan of sea otters in oiled areas remained lower than in clean areas, even over a decade after the spill. There is considerable ongoing controversy over whether effects are still occurring from this spill. Mark Harwell and John Gentile, scientists funded by Exxon, looked at the data and concluded that residual oil from the spill no longer poses any significant ecological risk to organisms in Prince William Sound. There was a $2.5 billion lawsuit that was heard by the Supreme Court in February 2008, nineteen years after the spill, and the Court's decision was to reduce the punitive damages considerably. Remedial actions after oil spills are controversial; and some of the cures, such as aggressive cleaning with large, heavy equipment, may be worse than the original problem, as was seen in some of the attempted clean up after the *Exxon Valdez* oil spill.

Polycyclic Aromatic Hydrocarbons (PAHs)

These chemicals are present in large amounts in oil. In addition to potential spills, polycyclic aromatic hydrocarbons are also released into the atmosphere through burning and can reach aquatic systems through atmospheric deposition. Large quantities of PAHs are also released directly into the water by chemicals leaching from creosote-treated wood that is used for bulkheads and docks placed in shallow estuarine water. While the wood is treated to prevent it from rotting while sitting in the water, the PAHs released are quite toxic to surrounding aquatic life. The rate of release is greatest when the wood is new and declines over time. There was an interesting case in which an unfortunate female herring was found by Carol Vines and her colleagues at the University of California, Davis, to have laid her eggs on a creosote bulkhead in California; all the eggs were highly abnormal or dead. This particular bulkhead was over forty years old and releasing far less creosote than when it was new, but it still was lethal to all the herring embryos.

Another major source of PAHs is runoff from paved surfaces. Parking lots and roads are often sealed with PAH-containing coal-tar sealants, and, especially after the paving has recently been treated, the PAHs leach out into runoff whenever it rains.

There are thousands of different compounds in this group, and the ones that have larger molecules are less soluble in water, more soluble in fats, and tend to be carcinogenic (causing cancer), mutagenic (causing genetic mutations), or teratogenic (causing embryonic malformations, as in the herring embryos). PAHs are readily metabolized and generally do not increase in concentration as they make their way through the food chain.

In aquatic environments, PAHs may evaporate or experience degradation by bacteria, but they generally become more toxic after exposure to light (*phototoxicity*), and they may also become incorporated into sediments where they degrade very slowly. High levels in sediments are associated with liver and skin cancers in fishes. They also can become concentrated in some animals when they are metabolized in the liver, and some of the intermediate breakdown products can be more toxic than the PAHs. Because mollusks cannot metabolize PAHs, they are useful for biomonitoring, a process where their bodies are analyzed to evaluate the levels of PAH pollution of a particular environment.

Metals

Metals are naturally occurring elements that can become contaminants when industrial activity concentrates them at higher than normal levels. When marshes were being filled in for development, household and industrial wastes such as metal cans and paint cans with pigments that are metal compounds were a common component of the fill material. Mercury, cadmium, lead, and copper used in pipes, boat antifouling paints, and CCA (chromated copper arsenate)-treated wood bulkheads and pilings were common contaminants. While copper is essential for some biological processes and is not generally a human health problem, it is extremely toxic to marine algae and invertebrates and is even used as an algicide.

Lead arrives in runoff from road surfaces during rain, a legacy of lead as a gasoline additive, even though leaded gas is not used any more. Lead remains in the environment and does not break down, so some otherwise fairly pristine marshes have elevated amounts of lead in the sediments as a result of decades of hunting ducks and other waterfowl with lead shot. Lead shot contaminates the marsh soils, and birds that normally pick up pebbles for grit in their digestive system (to grind up seeds) can consume the spent shot, sometimes resulting in fatal lead poisoning.

Other metals that can be environmental problems include cadmium, chromium, zinc, and mercury. Selenium can be found in different chemical forms and can bioaccumulate and cause deformities under some circumstances, although in other instances it can counteract the toxic effects of mercury. Knowing the chemical form of a metal is necessary in order to understand the risk it poses to the environment. In general, the free ion, for example, copper with two positive charges, is the most toxic form found in the water. Metals do not generally reach high concentrations in water; instead, they bind to sediment particles. Since smaller-sized particles have more surface area for binding metals, the fine particles of silt and clay in estuaries and marshes bind more to metal than sand, causing high contaminant levels in estuarine and marsh sediments that are consumed by benthic animals. Some of these bottom dwellers absorb the metal from the water that surrounds the sediment particles, known as pore water, while others directly eat the sediments. Once metals are taken up into an organism, they may be stored in significant quantities in non-toxic granules tucked away in their cells or attached to metal-binding proteins that keep the metals unavailable to the host, but they are transferred to a predator that eats the organism. This is the most important way that metals move higher up the food web into larger fishes and birds. Plants generally pick up metals from the soil in which they grow, and different species store different proportions in their roots, stems, or leaves and can pass the metals along to animals that consume the plants.

Mercury enters the environment from industrial operations and dental offices, and when it comes from burning coal, it can be transported long distances in the atmosphere before coming down to earth. Bacteria in bottom sediments convert the mercury to an organic form, methylmercury, which is taken up more rapidly and is much more toxic than inorganic mercury. It affects the immune system, alters genes, damages the nervous system, and is particularly toxic to developing embryos. Inorganic mercury and methylmercury tend to accumulate at much higher levels in sediments with marsh plants than in non-vegetated sediments, perhaps due to greater microbial activity in rhizosphere sediments. Common reeds are able to release a volatile form of inorganic mercury into the air, thereby removing some of it from a contaminated site.

In the late 1950s and 1960s, hundreds of individuals in Minamata, Japan, suffered from mercury poisoning. This community had a factory that discharged mercury into Minamata Bay, from which the people ate fishes that had accumulated the poison in their tissues. Local residents developed severe neurological and developmental defects, a condition now called Minamata disease, sending a wake-up call to the rest of the world that exposure to mercury can have life-long behavioral and neurological effects.

Berry's Creek Marsh, a highly contaminated Superfund site in the Hackensack Meadowlands of New Jersey, also has extremely high concentrations of mercury in its sediments as a result of industrial pollution. The area along the banks of the Hackensack and Passaic Rivers where they join at Newark Bay was one of the major centers of the industrial revolution. Paper, paint, and chemical factories as well as plants that manufactured gas were some of the early manufacturing facilities in the area, and the plants used the rivers and estuary for wastewater disposal, which at the time was quite legal. As a result, the entire system—not only Berry's

Weis Lab Research on Ecology of Salt-Marsh Species in Contaminated Marshes of Northern New Jersey

Mummichog Studies

Mummichogs (killifish) are one of the most abundant estuarine fish species along the Atlantic coast. In the metal-polluted estuaries of northern New Jersey, we have found that mummichogs are more resistant to methylmercury than those living in cleaner areas, but only in their embryonic stages. Embryos treated with methylmercury develop with cardiac, skeletal, and neural abnormalities. Those treated with lower concentrations of mercury looked normal when they hatched but had reduced activity and ability to capture food afterwards. This is a delayed effect of toxic exposure. While embryos from clean sites showed considerable variation in their susceptibility or tolerance of the contaminant, and different females produced eggs with different degrees of tolerance, embryos from the contaminated site were much less affected by the exposure. One can envision that fish at the polluted sites started out variable like those at the clean sites, and as these sites became more polluted the segment of the population that produced tolerant embryos persisted while those that produced susceptible embryos disappeared.

The mercury resistance we saw in the embryos was not seen in adults of the polluted population. The adults seemed stressed and did not live as long or grow as well as fish from clean sites. We later found a possible explanation for this. We found that their predator-prey behavior was altered in such a way that they were less able to capture live food (grass shrimp) than were fish from the clean sites. We did experiments where we "switched" environments and found that the predatory ability of fish from the clean sites was reduced after a month of living in a tank with mud from the polluted site and feeding on food (grass shrimp) from the polluted site. Fish caught from the field at the polluted site were found to be eating a lot of detritus and sediment and much less live food than fish collected from the clean sites. Although they ate a lot of detritus, it is known that this is not nutritious for mummichogs—it is the equivalent of junk food. So eating a lot of junk food can explain why these fish did not grow as well or live as long as fish from the clean sites.

In addition to being poor predators, fish from the polluted site were also worse at avoiding predators themselves, as Graeme Smith found out. When put in tanks with blue crabs, the polluted fish were much more likely to be caught and eaten than the clean fish. This can also partially explain why they do not live as long as fish from the clean site. The basic behavioral reason behind their poor predatory ability and poor predator avoidance

(continued)

was that these fish were just slower—slower to swim, slower to attempt to
catch the shrimp, and slower to escape from the predator. Tong Zhou found
that they have abnormal thyroid glands and reduced levels of serotonin in
their nervous system, which could be underlying reasons for their overall
sluggishness.

Grass Shrimp Studies

Grass shrimp from the polluted site were also more tolerant of the contaminants and, interestingly, were not impaired behaviorally like the mummichogs in that they were not easier to catch. Fish could capture grass shrimp
from the clean and polluted sites at the same rate. Celine Santiago Bass also
found, to our surprise, that the shrimp from the polluted site were more numerous and larger in size than those from the clean sites, unlike the mummichogs, which were smaller and less numerous at the polluted site. However, the actual rate of growth of the shrimp from both sites turned out to
be the same, so the fact that the shrimp from the polluted site were larger
can be explained by the fact that they were not eaten as frequently by their
impaired fish predators. At that site, the shrimp could live a long happy life
in comparison to the clean site, where they were much more likely to be
eaten. So the pollution turns out to be a benefit to these shrimp because
their major predator is impaired. This is an example of a "top-down" effect, where a species is affected, positively or negatively, by the ones that
eat it.

Fiddler Crab Studies

Mud fiddler crabs from the contaminated site were more tolerant to mercury than those from clean sites. One way that they deal with the high concentrations of metals in their environment and in their bodies is to move a
lot of the toxic metals, like lead, into their exoskeleton just prior to molting,
and then they get rid of it by molting—a very handy adaptation, as Lauren
Bergey found. She also found that population density of fiddler crabs at the
polluted site was smaller than at the clean sites, although individual crabs
were larger (like the shrimp). There was considerable loss of larvae and early
juveniles so that those individuals that survived past the vulnerable early life
stages were more resistant to the contamination and also had less competition. An interesting side observation was that the breeding season of crabs
from both sites was much longer than what had been reported in the 1970s.
Perhaps this is a response to climate change, the same as plants that flower
earlier in the season now than they did in the past.

Fiddler crabs do not have to capture prey because they only feed by processing sediments, and the sediments at the polluted marsh were enriched with nutrients from a sewage treatment plant. So those crabs that survived to adulthood benefited from having a rich food source and less competition. They were able to spend less of their time feeding at the surface and a greater percentage of their time safely down in their burrows where they were protected from predators. It is also likely that there were fewer predators at this site.

Blue Crab Studies

Blue crabs are predators in these polluted marshes, and it was of interest to see how their predator-prey interactions were affected. Since cannibalism is common in this species, it was possible to investigate predator and prey behavior in the same experiment.

Jessica Reichmuth has found that blue crab adults from polluted marshes (from the Hackensack Meadowlands—about which we will devote a whole chapter later) turn out to be poor predators on active prey (juvenile blue crabs and mummichogs) compared to crabs from clean sites, although they can prey on inactive prey like mussels equally well. Despite their poor predatory ability, these blue crabs are very aggressive, showing that aggressiveness is not equivalent to being a good predator. Crabs collected from the field at the polluted area appeared to eat a lot of detritus, algae, and sediment rather than live food. However, this diet of junk food does not seem to limit the size they can attain—there are some very big crabs out there. But maybe that is only because there is a fishing ban and one of their major predators (people) are not catching them—another top-down effect!

The juvenile blue crabs from the contaminated site are also more aggressive than those from the clean site; and, rather than being easier to catch, they are more difficult for the predatory adult blue crab to capture. Putting this all together, one would expect that there would be considerably less cannibalism at the polluted site, since the adult blue crabs are not good at being predators and the juvenile prey are less likely to be captured, perhaps because they are aggressive and fight back. Less cannibalism potentially might result in greater population growth. The ban on fishing and crabbing due to the contamination in the area also is probably helping the population growth of the crabs, an interesting way in which pollution can benefit an organism.

Bluefish Studies

Bluefish have a life cycle in which they breed and spend their embryonic and larval stages out in the ocean. In the late spring and early summer, the

(continued)

Weis Lab Research on Ecology of Salt-Marsh Species in Contaminated Marshes of Northern New Jersey (*continued*)

juveniles enter estuaries, where they spend the summer eating the rich food supplied by the estuaries and marshes. In the fall, the larger juveniles (called "snappers" and popular with recreational anglers) leave the estuaries and go back to the ocean. The question we tried to answer was whether those fish that spend their first summer in polluted estuaries are affected by eating the polluted food.

Bluefish were collected from the clean site and raised in the lab over the summer. They were fed a diet of mummichogs and menhaden from either the clean site or the contaminated site. Allison Candelmo has found that those that were fed contaminated prey (from the Hackensack Meadowlands) gradually showed a reduced appetite and less activity. As a result, they did not grow as well as bluefish fed prey from the clean site. They also accumulated very high levels of PCBs and mercury from their prey. Young bluefish caught from the polluted Hackensack Meadowlands area were not eating much—lots of them had no food at all in their stomachs, which is very unusual for this species. Also, they were generally smaller than those from the clean place, showing that what we saw in the lab was actually going on in the real world. It is likely that these fish will be at a disadvantage when they migrate back to the ocean, having to spend a long cold winter competing with better predators—larger bluefish that were lucky enough to spend their first summer in a clean estuary.

Creek—is highly contaminated with PCBs, dioxins, and PAHs as well as mercury.

Fortunately for local residents, the mercury has largely not become methylated and has not accumulated in Minamata-type levels in local fishes because of special circumstances. In this area, there is so much sulfide in the sediments as a result of years of accumulating wastes from sewage treatment plants that the mercury is chemically bound to the sulfide and is not available for bacteria to methylate. Nevertheless, mercury levels in the fishes in this area do exceed levels that are considered safe, with the result that fish advisories are posted throughout the Hackensack–Passaic–Newark Bay system, warning people not to consume fishes or crabs from the waters. While there are other estuaries in the country that are highly contaminated with toxic substances, this one was designated by EPA as the worst in the nation.

Effects of Toxic Chemicals

Aquatic animals take pollutants into their bodies through the skin, gills, and digestive tract, and they excrete them in their waste or expel them through the gills. When uptake is greater than removal, the net result is increased levels of the chemical in the body. Chemicals that have low solubility in water and bind to sediments tend to accumulate to greater concentrations in organisms, especially in their fatty tissues. Chlorinated hydrocarbon pesticides, PCBs, and methylmercury are among those toxic substances that are not readily metabolized or excreted.

Contaminants are transferred through food webs from prey to predator (*trophic transfer*), and some chemicals tend to become more concentrated during this process, a phenomenon called *biomagnification.* An animal in a polluted area accumulates toxic chemicals from each item of contaminated food that it eats, so the concentrations of the chemicals are higher in consumers than in their food and are highest in the top carnivores such as large fishes, fish-eating birds, marine mammals, and humans, particularly older individuals. Because of biomagnification, methylmercury levels can be quite high in large fishes like swordfish and tuna, even though they live in the open ocean far from any sources of mercury. It is recommended that people, particularly pregnant women and young children, not eat a lot of these fishes. Chlorinated pesticides, PCBs, and dioxin also undergo biomagnification, but metals other than methylmercury do not seem to do so.

The sex of a fish may affect how much of a contaminant is accumulated. Egg yolk is a fat-rich substance that can store large quantities of organic contaminants, and some females sequester large amounts of these fat-soluble chemicals in their eggs as a way of removing them from their system. This maternal transfer of contaminants is found in egg-laying birds and reptiles as well as in fishes. While this is a good survival strategy for the females, it certainly does not benefit their offspring to start out life suffused with toxic chemicals.

The effects on individuals can eventually cause changes in populations, resulting in a reduced population growth rate, lower population size, reduced birth rates, and higher death rates, resulting in a population dominated by younger, smaller individuals with reduced genetic variability. Reduced genetic variability happens when the more susceptible individuals disappear from the population and more pollution-tolerant ones become predominant, as has been seen with insecticide-resistant insects.

Whether in plant or animal tissue, toxic effects appear first at the biochemical level, then at higher levels of organization in cells, and later are manifested in the activity of the organism, the species' population, and eventually in the ecological community as a whole. Initial biochemical changes can be altered enzymes, changes in DNA and RNA, and synthesis of particular proteins to detoxify the chemical. At the cellular level, chromosome damage, cell death, abnormal structures, or cancer can occur. Some chemicals like the dioxins and PCBs have effects on the immune system and can increase susceptibility to infectious diseases. At the level of the organism, changes in physiology, development, growth, behavior, or reproductive capacity may occur; and at high concentrations the animal or plant can die.

Fortunately, we have seen in many locales that when the input of pollutants has decreased, or after toxic waste sites have been cleaned up, the incidence of diseases and other problems has been reduced. Tolerance to the contaminants may be lost as well. In a marsh in the Hudson River near a former battery plant that released cadmium for decades, Jeffrey Levinton and his colleagues from Stony Brook University showed that the worms in the sediments had become very tolerant to cadmium. Once the pollution was cleaned up by the Environmental Protection Agency, the scientists revisited the site and found that the worms gradually had lost their tolerance, over relatively few generations.

Endocrine Disruption

There is particular concern about certain chemicals that, even at very low concentrations, can affect reproduction and can alter the development and functioning of the endocrine system. These chemicals are called *endocrine disruptors,* a term coined by Theo Colborn, who focused attention on the issue. Known endocrine disruptors include DDT and other chlorinated hydrocarbons used in agriculture certain PCBs and dioxins, and some metals, plastics, detergents, and flame retardants used in industry. These chemicals have different mechanisms of action, depending on the life stage at which the animal is exposed, and they may have effects that are not seen for many years after exposure. The most commonly studied chemicals are those affecting reproduction or growth, and they may mimic natural hormones or inhibit them, so that reproduction may be disrupted, offspring may have intersex traits, and metamorphosis may be delayed, accelerated, or prevented.

The first documented examples of endocrine disruption in the estuarine environment were in dog whelks and mud snails that were affected by the use of tributyltin (TBT). This chemical was used in antifouling paints applied to boats to prevent algae and barnacles from attaching to the hull.

Previously, copper had been the main toxic ingredient in these paints, but in the 1960s and 1970s the organic tin compound TBT was found to be more effective and longer lasting. These tin-based chemicals, even at extremely low levels, caused female snails to develop male sexual organs and to become sterile. Geoff Bryan of the Plymouth Marine Biological Association and his colleagues demonstrated that this sterility was linked to TBT and was responsible for major decreases in the populations of snails around the coast of England. Extensive use of these chemicals also caused oyster shells to develop abnormally and eventually wiped out the oyster industry in parts of France.

TBT use is now prohibited for use in marine paints in most countries, and populations are recovering. Most boats are again being painted with copper-based paints that are far from benign but are much less toxic than TBT, and extensive research efforts are underway to find non-toxic methods to prevent fouling. One popular formulation being used is adding a substance called *irgarol* to copper-based paints to boost their effectiveness. Though not an endocrine disruptor, irgarol is highly toxic to plants, including phytoplankton, seaweeds, and sea grasses. It is fairly stable in water and sediment and has become a widespread contaminant in the vicinity of marinas and poses a continual risk to the environment.

Some other pesticides and industrial chemicals in very low concentrations also may affect hormone functions, and it is suspected that decreases in human sperm counts and sperm abnormalities may be a result of these chemicals. Alligators from Lake Apopka in Florida that were exposed to pesticides were found by Lou Guillette and his colleagues from the University of Florida to have reduced penis size and sperm abnormalities. Berkeley biologist Tyrone Hayes has shown that intersex frogs appear in areas where the herbicide atrazine is used. Steven Bortone, then at the University of West Florida, found that mosquito fish living in areas near paper mills have intersex conditions in which females grow an extended anal fin, called a gonopodium, typically seen in males and used to transfer sperm to females. The eggshell thinning noted in birds exposed to DDT was probably also an example of endocrine disruption, although that term had not yet been coined when the problem occurred. There is considerable concern that elevated levels of breast cancer in humans may be associated with prior exposure to some endocrine disrupting substances, but despite considerable study, no "smoking gun" has been found to date.

Pharmaceuticals and Other Emerging Contaminants

Waters near urban areas contain pharmaceuticals that are released through the sewage system, such as metabolized birth control pills containing estrogens, which can have endocrine effects on fishes and other animals. These chemicals are excreted by people and go through sewage treatment plants without getting broken down. Currently, there is considerable interest in investigating emerging contaminants, which include pharmaceuticals and personal care products that end up in aquatic ecosystems, and numerous studies have been finding endocrine effects in aquatic organisms in waters containing synthetic estrogens. It would not be at all surprising if the pharmaceutical pollution produces greater endocrine effects than the "usual suspect" pollutant chemicals because the biology of humans is very similar to that of fishes in this regard.

Tranquilizers, antidepressants, and other neuro-active pharmaceuticals may also affect the behavior of fishes and wildlife. Recent research on the effects of the selective serotonin re-uptake inhibitor (SSRI) fluoxetine (Prozac) on fishes has found that it alters the amount of the neurotransmitter serotonin just as it does in humans, causing the fishes to have reduced swimming and feeding behavior. It also has some toxic effects on algae. Commonly used cholesterol-lowering drugs (statins) are only about 20 percent metabolized in the body; the rest is excreted and finds its way into aquatic systems, where the effects are largely unknown. Also commonly detected are caffeine, nicotine, acetaminophen, ibuprofen, and many other familiar substances—a veritable drug cocktail. While they are not likely to be toxic in the traditional sense, they are certainly biologically active and likely to have effects on aquatic animals.

In addition to pharmaceuticals, personal care products such as cosmetics, lotions, sun blocks, and insect repellants (DEET) are not broken down in sewage treatment plants; and when they enter aquatic systems the chemicals contained by these products can have effects on aquatic plants and animals. Triclosan, for example, is an antibacterial used in personal care and household products, and it is now one of the most commonly found chemicals in waste water in the United States. It is a potent endocrine disruptor with effects on the thyroid gland, and it is toxic to aquatic plants. Other antibacterial compounds are released from sewage treatment plants, and wherever they have been looked for, they have been found. Antibiotics such as erythromycin and tetracycline can stimulate the evolution of (or selection for) antibiotic-resistant bacteria that can cause illness in wildlife and humans.

Other types of emerging contaminants are flame retardants that are used in a variety of consumer products including clothing, carpets, and toys. They have been found at very high levels in aquatic systems and appear to be ubiquitous in landfills and in the environment. Attention to this class of contaminants is only recent, since no one had bothered to monitor them before. These are chemicals called polybrominated diphenyl ethers (PBDEs), and their chemical structure is reminiscent of PCBs and dioxins, but with bromine attached instead of chlorine. Not surprisingly, they are also persistent, toxic, and bioaccumulative. They also have many neurological, endocrine, and developmental effects similar to PCBs and dioxins and are extremely potent thyroid hormone disruptors.

Nanoparticles are another emerging issue of concern for both the environment and human health. They are microscopic particles that are larger than molecules and have at least one dimension less than one hundred nanometers (a nanometer equals one billionth of a meter or one millionth of a millimeter). Nanoparticles can be made of different materials; some are combustion-derived like diesel soot, and some are manufactured. Because of their size, they have unusual properties which make them potentially useful for drug delivery, gene therapy, and other biomedical uses, as well as for applications in the optical, cosmetic, material science, and electronics fields. Nanoparticles pose possible dangers because they are very reactive and can pass easily through cell membranes, and their interactions with the body are poorly understood. They can cause inflammation in the lungs, and because of their tiny size they are very mobile and able to move from their original site (the lungs, from being inhaled) to other parts of the body. In the aquatic environment, nanoparticles tend to agglomerate, which means they will settle into sediments and be taken up by organisms. They accumulate in estuarine organisms, but their effects are largely unknown even though they have become ubiquitous. A limited number of studies have been performed, and these have shown toxic effects, but the effects are highly specific to the chemical nature of the nano-material and the species studied. Because of these limitations, scientists and regulators have been reluctant to propose broad or sweeping guidelines limiting their use.

The release of old toxic pollutants has been reduced and the amount of contamination by these chemicals has generally decreased as a result of legislation like the Clean Water Act of the 1970s. Estuarine sediments near the surface are less contaminated with these chemicals than are the deeper layers of sediments, where the chemicals were deposited decades ago. However, new chemicals are constantly being made and released into the environment, and much of what is released ends up washing into estuaries and marshes. While we do not know which new chemicals will emerge as problems in the future, we can be sure that some of them will cause problems, perhaps new kinds of problems that we haven't seen

The Precautionary Principle

Because the standards for scientific demonstration of cause and effect are very high, some people advocate that action should be taken, even in the absence of clear proof, when a chemical or activity is thought to pose a risk to the environment or to human health. For example, smoking was strongly suspected of causing lung cancer long before the link was demonstrated conclusively. By then, many smokers had died of lung cancer, but other people had already quit smoking because of the not-yet-conclusive evidence that smoking was linked to lung cancer. These people were exercising precaution despite some scientific uncertainty.

The precautionary principle is that when evidence gives us reason to believe that an activity, technology, or substance may be harmful, we should act to prevent harm rather than waiting for scientific certainty, by which time the natural world may suffer irreversible damage. The 1998 *Wingspread Statement on the Precautionary Principle* summarizes the principle this way: "When an activity raises threats of harm to human health or the environment, precautionary measures should be taken even if some cause and effect relationships are not fully established scientifically" (see http://www.gdrc.org/u-gov/precaution-3.html).

before. Toxic substances interact with each other, and in the natural environment there is probably no place contaminated with only a single chemical. It is important to know how they interact with each other and with aspects of the changing environment.

Garbage

Her river banks and sea shores
Have a beauty all can share
Provided there's at least one boot,
Three treadless tires,
Some oil drums
An old felt hat
And a broken bedstead there.
    —Michael Flanders and Donald Swann, *Bedstead Men*, 1963

Marshes have been smothered in trash by many coastal towns that used them as waste dumps. Bottles, cans, and plastic cups are dumped into the water by careless boaters, and they wash up into the marshes. Discarded fishing line, formerly made of degradable material and now made of non-degradable plastic, washes into marshes and entangles shorebirds.

Dumps were originally open places where waste was burned and vermin were abundant. The technology of modern landfill operations did not exist, no environmental controls were in place, and no one monitored the composition or toxicity of the material being dumped. Everything was dumped together with household trash—including oil and lead-based paints, waste with metals and oil-based solvents, industrial-strength cleaning products, other toxic liquids, tires, and construction debris. It wasn't until 1976 that the federal Resource Conservation and Recovery Act (RCRA) was passed by Congress, marking the beginning of damage control. Many landfills were eventually closed, but under the layers of dirt remains the legacy of decades of dumping toxic material.

Health considerations prompted the development of "sanitary landfills" in which the daily accumulation of garbage was covered with a layer of soil. In theory, biodegradable materials should be broken down in a landfill, but because material deep under the ground is in anoxic conditions and may not be damp enough for bacteria to function well, this breakdown is extremely slow. Readable newspapers over thirty years old have been excavated from landfills. RCRA also mandated that hazardous and toxic materials could not be mixed in with regular household trash, but must be disposed of in special landfills with thick liners to prevent leachate from oozing out into the groundwater.

Landfills are not devoid of life, however. They have a biota of their own, dominated by rats, mice, and herring gulls. Hawks and owls may visit to hunt the rodents, and raccoons and opossums may be found scavenging.

Leaching is an environmental problem caused by landfills. Rainwater percolating through the landfill picks up chemicals and generates a noxious liquid soup or leachate that contains decomposing organic matter along with a sprinkling of heavy metals, paints, pesticides, cleaning fluids, dissolved newspaper ink, and so forth. This chemical soup can percolate down to the groundwater, and if the landfill is located in a salt marsh, it can seep into the surrounding estuary.

The Fresh Kills Landfill on Staten Island has the dubious honor of being the largest landfill on earth. It is an artificial mountain covering three thousand acres, rising over 150 feet into the air, and containing 2.9 billion cubic feet of garbage. It was once a thriving tidal marsh with abundant life, but now it is inhabited only by gulls, rats, and feral dogs and cats. It was originally planned in 1948 to be filled with municipal garbage and then capped with topsoil and developed, but the increasing volume of garbage being generated by New York City made it necessary to keep the landfill open through several more decades, until it was finally closed in 1996. It is now being revegetated.

The Future

Many landfills and garbage dumps have been closed in the past decade. They have been revegetated so that parks, golf courses, and other facilities have been built on top of them, turning blighted areas into attractive landscapes—but they cannot become wetlands again.

Recycling and source reduction are making some dents in the amount of waste material being generated, but the issue of what to do with municipal solid waste is still a problem in this country. The amount of new pollution coming into marshes has greatly decreased as a result of environmental legislation, starting in the 1970s, which put limits on the amounts of pollution that could be discharged from pipes (point sources). Despite this progress, the non-point source runoff from agriculture, lawns, construction sites, and city streets remains a major issue that is a long way from being solved. In addition, the legacy of persistent contaminants in sediments will remain for many more decades as these chemicals continue to be cycled and recycled through food webs.

Low impact development (LID) principles are being recommended by the EPA to reduce pollution caused by storm water runoff. Some of the recommended techniques include green roofs and rooftop gardens that replace impermeable surfaces with soil and plants that capture water. These surfaces can absorb up to 75 percent of the water that falls on them, reducing the runoff speed and volume. Another technology is pervious pavement, which allows rain to be absorbed in the spaces between paving tiles and thereby replenishes groundwater instead of forcing the rain to become runoff. Vegetated buffer areas and highway shoulders capture suspended sediments and runoff and promote infiltration into the soil. These types of techniques will have economic as well as environmental benefits to adjacent bodies of water.

The dispersed sprawl typical of the suburban growth that began in the 1950s made walking between destinations impractical. There was little or no public transportation, and so people had to drive everywhere. New approaches called *smart growth* encourage higher-density development and the creation of traditional towns and neighborhood centers, similar to the way communities were built before cars became the dominant mode of transportation. This type of development includes more undeveloped open space and reduces the amount of paved surfaces in the watershed, resulting in less air and water pollution. People are much more efficiently served and have much less per capita impact on the environment when they are in high-density areas, and the challenge is to design high-density locales that are attractive. Although this movement is in its infancy, positive outcomes are already being observed.

6 Biological Alterations
Non-indigenous Species

We are waging a vigorous battle against invasive species, but I fear we are losing the war. The scope of invasions across the country is daunting.

—U.S. Representative Vernon J. Ehlers, at a House Science Environment, Technology, and Standards Subcommittee hearing on *Combating the Invaders: Research on Non-Native Species,* 2001

People have been traveling around the globe for centuries, and they have always brought home souvenirs. The first greenhouses and "orangeries" were built to house plants during the winter that were brought to Europe by explorers returning from trips to the New World. On a larger scale, plants and animals frequently get transplanted unintentionally or as stowaways, and they don't always settle easily into their new surroundings; sometimes they cause costly ecological and economic problems.

When non-native species arrive in a new location, most of them either are harmless or do not survive the changed conditions and the new threats they encounter. But some of the new immigrants do flourish, and the small percentage that thrive and reproduce may end up becoming invasive by outcompeting, eating, or parasitizing native species. If a non-indigenous species displaces or competes with a native species, the result is reduced diversity, especially of species that are dependent on the displaced native species. For example, if a particular plant that is habitat or food for certain animals is replaced by a different plant, the animals may be unable to survive. In this way habitat, nutrient dynamics, and productivity are altered.

Early ocean-going ships were made of wood, and their hulls became covered with a large variety of attached organisms such as barnacles and algae, native to foreign waters, which were then transported to other ports around the world. Ships formerly took on ballast in their home port in the form of rocks or sand in order to provide stability at sea, and terrestrial organisms contained in the ballast were dumped along with the rocks or sand to lighten the ship so it could enter a shallow harbor in a foreign port.

Nowadays, antifouling paints are used to prevent the attachment of organisms to a ship's hull, but some organisms still hitchhike around the world in the nooks and crannies of a ship. Water is now used as ballast, and millions of gallons of water, along with the small organisms living in it, are taken up into the ship at one port and released in another. Millions of planktonic organisms, including larvae, can be contained in the ballast water; and when the water is taken up, some sediments are sucked into the ballast tanks as well. In this way whole benthic communities are transplanted.

A type of invader that has a major impact at the new site is called an "ecological engineer." These are species that modify their habitat, for example, by changing the substrate, changing light penetration, making burrows, or elevating the marsh surface. Changing the substrate makes the habitat preferable for a whole new suite of species, and reducing light penetration harms plants that need to photosynthesize. When the marsh surface becomes more elevated, the amount of time during the tidal cycle that it is under water will be reduced, and this can affect the animals on the marsh. An organism that makes lots of burrows at the edge of a marsh can contribute to wearing away and loss of marsh area. These are just a few examples of major effects that can be caused by ecological engineers.

Invasive species can cause major economic problems. The invasion of zebra mussels into the Great Lakes in the late 1980s had an economic impact because they clogged up intake pipes for the water systems in the Great Lakes. It is estimated that aquatic and terrestrial invasive species cost the world's economy hundreds of billions of dollars annually; the cost for the United States alone is estimated at $128 billion each year. Much of this cost is due to the impact of invasive species on fisheries, boating, and coastal recreation as well as to the expense of controlling or attempting to eradicate the invaders.

In the fresh and salt waters of the United States, it is estimated that there are over 500 species of introduced organisms, including over 140 in the Great Lakes, over 200 in Chesapeake Bay, and over 240 in San Francisco Bay. By the time this book is published these numbers will certainly be higher. In San Francisco Bay alone, a new species is estimated to arrive every fourteen weeks. It is the most invaded aquatic region on Earth, and more than half of the area's fishes and most of its bottom-dwelling organisms are not native to the bay. Hawaii is another region with high levels of invasion, with 73 marine invasive species, 42 percent of which are considered harmful.

There is usually a lag period of several years between the arrival and establishment of an exotic species and its rapid population growth. Scientists think that stressed or disturbed environments are more susceptible to invasion, so that natural communities that have been changed by human impact may be more vulnerable to invasive species. When native species are reduced or impaired, it is easier for new species to succeed, and the relative scarcity of certain functional groups (filter feeders, for example) will make invasions by other species of that group easier. If there are unused resources, such as nutrients, an environment will be more susceptible to invasion by species that will use those resources. A community with filled niches and greater diversity should be more resistant to invaders, but we cannot predict when or where a species will become a problem in the future, a phenomenon that Williams College invasive species ecologist James Carlton has called "ecological roulette."

Why does a species arrive at a particular time? Why not last year or ten years ago? Sometimes the explanation is a change in the donor region, such as an increase in population, or a change in the recipient region, such as diminished water quality due to a new source of pollution. In addition, the possibility of invasion is increased by more and faster transport between regions that are climatically similar and by the use of bigger ships that transport more ballast water. Also, the number of individuals introduced at one time and the frequency with which they arrive, called propagule pressure, can play an important role. Sometimes sheer numbers can make the difference between success and failure of an introduced species, in which case persistence can pay off.

Many invaders become larger in size in their new location than they were in their native range, perhaps due to the presence of fewer predators at the new location. This is referred to as the "enemy release hypothesis." Parasites are often lost during the transition to a new location, and this can occur in a number of ways. For example, if a species arrives as planktonic larvae, it will not have brought along the parasites that are present in the adult animal. Parasites often have complicated life cycles that require more than one host, and if all the required hosts are not present in the new location, those parasites cannot survive. Invasive species can have severe impacts on salt marsh environments.

Invasive Species: Major Trouble-Makers

The Common Reed, *Phragmites*

The Web site of Shore Precision Engineering, a firm specializing in Phragmites control, offers this information:

The aggressive growth of phragmites is one of the major causes of the depletion of our wetlands. This billowing plant, if left to grow, will continue to smother the growth of beneficial grasses and overtake our pristine waterfront. Phragmites is a type of plant that can devastate a wetland environment. It has the ability to overpower the local wetland, reducing the diversity amongst plants. Phragmites does not provide adequate shelter for the common resident wildlife. The root system can alter a wetland environment by trapping sediments, which can lead to a drying out effect.

East Coast brackish marshes have been invaded by a new European strain of the common reed, *Phragmites australis* (see fig. 2.9 in chapter 2), which has turned out to be a problem. This species has been in North America for thousands of years, but until recent decades it remained a minor part of the high-marsh and freshwater marsh communities until the arrival of the new strain. This particular strain was probably brought from Europe as a stowaway in the dry ballast in the hold of a ship during the nineteenth century, and it produces more shoots and grows faster than the native variety, outcompeting and reducing the diversity of native marsh plants. It expands rapidly using rhizomes which can grow more than ten meters in a single growing season, and it is more tolerant of salt and low oxygen than the native variety. It also spreads easily in areas where salinity is low and tidal flow is restricted, and it is more dense and taller than native plants, crowding them and blocking their exposure to the sun. It produces dense litter layers that sit on the marsh surface and inhibit germination and growth of other species and thrives on high levels of nitrogen found in estuaries receiving sewage plant effluent or farm runoff, giving it yet another advantage over native plants.

A decade ago, when there were few ecological studies to demonstrate how *Phragmites* reduces wetland value, efforts were made to eradicate the plant. Managers relied on negative feelings (see quote above) rather than scientific evidence to declare that the plant was undesirable, and they established removal policies costing millions of dollars. In many areas where it was removed, the reed has re-invaded, and new studies have found that its effects on the marsh are not all negative.

While it does reduce plant diversity, many animals do not seem to be affected by its takeover of the marsh. On the negative side, it has reduced value as a nursery habitat for estuarine animals like killifish, so we find that larval and juvenile killifish are much less abundant in *Phragmites* because it smoothes out the marsh surface, removing the small puddles and depressions that the larvae and juveniles live in at low tide. Tish Robertson, working in the Weis Laboratory, found that the epifauna (small animals that live on the stems) on *Phragmites* are fewer in number and less diverse than those that live on *Spartina*. Differences in stem structure were thought to be in part responsible for *Spartina* providing a better home for these animals. On the positive side, other invertebrates such as fiddler crabs, ribbed mussels, grass shrimp, and benthic infauna thrive regardless of which species of marsh plant is dominant. Birds are mixed—some prefer *Spartina,* but some prefer *Phragmites*—and there are differences in the insect community associated with *Spartina,* compared to *Phragmites.* The detritus produced by decaying leaves of the reed provides nutrition comparable to that of cordgrass, and it enters estuarine food webs the same way cordgrass detritus does. The reed also provides good protective habitat, comparable to cordgrass. Most nekton use both types of marshes equally, and plenty of food is available for them in either setting.

Another way that the common reed changes the marsh is by increasing the rate at which sediment is trapped and fills in creeks and tidal channels, increasing the elevation of the marsh. The overall smoothing and filling of the marsh surface reduces its variability (the surface has been likened to that of a pool table) and reduces habitat available for animals. Ditches and creeks can become filled, reducing the tidal exchange with the high marsh and limiting access during the tidal cycle for aquatic organisms to spend up on the marsh surface. In some areas, the marsh may eventually become so elevated that it will be higher than the upper tide level and will dry out, ceasing to be a marsh. Ironically, given the forecasted rate of sea-level rise, it may be that only the *Phragmites* marshes will be able to keep pace and survive.

The reed is able to sequester pollutants more effectively than native cordgrass. It absorbs more nitrogen, which reduces the effect of the nitrogen on the rest of the marsh-estuary community. It retains more metal pollutants below ground in its roots, while *Spartina* puts more into its leaves and excretes them back into the water. Keeping the contaminants below ground, as *Phragmites* does, is beneficial to the ecosystem since the contaminants are not available to be taken up by other species, while contaminants that are excreted back into the water can then be taken up by other species. *Phragmites* also appears to be more tolerant of contaminants than other marsh grass species. Portuguese investigators (Valega et al. 2008) examined salt marshes in the Rio Aveiro, an area that was subjected to decades of mercury pollution from industrial sources. Over time, as mercury levels in the sediments increased, there was a decrease in plant diversity and increasing dominance by *Phragmites,* which became the dominant species in the more contaminated sites. After the pollution

Invasive Species Research in Weis Lab on *Phragmites*

We have investigated the role that the vilified common reed can play in marshes like the Hackensack Meadowlands where it is dominant. We studied animal populations at a site where *Phragmites* (common reed) and *Spartina* (cordgrass) were growing on opposite sides of a small creek. We also set up aquaria in our laboratory with either *Phragmites* or *Spartina* to see how marsh animals behaved toward the two plant species. We found that many marsh organisms, including fiddler crabs, grass shrimp, and benthic infauna, "don't care" which plant is on the marsh; but juvenile and adult mummichogs as well as small animals (epifauna) that live on the stems are more abundant on *Spartina*.

The *Phragmites* protected prey from their predators as well as *Spartina*, and when we investigated the nutritional value of detritus from the reed compared to that from the cordgrass, we found that they were equivalent as food for fiddler crabs and grass shrimp. Actually, for the grass shrimp, diets of detritus alone from whichever source were not adequate for survival longer than three weeks. These animals seem to also need some animal protein. We studied white perch (*Morone americana*) from the Meadowlands and found that their diet, consisting mostly of amphipods, was based on a food web with common reed at its base. So, clearly, this plant is not ecologically useless, though it appears to be inferior to cordgrass in a number of ways.

We also looked at how the common reed and cordgrass take up and deal with contaminants, specifically metals, in both field and laboratory experiments. While both species of marsh plants take up comparable amounts of metals from the sediments in which they grow, they differ in how they store and move the metals around, as Lisamarie Windham found. The cordgrass moves a greater amount of the metals to its leaves, from which it excretes them along with salt. This returns the metals back to the environment, where they can be taken up into other species and have negative effects. The reed stores more of the metals below ground in its roots, which is better for the ecosystem since they are less available to other species. When the plants die and decay, the litter from both plants gradually takes up metals from the surrounding environment and becomes highly and comparably contaminated. So while living *Phragmites* is better for the ecosystem by sequestering metals below ground, once the plants have decayed and turned into detritus, both species are equivalent.

ceased in the 1990s and sediment mercury levels began to decrease, the marsh started to show a gradual recovery and an increase in species richness of the marsh grasses.

Because of the controversy in the United States over this species, a conference entitled *Phragmites australis:* A Sheep in Wolf's Clothing? organized by Michael Weinstein of the New Jersey Sea Grant Program, was held in 2002 in New Jersey to focus on and review all the aspects of the invasion and effects of this plant. The plant's ecology was examined with regard to how it affects habitat quality in marshes. The conclusion was that it is neither a villain nor a hero. Given the scientific findings about this plant, managers should reconsider their automatic and expensive extermination programs and replace them with well-thought-out goals based on site-specific findings.

Cordgrass: *Spartina alterniflora*

In 2003, the U.S. Fish and Wildlife Service issued the *Draft Environmental Impact Report for the San Francisco Estuary,* which stated:

> In particular, the non-native cord grass species Atlantic smooth cord grass (*S. alterniflora*) and its hybrids, formed when this species crosses with native Pacific cord grass (*S. foliosa*), are now threatening the ecological balance of the Estuary. In the Estuary, Atlantic smooth cord grass is likely to choke tidal creeks, dominate newly restored tidal marshes, impair thousands of acres of existing shorebird habitat, and eventually cause extinction of the native Pacific cord grass.

Mudflats, rather than salt marshes, are considered the most biologically productive of the West Coast estuarine habitats because they are teeming with invertebrates of all kinds. Marine worms, crustaceans, and mollusks support the hundreds of thousands of shorebirds that inhabit the estuary. When Eastern cordgrass dominates marshes above the mudflats, it displaces native cordgrass and other native plants, creating a single ecological zone that eliminates the many transitional areas native species need. It reduces the species richness of benthic organisms and modifies benthic communities.

It is ironic that while *Spartina alterniflora* (cordgrass, see fig. 2.1 in chapter 2) is valued in East Coast marshes, in West Coast salt marshes it is considered a noxious, invasive species because it converts valued mudflat areas into marsh; it is a "weed" that is smothering San Francisco Bay's mudflats. It has displaced native flora, changed sedimentation, decreased invertebrate and algal populations, and eliminated foraging sites used by marsh birds and shorebirds. It is suspected that *Spartina* was introduced into Willapa Bay in the late 1800s or early 1900s as packing material for oyster shipments from the East Coast. From the middle of the twentieth century the plant spread rapidly throughout Willapa Bay. In the 1970s, the Army Corps of Engineers deliberately introduced it to stabilize flood-control levees on Alameda Island in San Francisco Bay because it grows much faster than the native cordgrass (*S. foliosa*). Unfortunately, *S. alterniflora* both outcompetes and hybridizes with *S. foliosa,* and the hybrid is particularly invasive, choking off small creeks in the marshes that are used by the endangered California clapper rails and covering mudflats that provide food for the rails and other shorebirds. By 2005, about 10 percent of the acres of tidal flats in the San Francisco Bay estuary had been invaded by the hybrid. In Washington State, it was accidentally introduced about one hundred years ago, but for some unknown reason it has not hybridized there.

Loss of mudflat habitat harms marine species such as the juvenile chum salmon, Dungeness crab, and English sole that rely on these habitats as food sources; about one quarter of the total foraging habitat of the Dungeness crabs has been lost because the rigid structure of the grass shoots seems to reduce the ability of the crabs to access their prey. The sediments around the *Spartina* hybrid have also reduced communities of invertebrates, and commercial oyster production has been threatened because culture beds are being invaded. At the Willapa National Wildlife Refuge in Washington, *Spartina* has displaced habitat for wintering and breeding migratory aquatic birds.

Costly efforts to spray and excavate are underway in San Francisco Bay and Puget Sound on the West Coast to remove and destroy the species that is so valued in East Coast marshes. A full-scale assault has been launched, with workers spraying many acres with the herbicide Habitat®. This herbicide kills the grass with minimal environmental effects on animals because it works by selectively interfering with plant biochemistry. Reading about the *S. alterniflora* eradication efforts in California, a staffer from the National Oceanic and Atmospheric Administration's Restoration Center on the East Coast mused, "We call it 'productive vegetation,' they call it an invasive weed." And on the East Coast, we plant *Spartina alterniflora* while we eradicate *Phragmites,* while in Europe they value *Phragmites* and are concerned about it dying back.

Furthermore, in the summer of 2007, a paper was published by researchers in China (He et al. 2007) about how the invasive *Spartina alterniflora* was threatening their valuable *Phragmites australis* marshes. It is highly invasive on the Chinese coast and is causing increasing concern due to its rapid expansion and damage to native ecosystems. Both tall and dwarf forms of the species are in China, and the tall form with its strongly invasive ability has expanded widely and is replacing native *Phragmites* in some sites. It does make you wonder if a certain amount of xenophobia is involved in our responses to non-indigenous species.

Dead Man's Fingers: *Codium*

Dead man's fingers (*Codium fragile* spp. *tomentosoides*) is a spongy, fuzzy, branched seaweed, native to Japan, that attaches to rock surfaces and mollusk shells. It arrived in Long Island waters in the 1950s coincident with the launching of Sputnik, so it was called Sputnik weed. In the early 1960s it was introduced accidentally to southern Massachusetts on shells of oysters transplanted from Long Island Sound. It has since invaded northwestern Europe, the Mediterranean, and New Zealand, living in intertidal pools and in the subtidal zone in both sheltered and exposed locations. It can grow quickly and it thrives with relatively little light. Because it can reproduce by regenerating from small pieces, known as fragmentation, it can spread easily. *Codium* is eaten by sea urchins, but they much prefer kelp and red algae, with the result that it grows quite successfully.

Green Algae: *Caulerpa*

A strain of *Caulerpa taxifolia* that had been developed for use as an aquarium plant was inadvertently released into the Mediterranean Sea from the Monaco Aquarium in the 1980s. It initially occupied only a few square feet, but it was not removed and subsequently grew so vigorously that it literally took over the Mediterranean. Like *Codium,* it can regenerate from fragments, so physical removal can make the problem worse. In areas where it grows, hardly any fishes and no other algae or invertebrates are found, and to make matters worse it contains toxic chemicals that keep grazing animals from eating it and inhibit the growth of sea grasses and other plants. It grows unchecked and is considered one of the most harmful marine invasive species.

Its presence was discovered in June 2000 in California in an eelgrass bed at Agua Hedionda Lagoon. Because of prior knowledge about its spread in the Mediterranean Sea, it had already been placed on the U.S. Federal Noxious Weed list. Alarm about its potential damage prompted rapid action and cooperation among governmental agencies, private groups, and non-governmental organizations. The San Diego Regional Water Quality Control Board deemed this invasion tantamount to an oil spill and provided emergency funding and mobilized crews of divers. California passed legislation prohibiting the possession and sale of *Caulerpa,* and it was successfully eradicated. California's integrated rapid response and the provision of financial resources resulted in effective containment, treatment, and eradication of the alga for the time being. But despite the concerns of ecologists and conservationists, amazingly, it is still possible to purchase *Caulerpa* from aquarium supply stores and through the Internet, so new releases may be inevitable. A similar response will undoubtedly be necessary in the future to eradicate other invasive species before they spread and become a big problem.

"Where can i get some *caulerpa*? It's illegal in California, cause people like to flush it down their toilets and then it runs into the ocean, and it grows like crazy. so does anyone know where i can get some of this? i tried an lfs store but they wouldn't sell it to me cause its illegal. any websites?" (direct quote of a posting on the Internet, *FishGeeks forum,* 2006).

Red Algae: *Eucheuma*

Eucheuma is an alga that is cultured throughout the Pacific. It is a major source of agar and carrageenan, which are used mainly as food additives for gelling and stabilizing, and small amounts are used by the pharmaceutical and cosmetic industries. The red alga was imported by the late Maxwell Doty's research lab on Kaneohe Bay, Hawaii, from the Philippines in the 1970s; and his research helped the Philippines and other island nations establish multimillion-dollar industries based on the algae (see http://128.171.57.100/libdept/archives/univarch/doty/index.htm). The methods developed made *Eucheuma* the world's most widely farmed seaweed, cultivated in twenty-three countries. However, open-cage experiments released the species into Hawaiian coastal waters, where it smothers and kills coral, creating underwater devastation. It has spread and smothered at least half the reefs in Kaneohe Bay on Oahu's east coast and has begun to spread to waters beyond.

An effective tool in combating invasive algae in Hawaii is the Super Sucker, an underwater vacuum cleaner that scoops up about eight hundred pounds of the invasive algae each hour. It sucks the algae off the reef and places it on a barge above water so that non-invasive marine life can be sorted out and returned to the water. The alien algae is packed into sacks and delivered to taro farmers for use as fertilizer. Skeptical coral expert Thomas Goreau thinks that this will give only temporary results unless the nutrient excess that promotes the rapid algal growth is removed. In a letter to *Science Magazine* Goreau wrote, "No amount of sucking them off will work when they grow right back because they are overfertilized. It is the suckers paying for this well-intentioned, but ultimately futile, effort who will be hosed unless the underlying causes of eutrophication are removed" (2008, 157).

A long-term solution may depend on increasing the population of sea urchins that eat the invasive algae. The sea urchin population around Hawaii has declined because of excessive harvesting for their gonads, prized by sushi eaters. Researchers are learning how to propagate them so that they can place baby urchins on newly vacuumed reefs to graze on little bits of algae.

Common Periwinkle Snail: *Littorina littorea*

The common periwinkle (see fig. 3.14 in chapter 3) was introduced from Europe to Nova Scotia around 1840 as a food, and it spread southward to Virginia, feeding on marsh grasses and on the algae that covered rocks at the shoreline. The snail's shell is usually dark with transverse black stripes on its tentacles, and it is so abundant that most people think of it as a normal part of the coastal habitat. It can be found on rocky shores in the Northeast as well as in marshes in intertidal and subtidal areas, where it has become so abundant that its voracious grazing has destroyed much of the intertidal algal vegetation. It has caused a gradual transformation of the New England coast from rocks with abundant seaweed cover to the bare rocks that most people think of as natural. The state of New Hampshire actually passed a law protecting this edible species from out-of-state poaching. In salt marshes, the snails are eaten by diamondback terrapins and by blue crabs.

The related periwinkle, *Littorina saxatilis,* is a more recent (1990s) invader in San Francisco Bay and probably arrived with bait worms for the sport-fishing industry. There have not been reports to date about their damaging the ecology of the bay or causing wholesale changes.

Asian Clam: *Potamocorbula amurensis*

In the late 1980s, the Asian clam became established in San Francisco Bay. It has replaced the native clam, *Macoma balthica,* as the dominant benthic macroinvertebrate in the area. It is a filter feeder, and its rapid spread has resulted in less phytoplankton in the bay, which means less food for zooplankton, which means less food for fishes. The invader is eaten by diving ducks and lives closer to the surface of the mud than *Macoma,* increasing its availability to the ducks. This clam has altered nutrient cycling in the bay and caused major ecosystem changes.

A related clam on the East Coast is *Corbicula fluminea,* which arrived in the late 1970s and is abundant in the Potomac River. When it was first discovered in the river, scientists were worried that it would cause major problems, like the zebra mussel did in the Great Lakes (attaching to surfaces, blocking intake pipes for water supply systems, etc.), but it does not attach to hard surfaces since it lacks byssus threads. This clam instead settled on sandy bottom sediments, and after it arrived there were increases in submerged aquatic vegetation and fish populations. The clam also serves as food for birds and muskrats, and after its arrival the water quality and clarity actually improved considerably, possibly caused in part by the filter feeding of *Corbicula*. The improvement in water quality may also have been due to improved sewage treatment and a ban that took effect on phosphorus in laundry detergents, but at the very least, this outcome means that not all invasions are ecological disasters.

Green Crab: *Carcinus maenas*

Called the "European green crab" in the United States and the "shore crab" in Europe (see fig. 3.5 in chapter 3), this uninvited visitor is native to the Atlantic coasts of Europe and Northern Africa, found on protected rocky shores, pebbly beaches, mud flats, and tidal marshes. It thrives in a wide range of both salinity and temperature and has already invaded numerous coastal areas, including South Africa, Australia, and both coasts of North America. Although it is called a green crab, large individuals (about three inches across) may be brownish red.

Its larvae can survive in the plankton for over two months, dispersing many miles up and down the coast. After the larvae develop in the sea, they are swept into coastal waters and estuaries by tides and currents; there they molt and settle out as juveniles in the intertidal zone. If conditions are suitable, they will survive and reproduce, establishing a new population and extending the species' range.

There have been two major green crab invasions of America, first beginning in the mid-1800s when they reached the Atlantic coast, probably in crevices of heavily fouled ship hulls. They found suitable habitat in coastal bays from New Jersey to Cape Cod. Then in the early 1900s, they began spreading north to Nova Scotia, and their arrival in Maine in the 1950s coincided with dramatic declines in the soft clam fishery. The second major invasion was detected in 1989 in San Francisco Bay, where they probably arrived as larvae in the ballast water of commercial ships. It is also possible that they were hanging onto the fouling on ships, or they could have been in with the sea grass and kelp used for packing and shipping lobsters and bait worms to the West Coast. Their arrival on the West Coast was associated with losses of up to 50 percent of the Manila clam stocks in California. The crab is an effective forager, able to open bivalves more quickly than most other crabs, which makes it a threatening competitor for the food

Green Crab Research in the Weis Lab

We did a number of behavioral studies investigating interactions between native blue crabs that are prized for food and the invasive green crab to see if the invader could potentially have negative effects on the valuable native species. We set up a competition in which a piece of food (a mussel) was put in the center of an aquarium, and size-matched hungry crabs of the two species were placed at either end and released simultaneously. We noted which crab got the food and how long it took. If there were any fights over the food, we noted who started and who won, winning meaning who got the food in the end. As James MacDonald found, invariably, the green crabs won these competitions.

Blue crabs, being both mean and nasty, saw the green crabs in the aquarium and typically went into an aggressive display with their claws spread out—typical blue crab behavior. Meanwhile, the green crabs generally ignored the displaying blue crab, scuttled in, and got the food. The blue crabs frequently then started a fight over the food, but the green crabs just hunkered down over the mussel, and eventually the blue crab gave up and the green crab ate the food. So being aggressive and nasty doesn't mean you win a competition for food!

MacDonald also measured shell strength and thickness of similar-sized crabs and found that the green crabs' shells are thicker and it takes greater pressure to break them—so they are more resistant to predators than blue crabs of the same size. On the other hand, blue crabs do grow considerably larger than green crabs, and once they are larger, they win the competition for food and also have stronger shells. But juvenile blue crabs that are of the same size as green crabs are definitely outcompeted by them.

Another study looked at the potential for learning in these two crab species. In these behavioral studies, only one crab was tested at a time. We had a piece of food (a mussel) hidden under the sand in the middle of the test aquarium and a ring of plastic "seaweed" on top of the place where the mussel was hidden. Individual (hungry) crabs were put in the tank for ten minutes and timed to see how long it took them to find the food. Each crab was tested for five days in a row to see if it improved its performance, and the green crabs found the food faster each day. As Ross Roudez found, many of the blue crabs did not get the food at all in the ten minutes they were given, and overall there was no decrease in the time they took time to find the food that would be indicative of learning. So it appears that the green crabs are also "smarter" than blue crabs, which would give them an additional advantage as a successful invader.

sources of native crab, fish, and bird species. It feeds on many organisms, including clams, oysters, mussels, marine worms, and small crustaceans. It also appears to learn and remember better than native blue crabs and is an able colonizer and an efficient predator, possessing the characteristics that make it likely to alter any ecosystem it invades.

Green crabs threaten Dungeness crab, oyster, and clam fisheries and aquaculture in the Pacific Northwest as they move up the West Coast. On the East Coast, the snails and mussels that have been living with green crabs for over a century have developed thicker shells as a defense against this invasive predator, becoming harder to crush than shellfish that have not been exposed to green crabs. The green crabs we see in North America have fewer parasites and grow considerably larger than they do back home in their native European waters, traits that may be contributing to their success in the New World.

Chinese Mitten Crab: *Eriocheir sinensis*

The Chinese mitten crab (fig. 6.1) is a burrowing crab native to the Yellow Sea in Korea and China. It has dense patches of hairs on its white-tipped claws, hence the name mitten crab. In Asia the crab is a delicacy; it has been imported illegally into seafood stores in California for the Asian

Fig. 6.1. Invasive Chinese mitten crab in Pacific and, as of 2007, Atlantic coast marshes. Barnacles are on its carapace. *Photo courtesy of the Smithsonian Institution.*

market, and this suggests that the crabs were probably introduced by the deliberate release of leftover crabs. They could also have been accidentally released in ballast water, which seems to be what happened in the early 1900s in Germany, with the result that in the 1920s and 1930s the population exploded and the crabs rapidly expanded into many northern European rivers and estuaries. Recently, the Thames River in England has had a population explosion of the crabs, again, possibly released from a Chinese restaurant.

Mitten crabs have become established on the West Coast of the United States, posing a potential threat to native invertebrates, to the ecological structure of freshwater and estuarine communities, and to some commercial fisheries and shrimping operations. In 1992, shrimp trawlers collected the first mitten crabs in San Francisco Bay, and they have become established in the bay and have spread upstream. By 1998, they were found far up in the Sacramento River system and throughout the delta. They may imperil the state's threatened and endangered salmon populations due to their appetite for salmon eggs, and there is concern that they will next invade Oregon, Washington, and British Columbia.

Mitten crabs can walk on land, and in California they have been found on roads and in parking lots, yards, and swimming pools. Their phenomenal ability to disperse is of concern to scientists because they can leave the water and cross dry land and easily enter new rivers. In the summer of 2006 the crab was found in part of the Chesapeake Bay, and in 2007 some were spotted in Delaware Bay.

Adults migrate downstream to reproduce in estuaries, and after one or two months as planktonic larvae, they settle out in brackish water in late spring and then migrate upstream to fresh water. Juveniles primarily eat vegetation, but as they grow they prey more on animals, particularly worms and clams. Many animals prey on them, including bullfrogs, raccoons, river otters, wading birds, and fishes, including sturgeon, striped bass, and channel catfish; but they apparently do not have enough predators to slow down their invasion.

In Europe, the primary economic impact has been the damage to commercial fishing nets and to the catch if the crabs are caught in large numbers. In San Francisco Bay, one trawler reported catching over two hundred crabs in a single tow on several occasions, a time-consuming and costly diversion. Another problem in California is the impact on water diversion and on fish salvage facilities. Crabs followed the moving water into a salvage facility in the late 1990s and clogged holding tanks full of the fishes that were the object of the salvage attempt. Many fishes suffocated because it took too long to separate them from the crabs, and the fishes that survived were put in transport trucks, but most of them also died. Facility operators and biologists were surprised at the magnitude of the invasion—they had expected a population boom but not ten thousand crabs a day clogging up systems throughout the facilities' infrastructures and creating long delays in what is normally a standard process.

In tidal areas, mitten crabs burrow into banks during low tides, and there is concern that this will eventually increase erosion and make the levees and riverbanks unstable. It is interesting to note that when there are native burrowing species like fiddler crabs, their burrowing is considered a positive attribute, aerating the soil and contributing to the growth of marsh plants; but when an exotic burrowing animal arrives, concerns arise about it causing destabilization and erosion of creek banks. Like the response to invasive grasses, perhaps there is a bit of subjectivity going on here?

Since the crabs are edible, some scientists encourage people to eat them to minimize potential problems. Philip Rainbow of London's Natural History Museum has called on commercial fishermen to target the species, as reported in *National Geographic News:* "The Chinese love them, especially when they're full of gonads during the breeding season. The carapace of a large one measures eight centimeters (about three inches) across—that's a decent-sized meal." Joe Franke's *Invasive Species Cook Book* is available ("If you can't beat 'em, eat 'em"). The idea of the cookbook is to increase interest in the issue of invasive species and to reduce their populations by harvesting them as food sources and finding interesting ways to eat seaweeds, crabs, clams, mussels, fishes, and snails.

Asian Shore Crab: *Hemigrapsus sanguineus*

This small species was first observed in New Jersey in 1988, probably having arrived in ballast water, and it has extended its range from Maine to North Carolina, becoming very abundant in intertidal and shallow water habitats where rock cover is available. Characteristic of a successful invader, they have a long breeding season and reproduce readily in a wide range of environmental conditions. They are found in very high densities and actually seem to have displaced green crabs from some areas. Control of this species by predators seems unlikely as there is little evidence that they have major predators, supporting the "enemy release hypothesis" of invasion biology.

Killifish in Spain

The invasion of estuarine and marsh habitats is not a one-way street that only brings aliens to our shores, since a number of species native to the

An Invasive Species in Japan

Emperor Akihito received a gift of bluegill fish (*Lepomis macrochirus*) from Mayor Richard J. Daley of Chicago during a visit to the United States in 1960. The bluegill, a freshwater fish, is Illinois's state fish and is considered a delicacy in the state. The emperor donated the fish to a research agency with the hope of raising them for food, and some of the fish escaped into Lake Biwa, where they have been outcompeting native species in rivers and lakes. They have eradicated the royal bitterling (*Rhodeus sericeus*) and caused near-extinction of other native species.

The government of Shiga Prefecture (the area of Lake Biwa) has called on the public to catch and eat enough bluegill fish to eradicate them, and it has set up a Web site offering recipes for deep-fried, marinated, and chili-sauced bluegill. A local university will soon start selling bluegill burgers. A previous campaign to use the fish as fertilizer and chicken feed had only limited success.

United States have invaded other parts of the world. For example, the common killifish or mummichog, *Fundulus heteroclitus* (see fig. 3.19), arrived on the shores of Spain some time in the 1970s and became established in marshes in southwest Spain in the 1980s, where they were originally misidentified as another species in the same family. They have recently spread and become successfully established in the Ebro River delta in the Mediterranean, where they are now the most abundant fish species in the area's salt-marsh habitats. Their small size, short life span, early maturity, and very high tolerance for fluctuating and stressful environmental conditions that are low in oxygen and high in pollutants make them very successful invaders. Sharing the marsh habitats with the invaders is a native species in the same family (*Aphanius baeticus*) which is ranked as endangered. This species is likely to have an even tougher time surviving with an army of mummichogs taking over their habitat.

Mute Swan: *Cygnus olor*

Mute swans (see fig. 3.31) are very large birds, growing up to five feet long. Adults have a wing span of about six feet. Adults are white and quite dramatic in appearance, with an orange bill that has a characteristic black knob where the bill meets the swan's face. Originating from Eurasia, the birds were transported to northern Europe in the Middle Ages and, subsequently, to North America for use on estates because of their decorative value. They can live in a variety of aquatic habitats, including ponds and lagoons and freshwater to saltwater marshes. In warmer months they spend most of their time in shallow water, and as the water cools in the fall, they move to deeper water.

Their population growth has been very rapid. From 1989 to 1999, the mute swan population grew 68 percent in Massachusetts, 79 percent in Rhode Island, 159 percent in New Jersey, 78 percent in Pennsylvania, and 713 percent in Virginia. Flocks of six hundred to one thousand birds have been recorded. They are not migratory, and breeding pairs tend to remain in the same territory. When they reach about three years of age, they nest on small islands and isolated shorelines or in shallow marshes in nests made from rushes and coarse grasses placed one to two feet above the high-tide line. Nesting begins in March or early April and pairs often use the same nest sites over multiple years.

Their preferred food is submerged aquatic vegetation (SAV) that, unlike marsh plants, have adapted to living submerged in water 100 percent of the time. A large, resident mute swan population feeding on SAV all year could jeopardize the ability of the vegetation to recover from winter waterfowl grazing, making it less available for waterfowl the following winter. Declines in SAV abundance correlate with declines in black duck and canvasback populations. Swans consume and disturb SAV beds in impoundments and sheltered coves that people use for crabbing and fishing, and aggressive ones can keep people away from the shoreline. A particularly aggressive swan that resides in the Georgica Pond in East Hampton on Long Island, New York, has been named George, and it has been reported that the swan jumps into canoes, causing alarmed paddlers to spill out. Local residents will probably be disappointed to learn that Franke's *Invasive Species Cook Book* does not have any recipes for roasted swan, especially since marsh ecologist Scott Warren claims they are "pretty tasty."

The swans' high rate of population growth, year-round presence, and preference for feeding on SAV are reasons for concern. Dense concentrations of mute swans defecating in the water contribute to water quality problems. Elevated counts of coliform bacteria have been detected where mute swans congregate, and coliform counts are widely used to determine whether waters may be used for drinking, swimming, and shell fishing. Large amounts of bird excrement can also contribute to eutrophication and cause algal blooms.

Nutria: *Myocaster coypus*

An article in the *Washington Post* on November 17, 2004, stated:

> For the nutria, which resemble waddling beavers with naked tails, the area turned out to be a garden spot. There were huge expanses of a

marsh plant they love, called three-square bulrush. Nutria act like a "mammalian lawn mower," in the words of scientist Robert A. Thomas, a professor at Loyola University in New Orleans, "eating the plants, roots and all, and leaving huge stretches of bare mud. Without roots to hold it, in many places the mud simply washed away. About half of the refuge's marshland, a crucial pollution filter that scientists call the "kidneys" of the Chesapeake, had become open water by the 1990s.

Nutria (fig. 6.2) are large rodents weighing from eight to eighteen pounds. They were introduced from South America in the 1940s for their attractive fur, and they have become numerous in southern marshes from the Gulf Coast to the eastern shore of Maryland. They breed all year and have litters of up to nine babies. They become sexually active at four months of age and the gestation period is only four months, promoting rapid population growth. They are basically herbivorous, consuming huge quantities of marsh vegetation and totally removing cattails, rushes, and sedges. Their ability to excavate the root mat of the marsh for feeding makes them directly responsible for marsh loss, since when they remove marsh vegetation, soils erode through tidal action; and if damaged areas do not get revegetated quickly, they become open water as tides remove

Fig. 6.2. Nutria with babies, invasive rodent in southern marshes. *Photo courtesy of U.S. Geological Survey.*

the wetland soil. By disturbing the balance of the native plants, they provide an advantage for non-native plant species to become established.

The destruction of marshes by nutria has escalated due to a decline in the fur industry and a resultant overpopulation of nutria. As nutria chew up the marsh, they also displace native muskrats and reduce the area of wetlands available for birds, including migratory waterfowl, and the marsh loss affects the nearby estuary. Since fewer marsh plants are available to filter out pollution and sediments and to produce detritus, the estuarine ecosystem is impaired, reducing its population of commercially valuable crabs and finfish.

Eradication programs have been started in some nature reserves. In Maryland's Blackwater National Wildlife Refuge, which had been losing one thousand acres per year, a team of trappers was hired to catch and kill the nutria; and in 2004 the refuge was declared free of nutria at a cost of two million dollars. Whether this result will be permanent is an open question. Large-scale eradication also is taking place in the whole Delmarva Peninsula using traps, dogs, and guns. Franke's *Invasive Species Cook Book* contains a recipe for "heart healthy crock-pot nutria," which is supposed to taste like turkey.

A Dilemma: Should Non-native Oysters Be Introduced to the Chesapeake Bay?

Given the extensive harm that some non-indigenous species have caused, it is no wonder that a proposal to introduce a non-native species of oysters to Chesapeake Bay has caused considerable controversy. Since native oyster populations have collapsed due to a combination of overfishing, habitat loss, poor water quality, and two devastating diseases (one of which, MSX, was itself inadvertently introduced by a Rutgers scientist working with non-native oysters from Japan), it has been proposed that an Asian oyster, *Crassostrea ariakensis,* be introduced to replace the native oyster *Crassostrea virginica,* so that water purification through filter feeding can continue in those waters. Research is underway to learn more about the biology of the Asian oyster to evaluate its potential to either be a functional replacement for native oysters or become an invasive problem if it is introduced.

The two species' larvae are both attracted to adult oyster shells as sites for settling and metamorphosis, suggesting that they would settle in the same places and could compete for limited habitat and as a result could grow more slowly. But the Asian oysters might also provide future habitat for the native species, since larvae will settle on their shells. The Asian oysters grow faster than the native ones and have their maximum growth in early spring and in the fall when the native species is dormant (Paynter et al. 2008). There are concerns that it could outcompete and contribute to further reductions of the native species. On the other hand, the Asian oyster has less salinity tolerance and should, if introduced, have a more limited distribution. Its weaker shell may make it more vulnerable to predators like crabs. The two species can hybridize, but the hybrid larvae die—this could be considered a "waste" of valuable gametes that could have fertilized other *C. virginica*. This hybridization could contribute to reduced reproductive success of the native species. Will the Asian oyster build reefs like the native oysters to provide habitat for a variety of other species? Will it filter water to the same degree? Could the Asian oysters be infected with the same diseases that have wiped out so many of the natives, although they seem more resistant? Or could they potentially introduce new diseases into the system?

The long-term outcome of these interactions is unknown. Once all the information is integrated and assessed, an environmental impact statement will be produced and, ultimately, a decision will be made on whether to undertake this purposeful, potentially valuable, but risky introduction.

Control of Invasive Species

Over three hundred species of non-native invertebrates and many fishes have established themselves in North American waters as a result of human introduction; and the rate of introduction has been accelerating in recent decades, probably because of increased shipping due to larger ships and faster transoceanic voyages. Biological invasions have caused extensive ecological changes in salt marshes and other coastal habitats, and it is, of course, more cost-effective to prevent invasive species from establishing themselves than it is to try to eradicate them once they have become established.

A plan to prevent future introductions should include understanding the pathways or vectors through which introductions take place. This awareness has led to some steps to reduce the major vector of transport, which is ballast water. Ships are now required to exchange ballast water in the middle of the ocean, which releases organisms from the port of origin where they are unlikely to survive. The ships then take in ocean water with its collection of planktonic organisms which are released in the destination port. Oceanic plankton are not likely to be able to survive for long enough to establish themselves in the variable environmental conditions in a port. Studies have shown that this exchange is practiced by about 80 percent of foreign vessels entering the Chesapeake Bay, but it is not performed in stormy seas when the release of ballast water could de-stabilize the vessel. But with these new procedures, concentrations of zooplankton in the ballast water can be reduced to one-tenth of the previous levels, which should reduce the number of invasions in the future.

In addition to ballast water, sea chests, which are the intake areas for ballast water, can house diverse organisms. They have grates or screens to prevent large organisms from coming in with the water, but small ones can come in and survive and grow inside the chests. A wide variety of species including sponges, sea anemones, worms, mussels, oysters, scallops, barnacles, crabs, sea urchins, and fishes have been found in sea chests. Although antifouling paints have decreased hull fouling, many nooks and crannies, including rudders, gratings, holes, and sea chests, remain difficult to paint and are subject to high levels of fouling. So while a ship might be 99 percent free of fouling organisms, the remaining 1 percent that remains is all that is needed to introduce a species to a new habitat.

Anchors and chains are another source of moving species around the world. Fouling organisms can settle on the anchor or chain as juveniles and grow into adults that are transported to a new region where they reproduce or drop off. Also, mud accumulates on anchors while they sit on the bottom, and organisms living in the mud remain on the anchor as it is hauled aboard ship. If it is not washed thoroughly, the stowaway organisms may survive in the damp mud until the anchor is dropped at the next port, and then they may invade the new habitat.

Non-indigenous species are a problem in the Great Lakes and in fresh water in general, and increased public awareness of this problem led to a 2007 Michigan law that required all oceangoing ships sailing into Michigan's ports to obtain permits showing that the vessels will not discharge ballast water into local waters. If they do plan to discharge water, they must treat it first to remove any non-native species. Efforts are underway to develop treatment techniques to kill the organisms in ballast water. These techniques could potentially be harmful to the environment if they involve toxic chemicals. Studies have tested the ability of ozone treatment to kill the organisms, and the approach appears promising. A lawsuit challenging the law by a coalition of shipping interests was dismissed.

Another problem is that the mud on the bottom of the ballast tanks, with its resident organisms, is not removed during ballast water exchange. One of us was once privileged to climb down into the ballast water tank of a large tanker when it was in port. Although it had been classified as "no ballast on board," a foot of water was observed in the tank, under which was a several-inch-thick layer of mud that contained populations of marine worms that must have been living there and cruising around the world for many years. There were also live adult barnacles on the walls of the tank.

Another approach to controlling invasive species is to evaluate those species that have become established to see if they can be contained and, if they cannot, to attempt to eradicate them in an organized manner. Such is the case with invasive marsh plants in the East and West coasts, where *Phragmites* and *Spartina* removal, respectively, is common.

Despite these efforts, it is likely that continued environmental changes in the twenty-first century will alter both the availability of species for transport and the degree of susceptibility of the habitat to invasions. In addition to human-caused modifications in the local environment, climate change will interact with the arrival of non-native species in new areas to modify diversity and to alter the functioning of ecosystems around the globe.

7 Marsh Restoration and Management for Environmental Improvement

In the southeastern reaches of the Garden State, a ten year effort to restore some of New Jersey's most bountiful "gardens" has paid off in acres upon acres of newly healthy salt marshes, their wavy grasses bending and stretching along miles of winding, high-banked creeks that lead to the Delaware Bay. Long blades of grass tipped autumn gold rustle in the breeze here, their murmurings insistent in fall's stiff winds.

—Cheryl Lynn Dybas, *Washington Post,* 2003

Restoration

When ecosystems are destroyed or degraded, a great deal is lost. Water purification services and seafood are drastically affected, and many other less obvious ecological functions suffer and cause serious consequences for the surrounding area: nursery habitat for juvenile fishes and crustaceans is lost, the accumulation of sediment is affected, protection from coastal erosion is reduced, the recycling of nutrients and detoxifying and trapping of pollutants diminishes, and opportunities for relaxation and recreation disappear. It is clear that if people want to have these services, attention must be given to protecting and restoring the natural systems that provide them.

A national goal of no net loss of wetlands was established for the United States in the late 1980s; and, as a result, when wetlands are lost as a result of development, efforts must be made by the developer to improve or create wetlands elsewhere to mitigate or compensate for the loss. Returning a degraded habitat to a healthy condition similar to the way it was prior to being disturbed is considered *restoration,* which reinstates important functions and services rendered by the habitat. Restoration also often involves altering the elevation and hydrology of a marsh, planting desired species, removing invasive species, and hoping that the rest of the marsh organisms will come on their own (the "if you build it they will come" philosophy). Efforts of this type have had mixed success, and after a couple of decades, marsh restoration still remains more of an art than a science.

The Estuary Restoration Act of 2000 established a national policy for implementing estuary restoration, including salt marshes, with the dual goals of creating healthy ecosystems and providing flood control. The legislation emphasized partnerships between the public and private sectors using the best science and technology along with careful monitoring and evaluation. Public education to increase awareness and sustain support was built into the policy.

Restoration projects should have clearly defined goals and objectives, and endpoints that define the success of a project should be clearly defined. Is it a certain species composition? The right vegetation? Canopy architecture? Fishes? Diversity in the system? Productivity of the system? In some cases, with the "if you build it they will come" approach, the species that come are not necessarily the ones that were anticipated.

Phragmites Removal

Phragmites is that tall reed that has been taking over low-salinity marshes on the East Coast. Some projects take functioning *Phragmites* wetlands and bulldoze them, turning them into vegetated islands that they hope will improve when *Spartina* takes root. This results in a net loss of wetlands, at least in the short term. Other mitigation projects in the Northeast involve removing *Phragmites* and then physically planting *Spartina,* which makes changes in existing marshes; but it does not involve a net increase in marsh to compensate for the loss of other marsh area.

These projects are simply habitat enhancements and conversions rather than real restorations, primarily because it is clear that *Phragmites* marshes, while of less value than *Spartina* for East Coast marshes, are not ecologically useless. They are functioning, productive systems that contribute to aquatic food webs and provide habitat for fishes, shrimps, crabs, and birds. Many species of birds, including bitterns, black-crowned night herons, egrets, mallards, gadwalls, harriers, coots, moorhens, rails, red-winged blackbirds, and marsh wrens, utilize *Phragmites* marshes.

"Phragmites. It's green most of the time, and it ain't condos" (Bill Sheehan, the Hackensack Riverkeeper, quoted in the *New York Times,* July 16, 2005). This emphasizes, with typical Sheehan-esque style, that *Phragmites* marshes are functional wetlands and preferable to a paved-over development. In *Phragmites*-dominated marshes, restoration involves removing the unwanted reeds by bulldozing, burning, and using an herbicide such as glyphosate. Glyphosate is a broad-spectrum herbicide that is toxic to other plants as well as to invertebrates, so it cannot be said to be good for the ecosystem. Repeated applications are generally needed to kill all the reeds, but frequently the unwanted reeds return because their underground rhizomes are insulated from the herbicides and burning, so they can revive if they have not been located and destroyed.

In a recent study by R. J. Howard and colleagues, the native variety of *Phragmites* and the invasive Eurasian variety were planted along with three other native marsh plants at similar densities in a restored brackish marsh in Louisiana and monitored for growth. After fourteen months, the invasive Eurasian type had spread to cover 82 percent of the area, more than four times the coverage of the native type, showing the potential of the invasive variety to grow rapidly at newly restored sites.

There is ongoing research into finding methods of biological control by, for example, introducing insects that eat the plant. But before any herbivore species is introduced, a lot of research should be done to make certain that the insect does not eat anything else, especially native plants. If something is introduced to control an undesired invader and it ends up eating the desired native species, the "solution" can turn into a problem itself.

Replanting

There are a variety of complex problems that can be encountered in the course of attempts at restoring indigenous vegetation. For example, various techniques are used when planting new areas with *Spartina;* sometimes seeds are planted, and at other times cores containing a shoot and rhizome are taken from existing marshes and transplanted in the new site. If the salinity of the water is too high or the soil has the wrong texture or chemistry, the effort can fail. If the water flow is too rapid or the wave action is too intense as the tides rise and fall, seedlings and young plants without well-developed root systems are vulnerable to erosion. Problems may occur if the hydrology or elevation of the created marsh is not quite right, and inadequate drainage can kill the plants. If the elevation is too low, the marsh will be flooded too much of the time and the plants will not survive. In the Northeast, ice rafting in the winter is another problem that can damage marsh vegetation.

People on the West Coast are attempting to eliminate the invasive *S. alterniflora* and replace it with the native *S. foliosa;* and because *S. foliosa* does not readily grow from seeds, transplanting soil plugs has been the approach most often used. A West Coast problem is getting the *S. foliosa* to grow tall enough for clapper rail nesting. If the level of nitrogen in the sediment is not adequate for plant growth, nitrogen can be added, but it should only be applied to pure stands of *S. foliosa* since it will also encourage growth of the superior competitor *S. alterniflora.*

Another problem arises when geese and other animals eat the young, tender plants. Geese can graze heavily on marsh vegetation, including the underground rhizomes. Protective tubes may have to be placed around seedlings, or it may be necessary to set up fenced enclosures for newly planted vegetation in order to reduce the impact of the geese.

Aspects of the plant community that affect the use of the marsh by animals include stem density, plant height, species composition, percentage of cover, and amount of edge that is adjacent to open water. During restoration projects, these characteristics must all be taken into consideration because while restored marshes may look superficially like natural marshes, they may lack many structural and functional aspects of natural marshes, and animal species typical of natural marshes may not return to restored marshes for many years. Ecologist Joy Zedler, now at the University of Wisconsin, has found that endangered clapper rails did not return to restored marshes on the Pacific Coast because the grasses did not grow tall enough for them, probably because the soil did not have enough nitrogen. Nutrient cycling in restored marshes may be very limited because of the reduced populations of important microbes, with the result that the soils may not be as rich as those of natural marshes for many years.

Mitigation Banks

A mitigation bank is an aquatic resource area that has been restored, established, enhanced, or preserved in order to provide compensation for the degradation of aquatic resources that was officially permitted at another site. It is considered an option only when mitigation on the site itself is not possible. Banks can be set up in advance of permitted impacts. Based upon the type, size, and function of the improvements, the bank is authorized by the regulatory agencies to sell a certain number of credits, comparable to a bank that has money to lend, except it is providing restored pieces of marsh rather than financial capital. The concept is related to that of carbon offsets or credits.

This concept is rather new, and it is controversial because of the length of time it takes for a created marsh to acquire all the functions, biodiversity, and value of a natural marsh. The National Academy of Sciences has stated, "Wetland restoration should not be used to mitigate avoidable destruction of other wetlands until it can be scientifically demonstrated that the replacement ecosystems are of equal or better functioning" (National Research Council 1991). Opponents are concerned that banking allows additional wetland destruction and minimizes the difficulties involved in truly creating or restoring wetlands as viable ecosystems and that wetland losses are sometimes allowed before the bank is fully functional. The concept of mitigation banking is criticized for creating a false sense of security and for doing little more than promoting development at the cost of further loss of wetlands.

Supporters claim that mitigation banking, compared with on-site mitigation, provides better-organized planning, greater commitment to long-term wetland protection, and better habitat for wildlife. They see large wetland banks as more beneficial than numerous small wetland mitigation sites of equal acreage because the larger banks provide greater function and ecological value and can be monitored and maintained more easily and effectively. The fact that banks provide mitigation *in advance* of impacts is of significant benefit to the environment and it has the additional benefit of reducing the permit-processing time, thereby increasing the effectiveness of the regulatory agencies.

Re-establishing Tidal Flow

When roads and railways were built through marshes, culverts (conduits) were placed at road crossings to direct the flow of the water beyond the road and into the marsh. If the culverts were too small to begin with or if they have collapsed over time, the tidal flow into the marsh can be blocked. The marsh can become semi-impounded, the salinity level goes down, and *Phragmites* replaces the cordgrass. The simplest form of restoration involves re-establishing tidal flow when it has been lost by enlarging the size of the culverts. When the tidal flow has been restored, the increased salinity of the tidal water will kill the *Phragmites* and desirable salt-marsh vegetation and fauna will return over a number of years. An example of this type of project is the removal by Amtrak of 175-year-old culverts from along its railroad tracks in Connecticut in areas the water could no longer reach. Once the culverts had been replaced and enlarged, the tidal flow was no longer blocked and the *Spartina* returned.

More complex projects involve breaching dikes on unused agricultural lands or impoundments, after which the salt-marsh vegetation is expected to return naturally to the area, followed by increases in the invertebrate, fish, and bird populations. Over time the organic matter in the soil should increase to resemble that of a natural marsh. In a project of this nature in the Bay of Fundy in Nova Scotia, Canada, despite the huge tidal variations that are normal in the bay, when the dikes of a former impoundment for ducks were breached, the *Spartina* recolonized.

Sediments in tidal marshes that have been diked for a long time undergo compaction and subsidence, and if the marsh surface has dropped too far below sea level, breaching the dikes to introduce tidal flushing will result in the area becoming open water rather than a marsh. Efforts must first be taken to increase the elevation of the marsh surface in order for the marsh to be restored under these circumstances. Another possibility would be to design the restoration so that the tidal range is reduced, for example, by using self-regulating tide gates. Another problem with restoring marshes that have been diked for long periods is that the sudden influx of oxygen-rich water can alter the soil chemistry. High concentrations of nutrients such as phosphate and iron can suddenly become mobilized from the soil and then washed away by the tidal flushing, leading to detrimental nutrient enrichment downstream.

Currently, one of the world's largest restoration projects involves over twelve hundred acres of diked former salt hay farms in Delaware Bay that have been invaded by *Phragmites*. They are being restored by breaching dikes and digging large channels to promote tidal flooding. In addition, the *Phragmites* have been burned and sprayed with the herbicide Rodeo. The project is being carried out by the Public Service Electric and Gas Company, a major utility in New Jersey, in order to offset the effects of their Salem Nuclear Power plant, where it has been estimated that the cooling system of the power plant causes the annual loss of one billion eggs, larvae, and juveniles of various estuarine and marine organisms in the Delaware River. The success of this project is still being evaluated, and whether it can ever make up for anything near the number of juvenile organisms destroyed by the nuclear power plant seems unlikely. However, my Rutgers colleague Ken Able has already demonstrated major increases in fish abundance and diversity in these restored marshes.

In San Francisco Bay, where 80 to 90 percent of the original marsh area has been lost, there is an ambitious restoration program in the works. Over sixteen thousand acres of salt evaporation ponds, formerly used by the Cargill Corporation for salt production, are being restored by a coalition of government agencies, local communities, and environmental groups. The restored wetlands will be in a highly urbanized landscape, and the healthier, richer environment will provide recreational opportunities for many people. The initial steps involve opening the gates to the pond system, allowing the tides back into the system, and restoring the natural hydrodynamics. Turning the impounded ponds into wetlands will require an enormous amount of clean sediment in order to raise the elevation up to the natural intertidal marsh levels, and while some of this sediment will be imported, a lot of it will have to come in naturally with the tides. Planners are aware of the potential for exotic species to invade the new wetlands, and they are planning controls for *Spartina alterniflora* and invasive crabs. They are also aware of the potential problems of mercury methylation since some South Bay sediments are rich in mercury. Using research, monitoring, and the results of pilot projects to plan future steps in the restoration, the keystone of this project is adaptive management (see http://www.southbayrestoration.org).

Another ongoing restoration project in northern California involves knocking down levees at a ranch in Point Reyes. While the levees kept flood waters out of the property for sixty years, flooding was accentuated in nearby areas. The demolition of the levees will reduce future flooding in adjacent areas along with allowing the return of natural marsh communities to the ranch and diverting flood waters into the historic floodplains of the ranch, dropping flood levels by as much as 20 percent in the nearby creek during small, biannual floods.

In Huntington Beach in southern California, about 140 acres of marshes along Pacific Coast Highway that are home to endangered birds and other wildlife will be restored, requiring the removal of about twenty-nine thousand truckloads of material. Levees will be demolished to allow seawater to replenish the marshes and restore nutrients to the marsh soil, with the expectation that the restored habitat will revitalize a resting spot for migratory birds and restore the home of the endangered Belding's savannah sparrow and California least tern.

A major wetland restoration seeking to restore tidal flow is going on in Iraq. The Mesopotamian marshlands at the junction of the Tigris and Euphrates rivers were at one time the largest wetlands in the Middle East, covering over seventy-five hundred square miles, and they served as habitat for millions of permanent and migrating birds. They contained fishes that were an important food source for local people, and they were populated by other vertebrates such as water buffalo, wild boar, and smooth-coated otters. Sometimes considered the site of the Garden of Eden, they also served as home for Marsh Arabs, who lived on islands in houses built of common reeds, where they fished and raised water buffalo in close harmony with their environment for several millennia.

The government of Saddam Hussein drained the marshes, starting in the late 1980s, as a way to gain greater control of the people in the area. By upstream damming, draining, and diverting the flow of the rivers away from the marshes through a series of dikes and canals, in less than a decade he turned most of the marshes into a salt-encrusted, dry wasteland where only 10 percent of the original marshes survived. Dairy production and rice cultivation became impossible, and desertification and pollution increased.

Efforts are underway to restore the marshes and to return the Marsh Arabs to their homes, using a hydrological model that has been developed to determine how much water will be needed to restore the marshlands and to wash out the accumulated salts and pollutants. Initial results suggest that enough water is present in southern Iraq to partially restore the marshlands if the water diversion structures are removed, and local people have begun breaking the existing dams and canals; this has already resulted in 20 to 30 percent of the dried land becoming wetlands again. One year after this reflooding began, species recovery was already taking place, and a survey of the marshes indicated that most plant, invertebrate, fish, and bird species are returning to the restored marshes, but their density is low compared to historical records. The site with the highest number of fish species had 72 percent of the historic number, and 66 percent of the bird species had also returned, as described by Curtis Richardson and Najah Hussain. The early return is probably related to reintroduction directly from the waters of the Tigris and Euphrates rivers that flow into the restored marshes. Studies on the function of the ecosystem with regard to water flux, productivity, nutrient cycling, decomposition, and wildlife habitat found that at least one of the restored marshes had nearly recovered all its key functions, as indicated by plant production that was measured at 83 percent of a comparable remaining natural marsh. The high quality of the water, the soil conditions, and the existence of native species indicate that the restoration potential for a large portion of these marshes is good, but it is unclear if the culture of the Marsh Arabs will ever be reestablished in the area.

Increasing Elevation

In Jamaica Bay, near New York City, the marsh has been sinking and the marsh islands have been shrinking and disappearing for years. A restoration project is starting to rebuild the marshes by adding sand to raise the surface. Tons of sand dredged from nearby areas are being pumped through a pipe on the bay floor to the area being reclaimed, and cordgrass will be planted on the new mudflats. In this case, the term *reclamation* is, for once, appropriate. The project manager for the Army Corps of Engineers, Scott Nicholson, was enthusiastic: "What we're going to see out there is a high density marsh island with grass that will bend and wave in the wind. The birds will be attracted to the kinds of shellfish and fish that thrive in that sort of marsh environment. . . . It will be really beautiful."

Using Dredged Material

Another type of restoration uses dredged material to create new marshes by placing the material on bay bottoms to stimulate the growth of intertidal *Spartina* wetlands. This does two good things at once since, in addition to creating new wetlands, it also derives beneficial use from the dredged material. Dredged material tends to have a different chemistry than natural marsh, usually higher in ammonia and lower in sulfide, but once many plants are growing on it, the ammonia levels drop. Studies on marshes created from dredged material have shown that they acquire some characteristics of nearby natural marshes rather quickly and acquire others much more slowly. Generally, these marshes continue to have a lower density of benthic fauna and nekton than a natural marsh.

Dredged materials were used to raise the elevation of marshes that have been restored in Galveston Bay in the Texas Gulf Coast after they were lost due to subsidence and nearby construction. *Spartina* was planted in different configurations, and while the stem density and biomass was not as great as in the natural marshes, the characteristics of the restored marshes are improving over time. A marsh in the Blackwater National Wildlife Refuge in Maryland was created from dredged material into which *Spartina* was planted, but the outcome was not as good. Even though the restored marsh was at the same elevation as a reference site, it developed different vegetation patterns and began sinking despite an accumulation of five millimeters of sediment each year.

Restoring Bivalves

Natural oyster beds can filter huge amounts of water: one adult can filter from five to fifty gallons of water in a day, absorbing nitrogen, algae, and bacteria from the water and depositing them on the bottom in its feces, thus improving water quality. The oysters also serve as habitat for other species because they form reefs with three-dimensional structure on the bottom and serve to attract a whole suite of other species that like hard substrate, with the result that even fishing is better in areas with viable oyster reefs. As with marsh grass restoration projects, good monitoring is an essential follow-up.

Oyster reef restoration involves "planting" oyster shells or other hard substrate. While free-swimming oyster larvae will settle on virtually any available hard surface, their chance for survival is much greater when they settle on other oyster shells because they provide small oysters with the best protection from predators. Shellfish restoration projects have been started in many coastal states, and they often have both educational and ecological benefits, serving as a model for establishing partnerships between communities, conservation organizations, and state and federal government agencies for achieving environmental restoration. Students and volunteers frequently participate in the plantings and learn about the biology of oysters and their associated reef communities as well as about the factors affecting the overall health of their local waterways. They have the opportunity to apply concepts in science and math to a real-world problem.

In Long Island's Great South Bay, populations of hard clams have plummeted since the mid-1970s, when more than half of the hard clams eaten in the entire United States came from the Great South Bay. When clams were abundant, they filtered 40 percent of the water in the bay every day. Natural and manmade problems have caused a great decline in shellfish populations, and now there are only enough hard clams to filter about 1 percent of the bay's water daily. Scientists believe that lowered populations of filter feeders have disrupted the food web, allowing harmful algae blooms (brown tide) to shade out sea grass meadows, probably causing further harm to the shellfish population. Volunteers from the Nature Conservancy and other partners are working together to restore these filter feeders to the bay, which should make a major impact on improving water quality. They are creating "spawner sanctuaries" and shellfish nurseries where clams and scallops can grow, reproduce, and live safely, monitoring the role shellfish play in improving water quality, controlling harmful algal blooms, and enhancing habitat for other marine life. As of 2007 they had "planted" nearly two million clams in the Great South Bay, but the results are not in yet (see http://www.nature.org/wherewework/northamerica/states/newyork/science/art21714.html).

Oysters disappeared from the New York Harbor area over one hundred years ago, but a study of the potential of oysters to survive and grow in the Hackensack River is underway led by Beth Ravit of Rutgers. Results indicate about 30 percent survival over the first winter at the optimum location. A project starting in New York City in 2009 will investigate the ability of planted oysters and ribbed mussels to improve water quality in a creek in Brooklyn that starts at an output pipe of a wastewater treatment plant and empties into Jamaica Bay. One concern with both of these projects is that the oysters, assuming they survive, will be too contaminated to be eaten safely, and it is important that people are notified of that fact (see http://www.nynjbaykeeper.org/pdffiles/bkoppdoc.pdf).

Status of Restored Marshes

In general, population densities and sizes of various fish species tend to be smaller in restored or created marshes compared to natural marshes, but in time they may approach the levels in natural marshes. Fishes in restored marshes have been found to consume less food, perhaps because there is less food available, and many benthic invertebrates in restored marshes have smaller populations for decades than is normal in natural marshes. From the detailed work of Joy Zedler of the University of Wisconsin and her colleagues, it appears that the full recovery of animal populations and marsh functions after restoration may take two decades or even longer. This work put an end to the view of developers that all they needed to do was make a new acre of marsh somewhere to compensate for each acre they had filled or paved over somewhere else. Different species recover at different rates on each marsh, and the time required for the recovery of a particular species can vary greatly from marsh to marsh.

Juan Gallego Fernandez and Francisco Garcia Novo from the University of Seville did a study comparing adjacent restored marshes in southwestern Spain which had had very different levels of effort applied to the restoration. The high-intensity area, in which they opened up channels and created a ditch network, was immediately colonized by fishes; and the low intensity area, in which they allowed erosion to excavate the channels gradually, entailed much less expense. Both marshes attracted many birds, and in three years, the mudflats in the high-intensity area were covered with vegetation dominated by *Spartina,* while the low-intensity area had *Sarcocornia* (a succulent) communities with limited *Spartina,* indicating a slower return to the desired condition. After five years, species composition was similar at both sites and similar to natural vegetation, suggesting that, in this case, both approaches worked equally well in the long term.

As a natural community gradually returns after a restoration, interspecies relationships and food web connections get re-established, involving competition, mutualism (where both species benefit), predator-prey interactions, and parasite-host relationships. It is interesting that as the natural community returns after a successful restoration, parasites, which are natural components of all communities, return along with the other plants and animals, despite the fact that some parasites require a sequence of different hosts in order to go through their whole life cycle. For example, many trematode parasites initially live in a snail, then leave the snail, change form, and enter a fish in which they live in a particular tissue, generally in an encysted (dormant) form. In order for the parasite to complete its life cycle, the fish must eventually be eaten by a bird, which is the final host, in which the trematodes become adults and can reproduce. Once they reach the adult stage in the bird, the offspring are released in the bird's feces, enter the water, and live inside snails, and the cycle starts all over again.

Parasites can affect the behavior of their fish host in order to increase the chances that it will be eaten by a bird so that the parasite can continue its life cycle. It has been found that fishes with more of these parasites tend to swim higher up in the water and have more conspicuous behaviors, like jerking and twitching, which increase the chances of these fishes being spotted by a bird who will be the future host of the trematode parasites. It is amazing to think how these tiny parasites can alter their host's behavior to reduce its odds of survival and at the same time increase their own odds. In restored marshes, as the fishes, birds, and snails become more abundant, the parasites become more abundant too, and the animals become more highly parasitized.

Descriptions of food webs rarely include parasites as links between species because of the difficulty in measuring them by standard ecological methods. Parasites are small and invisible, hidden inside their hosts, but they affect the structure of the food web in important ways, as described by Kevin Lafferty and Armand Kuris. A link in a food web occurs when a particular predator eats a particular prey, or in this case when a particular parasite infects a particular host. They found that parasites dominated the food web links between species, and the salt-marsh food web, on average, contained more links between parasites and their hosts than between predators and their prey. To put it another way, a species has lots more parasites than it has prey or predators.

Policies

Ecosystems are all about food webs, interspecies connections, and balance. Can humans, who have played the major role in disturbing the intricate and balanced relationships of plants, animals, soils, and water, be trusted to take over from nature once again and help marsh systems to recover? How do we know when a marsh is healthy? How can we measure the success of a restoration project? A well-designed restoration project should have a clear goal and a reference site in a comparable area to provide a model of a reasonably healthy marsh. By studying the reference marsh over time, the normal conditions and fluctuations in the local systems can be understood and used to set realistic goals for the restoration project.

To determine the restoration potential of a degraded site, we have to understand its history, the nature and degree of disturbance, its connections to other natural habitats, the surrounding land uses, and other ecological and social factors. A site's history reveals the long-term factors such as climate, hydrology, and natural disturbances that have affected that site and helps map out restoration goals. If the site is contaminated, the pollution should be remediated as part of the restoration project. The overall design should promote the exchange of materials between the marsh and the open waters of the estuary by providing many small, branching, sinuous creeks and high drainage density so that fishes can quickly colonize the restored marsh. There must be enough vegetation to protect them from predators. The low marsh should be flooded for four to five hours

The Everglades Restoration

Everglades National Park was established in 1947 and now covers more than 1.5 million acres of wetlands and wildlife habitat. The park is a huge subtropical marsh, fresh water in the upper part, salt water in the estuary to the south. Half of the original area has already been developed for farmland and for residential communities. The Florida Everglades restoration project is an example of how complex it can be to protect and restore threatened marshland.

In 2000, a bipartisan, four-decades-long, $8 billion effort was agreed upon to restore the flow of water from Lake Okeechobee in south central Florida into the Everglades, including new reservoirs and other storage systems to guarantee an adequate water supply for the farms and cities in the area. In 2003, the Florida legislature, under pressure from the sugar industry, postponed enforcement of more stringent pollution regulations in the Everglades until 2016. Nevertheless, federal legislation authorizing $23 billion in water infrastructure projects, including $2 billion for the Everglades, was passed in Congress in 2007, overriding a presidential veto. The cost of the restoration was to be split equally between the state and the federal government, but by the end of 2007 the state had spent about $2 billion and the federal government had spent only $358 million.

There are several factors that threaten the future of this effort.

- In June, 2007 the Department of the Interior asked the United Nations to remove Everglades National Park from its list of endangered World Heritage sites, sending the confusing message that everything is OK in the Everglades.
- In September 2007, the Everglades were damaged by Hurricane Katrina.
- Florida has purchased 55 percent of the land needed for the restoration, but it continues to permit development in environmentally sensitive areas.
- In 2007, the South Florida Water Management District reported that farmers had missed a phosphorus reduction target for the first time in eleven years, despite the recent construction of forty-five thousand acres of filter marshes, which were designed to reduce contaminants in agricultural runoff.
- The Army Corps of Engineers, which typically executes projects like this, has been accused of being dysfunctional.
- Questions and criticism of the plan's ultimate effectiveness by scientists have surfaced.
- Projected land and construction costs have increased to over $10 billion.

The GAO (Government Accountability Office) Report

In December 2007, the GAO issued a report on lessons learned from past efforts to protect coastal wetlands in Louisiana, hoping to use the findings as a guide for future restoration and protection efforts. The report focused on Louisiana because it has lost over 1.2 million acres of wetlands since the 1930s, and it is anticipated that the state will continue losing wetlands due to subsidence, sea-level rise, and flood-control structures. A review was conducted of 147 projects in the state that had been undertaken as a result of the Coastal Wetlands Planning, Protection, and Restoration Act of 1990, part of the effort to restore and protect 120,000 acres of coastal wetlands that represent about 3 percent of the state's coastal area. Projects that had been undertaken include promoting marsh elevation by reintroducing fresh water and sediments, creating marsh using terracing to trap sediments, restoring natural drainage patterns using dredged sediments or hydrological restoration, restoring barrier islands to protect the mainland from storm surges, planting marsh vegetation and removing invasive species (nutria), and constructing shoreline barriers to protect the coastal landscape.

The reviewers came to several conclusions, including that increasing costs delayed the completion of projects and that without an integrated monitoring system they could not determine if goals and objectives were being met. Dealing with private landowners was found to have frequently been a problematic issue, and some projects simply failed to perform due to landscape or structural causes. Storms were found to potentially cause significant setbacks because large areas of both natural and restored wetlands can be destroyed quickly in a powerful storm. It is hoped that the lessons learned from the past as well as ongoing efforts can help to improve the prospects of future projects.

---

during mean tides to provide fishes and other nekton enough time to access the marsh surface; and in a year or two, fish abundance, density, number of species, average size, and community composition may equal that of nearby reference marshes.

Research can and should be a vital component of restoration. A large field experiment at Tijuana Estuary in California, published by Joy Zedler in 2005, showed that planting many species at once accelerated the development of ecosystem structure and function over single-species plantings. When six species were planted, more complex communities developed that accumulated more biomass and nitrogen than in areas with single-species plantings and in unplanted plots.

Bird density and species richness in restored marshes depends on an adequate supply of water, the connection of vegetation with open water, and the diversity of height provided by different types of vegetation. When muskrat populations are not high, they can be beneficial to the functioning of the restored marsh by opening gaps in the vegetation and increasing the diversity of the marsh substrate, leading to a greater variety of plant species. But too many nutria and muskrats can destroy a new marsh.

In establishing new marshes, care should be taken to create the optimum shape, edge, and elevation. It is important to pay attention to marsh surface topography and to include shallow depressions on the surface of the marsh to create small pools and tidal creeks that will accelerate the development of algae, aid plant survival, increase species diversity and fish use, and provide the restored marsh with features closer to that of a natural marsh.

In general, the marsh grass should be tall and dense enough to support key marsh species, the soil particles should be of a size appropriate to retain nitrogen to promote plant growth, and the stems should be close together to provide shading and reduce stress. Even if the marshes remain less productive and diverse than natural marshes, cordgrass can be established and the marshes do provide habitat for some animals. Monitoring is necessary until the new marsh appears mature and self-sustaining, and systematic data collection can assess whether the restored marsh is approaching or meeting the goals of the project. Aspects that should be monitored are surface topography and elevation, tidal creek cross-sections, water-table depth, surface and groundwater quality, soil organic matter, sediment accretion, plant species distribution and cover, benthic invertebrate communities, and utilization of the marsh by fishes and wildlife. Research and monitoring programs can help answer questions about which sites should be prioritized for restoration, what is the most cost-effective approach, and how the success of a restoration project can be measured. This type of monitoring can be done by government agencies or other parties involved in the project, or by university scientists or consultants, but good science is necessary for developing successful restoration projects.

Unfortunately, monitoring after restoration is often conducted for only three to five years, which is too short a period of time to evaluate the progress of many important attributes of a new marsh. Soil organic carbon, soil nitrogen, and biological communities probably require two decades or more to reach a level that is roughly equivalent to a reference marsh, so marshes should be evaluated based on their *progress* toward ecological goals, rather than by attempting to declare them a success or failure. Adaptive management allows a restoration plan to change whenever problems occur or new information is obtained, because a developing marsh system may evolve along pathways that diverge from the original plan. While restoration is being developed as a tool for improving salt marshes, restoration will never be more effective, cheaper, or easier than protecting existing healthy marshes in the first place.

Using Marshes for Wastewater Treatment

After the normal steps of primary and secondary sewage treatment (see chapter 5), some communities use created marshes (fig. 7.1) for tertiary treatment, to reduce the amounts of suspended solids, nitrogen, phosphorus, and other pollutants from wastewater or sewage. Constructed wetland systems (usually fresh water) are modeled after the ecological functions of natural wetlands, particularly their ability to decompose and convert organic and inorganic matter. The use of *reed beds,* the common European term for treatment wetlands, is widespread in northern Europe, where they use none other than our friend *Phragmites.*

There are now over six hundred constructed treatment wetlands in North America, most of them freshwater rather than brackish-water systems. Treatment wetlands may have free surface flow, with water flowing over shallow rooted or floating plants, or vegetated subsurface flow, in which the water flows in gravel beds below the surface of the treatment system in contact with the roots of the plants. In the United States, treatment wetland technology is not yet nationally recognized because people don't really understand exactly how the wetlands work. Since they are natural systems, their performance is variable, and because temperatures vary seasonally, affecting plant and microbial growth, the ability of wet-

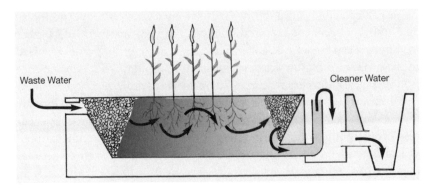

Waste Water

Cleaner Water

Fig. 7.1. Constructed wetland, consisting of a gravel bed on which wetland plants are grown. As water passes through, it is purified through the activity of bacteria, plant roots, soil, and other particles. *Courtesy of the U.N. Environment Program (UNEP), modified by John Laudando.*

lands to improve water quality varies as well. Many detailed questions are yet to be answered about how wetlands function, including their removal of biological oxygen demand (BOD), the effects of different plant species on a wetland's performance, the role of the plants' transport of oxygen to the root zone to promote nitrification, and the best ratio of open water to vegetated areas. We know that high levels of dissolved oxygen are beneficial to a wastewater treatment wetland, and dissolved oxygen may be increased by physical aeration at the surface as well as by the photosynthesis of the plants in the wetland system. The release of oxygen by plants to their root zone can enhance the growth of bacteria that improve wastewater treatment and promote nitrification (conversion of nitrate to nitrogen gas), and perhaps the release of oxygen from the roots may also help detoxify hazardous substances. Long-term field studies are investigating the workings of treatment wetlands and their capabilities in order to learn how to design more effective treatment systems.

Constructed wetland systems in North America have been designed predominantly for the large-scale treatment of municipal wastewater, capable of effectively removing a wide variety of pollutants including suspended solids (from fecal, food, and paper-product wastes), nitrogen, phosphate, ammonium, organic chemicals, metals, and bacteria. When the water enters the wetland, it spreads out into a slow, even flow, and heavy particles drift to the bottom. More buoyant particles may stick to each other as the water flows through the wetland (flocculation), or they may react chemically, forming heavier particles that also sink. The presence of rooted plants like common reeds creates a structure that improves the flocculation and settling of the suspended particles, and the intricate root systems provide good surfaces for large microbial populations that can remove large amounts of nitrogen and phosphorus from the wastewater. The plants themselves are also important in removing the nutrients, but to a lesser degree than the microbes. Removing the nutrients prevents eutrophication when the wastewater enters nearby bodies of water, but nutrients taken up by the plants contribute to their growth, and after the plants die, their decomposition can release the nutrients back into the system to be cycled again. It is generally impractical for rooted wetland plants to be harvested to prevent this recycling, but floating plants can be much more easily harvested. In contrast, denitrification by microbes has the advantage of not producing material that can be recycled in the system, as this process produces nitrogen gas that is released into the air.

The Arcata Marsh and Wildlife Sanctuary in California has been treating millions of gallons of municipal wastewater every day since 1986, and it is a very successful estuarine treatment wetland. The marsh serves as the final step in cleaning the water before it is released into nearby Humboldt Bay. Wastewater circulates through a six-marsh system which purifies the water by removing excess nutrients that "feed" plants with nitrogen-rich organic matter. The treatment marshes, constructed in the late 1970s at the site of a former landfill, were planted with native bulrush (*Scirpus acutus*) and other aquatic plants. Their roots and stems form a dense filter that removes suspended solid materials, and algae, fungi, bacteria, and micro-organisms on the roots feed on these solids. The marsh was intended not only to treat wastewater, but also to be a place for enjoying nature. The wetland is located along the Pacific Flyway, one of the nation's most important bird migration routes, and it provides a place for numerous birds to rest and feed during their seasonal journeys.

This treatment wetland is successful because the water flowing into it is not too dirty, since most of the pollutants and solids have been removed from the wastewater by a traditional treatment plant before they ever get to the marsh. The water is sent to an aeration pond for secondary treatment, and microscopic organisms feed on and break down the contaminants that remain in the water; then the water goes to a small wetland that provides further treatment but is not designed to support wildlife. Finally, the water is treated with chlorine and sent into the Arcata Marsh and Wildlife Sanctuary, which consists of three marshes in sequence. The water entering the marsh looks and smells clean, but it is still likely to carry small amounts of some pollutants as well as some residual chlorine from the sewage treatment plant, and it is likely to contain elevated levels of dissolved nutrients, which, if released directly into nearby Humboldt Bay, could damage the ecosystem. The water flows through the Arcata Marsh and Wildlife Sanctuary, where microorganisms and plants remove the remaining pollutants before it reaches the bay. To reduce the chance that wildlife will be harmed by the wastewater, pollutant levels are regularly monitored.

Arcata's waterfront is now one hundred acres of freshwater and saltwater marshes, brackish ponds, tidal sloughs, and estuaries. As a home or rest stop for over two hundred species of birds, the Arcata Marsh is considered one of the best birding sites along the Pacific Coast, and it is a model of wastewater reuse and wetland restoration that is so attractive that it is used by the public for recreation.

Wetlands can also be constructed to treat storm-water runoff from lawns and golf courses that is highly contaminated with pesticides and fertilizers. Urban runoff is highly polluted with suspended sediments, nutrients, and organic compounds from impervious surfaces like sidewalks and roads, and this can cause considerable toxicity to aquatic organisms.

For example, coho salmon migrating from the ocean into urban streams near Seattle exhibit neurological symptoms, and many of them die before they can migrate up to their spawning grounds. Those that survive can release high levels of contaminants when they die after spawning, and the contaminants can be taken up by grizzly bears that eat the salmon. Although the exact cause of their symptoms has not been determined, they are more prevalent in urban areas where there are large numbers of roads, resulting in a lot of runoff.

The initial runoff during the first hour of a storm tends to be the most highly contaminated, since much of the pollution on the surfaces is removed during the first period of rain. Wetlands are very efficient in removing pollutants from the runoff before it enters bodies of water; but, unfortunately, if there is inorganic mercury in the water, wetlands tend to convert it to the more toxic methylmercury. While total mercury decreases as the water passes through the wetland, the concentration of methylmercury increases, and this is the form that is more likely to biomagnify in food webs. If the oxygen level in the water can be kept higher this problem is reduced.

Marshes for Cleaning up Toxic Contaminants: Phytoremediation

While treatment wetlands are designed primarily to remove nutrients from the wastewater, wetlands have also been built to treat non-point runoff and other types of water that may contain large amounts of toxic materials, including acid mine drainage, industrial wastewater, agricultural and storm-water runoff. These wetlands provide *phytoremediation* of contaminated soils, which refers to the use of plants (phyto) to treat or remediate pollution. Organic chemicals and metals are taken out of the water by microbes and plants.

Processes that can be used by plants to deal with metals include *phytoextraction* of the contaminants from soil into the shoots of the plants for subsequent recycling; *phytostabilization* of metals in the soil into forms that are not available to living organisms; *phytovolatilization,* in which the plant removes metals from soil, passes them through its tissues, and releases them into the atmosphere; and *phytofiltration,* also called *rhizofiltration,* in which plants are grown hydroponically (with roots in water) and then transplanted into metal-polluted waters to absorb and concentrate the metals.

With phytostabilization, the mobility of pollutants is reduced by being concentrated in the roots, adsorbed onto roots, or precipitated in the root zone. Plant secretions into the rhizosphere precipitate the metals and bind them to soil particles, and the process works well for keeping metals bound to the soil. With rhizofiltration, plants growing in a hydroponic system are used to absorb, concentrate, or precipitate metals, which remain in the roots, and there is some environmental risk if the plants enter the food chain in the ecosystem. With phytovolatilization, wetland plants such as cordgrass and salt-marsh bulrush can remove chemicals like selenium from wastewater and drainage water; and they turn selenium salts into the gas dimethyl selenide, which is released into the air. Eventually, the selenium will come back down to earth, but since it is only harmful at very high concentrations, this is generally not considered a problem.

Wetlands have long been considered sinks for contaminants because the contaminants tend to be adsorbed onto sediments in the marsh and may become buried for long periods of time. Wetland plants provide a litter layer that provides habitat for microbes and a source of organic carbon so they can decontaminate the upper layer of sediments. Sulfide is abundant in wetlands due to the decay of sulfur-containing proteins in anoxic, waterlogged conditions; and metals rapidly combine with the sulfide, forming precipitates that are very stable under these conditions. This approach, in which the wetland immobilizes and stores the contaminants in the soil, is *phytostabilization*. In a system designed to treat mine wastes, Lesley Batty and colleagues found that iron was removed initially by chemical oxidation to form iron hydroxide precipitates in the beginning of the treatment system in oxidation ponds and in the initial reaches of the wetland, whereas in subsequent parts of the system, waste removal by plants became more important.

When phytoremediation is done on metal-contaminated soils on land, the species that are used are *hyperaccumulators*, and the process is phytoextraction. These land plants take up huge amounts of a particular metal, store most of it in leaves and stems, and then can be easily harvested. But since they have acquired such high metal concentrations, they must be carted away to a licensed hazardous-waste landfill. Marsh plants, however, cannot be harvested without doing great damage to the marsh, and they are not hyperaccumulators for any specific metal.

Metals tend to concentrate in the roots of wetland plants, and because they are stored below ground in deeper sediments, they will generally not cause trouble because they are unavailable to the rest of the ecosystem. Different species of marsh plants have different degrees of uptake and distribution of metals they take up. Cordgrass roots actively take up metals from the sediments, but some amounts are transported upwards through the stem and released from leaves back into the water to become available to the rest of the ecosystem. *Phragmites* stores more in its roots, thus the common reed would seem to be a preferable species for phytoremediation of metals. A genetically engineered variety of *Spartina alterniflora* has been developed that converts mercury into a gas that is released into the air (phytovolatilization), and it has recently been found that without any genetic engineering, *Phragmites* can release mercury gas into the air. While these plants will remove mercury from the soil, the airborne mercury will eventually come down somewhere else, so merely moving pollution from one place to another is not a satisfactory approach because even small concentrations of mercury are dangerous; and concentrations can build up through the food chain to dangerous levels in large fishes, as we already see in the warnings about limiting the consumption of tuna because of its high mercury content.

Pollutants may be released from treatment wetlands during seasonal cycles or if the wetland's capacity has been reached or exceeded, and if the excess contaminants are released into a nearby body of water, they threaten the nearby aquatic ecosystem and potentially damage the treatment wetland itself. If not properly monitored and managed, treatment wetlands can become "attractive nuisances" that could subject wildlife to risks of contamination. There is a considerable amount of political wrangling over this topic.

It is likely that natural wetlands that have been lost will never be adequately replaced. Despite the controversy surrounding them, the continued loss of natural wetlands is one reason for building and improving the design of treatment wetlands like Arcata. Natural wetlands should be protected and never used for waste treatment, and waste treatment should be left to the wetlands that were designed and built for that purpose and that represent a creative way to benefit nature while solving some of our pollution problems.

8 Death and Rebirth of an Urban Wetland
The Hackensack Meadowlands

In spite of the abuses heaped on them over the past two centuries, the meadows *have* survived, surprisingly intact. Today the Hackensack meadows and estuary epitomize the travails and the tarnished glories of urban ecosystems everywhere; like Lake Erie, the modern Meadowlands have risen, Lazarus-like, from the tomb of their own destruction and can now be said to be in a state of healing, of regeneration.

—John Quinn, *Fields of Sun and Grass,* 1997

For most of the American public, the name "New Jersey Meadowlands" does not signify a tidal wetland at all, but is associated with network broadcasts of sporting events from the Meadowlands Sports Complex. This 715-acre complex was built in the 1970s on filled former tidal wetlands located within the Meadowlands District, and it is now also the site of a shopping mall and entertainment center, the Xanadu project. The national media have offered glimpses of the New Jersey Meadowlands in films and on television in *Broadway Danny Rose, Being John Malkovich,* and, of course, *The Sopranos.*

The Hackensack Meadowlands is a 21,000-acre estuarine area of freshwater and saltwater marshes and meadows in the lower Hackensack River basin in northern New Jersey, about 17,000 acres of which were originally wetlands and open water. With its eastern edge just three miles west of Manhattan, it is the largest brackish marsh system in the New York–New Jersey harbor area and one of the largest in the northeastern United States. As a legacy of the days when shipping was the main mode of transport, most large metropolitan areas, including New York, are located on coasts or major waterways, and urban expansion has greatly altered the tidal wetlands. These blighted wetlands are devalued by the people responsible for their demise.

At one time, the Meadowlands covered thirty square miles from Oradell, New Jersey, on the north, down to Elizabethport at the south end of Newark Bay. The wetland system was subdivided into ten square miles that became the Newark Meadowlands, located on the western edge of Newark Bay, and twenty square miles that became the Hackensack Meadowlands, located above the mouths of the Passaic and Hackensack rivers. The Newark Meadowlands has been almost entirely converted to upland, as has one half of the Hackensack Meadowlands, so only approximately ten square miles of more-or-less undeveloped wetlands still exist in a patchwork pattern (fig. 8.1).

As part of the most densely populated region of North America, the area's natural ecological processes have been disturbed by extensive development, drainage, diking, filling, garbage dumping, and sewage pumping, The wetlands that have not been filled in are surrounded by urban development. Because the wetlands have been considered useless for many years, extensive areas have been polluted with industrial wastes, covered by asphalt, and used as legal landfills and illegal waste dumps.

Origins

The Hackensack Meadowlands are located in the basin of a glacial lake, Lake Hackensack, which was formed thousands of years ago during an ice age by the retreat of the Wisconsin Glacier. As ice melted and withdrew, debris and rocks that the glacier had carried down from the north were left behind in rows of rubble called *terminal moraines,* and the lake was formed when melt water was trapped behind a terminal moraine of rock and earth. Later, when sediments were deposited in the lake bed, vegetation took root in the lake's shallow regions, and between eight thousand and ten thousand years ago, when sea level rose and water flowed over the moraine, tidal water mixed in with the fresh water and an estuary was created. Plant communities came and went, responding to sea-level changes that altered salinities.

In the eighteenth century, the harvest of salt hay was of great economic importance in the lower reaches of the Hackensack River; and in the nineteenth century, the Hackensack Meadowland was a boggy area dominated by Atlantic white cedar (*Chamacyparis thyoides*). The cedar was harvested and used for boat masts, bedding, bowls, and logs for building. The cedar forests eventually declined due to harvesting as well as to land subsidence or sea-level rise, and fires were also common.

Widespread agricultural activities along with sea-level rise resulted in the decline of freshwater wetlands and an increase in brackish and salt-marsh communities. Small-scale reclamation projects involving diking and draining were common ways to try to increase the amount of agricul-

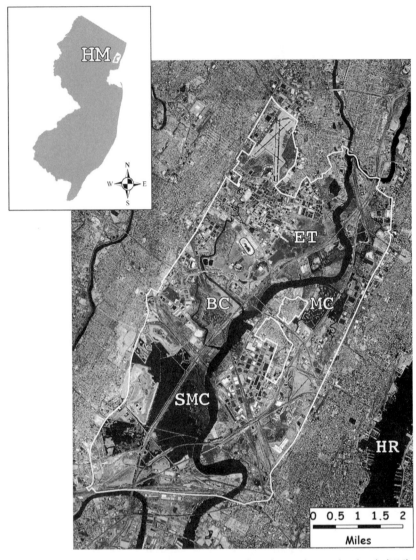

Fig. 8.1. Map of New Jersey showing location of Hackensack Meadowlands (HM) and map of the Hackensack Meadowlands (SMC = Saw Mill Creek, MC = Mill Creek, BC = Berry's Creek, ET = Empire Tract, HR = Hudson River, for reference). *Courtesy of the New Jersey Meadowlands Commission, modified by Ildiko Pechmann.*

tural land, but a number of these new areas subsided below sea level and failed. As the region's population grew, railroads and roads were built that crossed the marsh and fragmented it, so that by 1896, twelve important railways crossed the Hackensack and Newark meadows, going east-west as well as north-south. The filling and grading of railroad rights-of-way disrupted the natural tidal cycle of the estuary and altered the distribution of fresh and salt water, and the cedar forests were further reduced by the increased inflow of saltier water.

As early as the 1860s, ditching as an attempt to control mosquitoes and diking to make land more suitable for development became important activities. The area was further ditched and diked for mosquito control in the first half of the twentieth century using mechanized equipment, and the altered hydrology as a result of over seventeen thousand acres being ditched and diked led to additional changes. In the early part of the twentieth century the area was a brackish tidewater marsh with *Spartina, Juncus, Distichlis, Salicornia,* and *Limonium* growing in the higher-salinity areas. The lower-salinity areas had *Typha* (cattails) and *Phragmites*, which was the most common plant on the marshes. Reduced tidal flow and salinity led to *Phragmites* increasing its territory, but it was not yet considered a villain.

Another major change in hydrology that further diminished the freshwater wetlands was the construction of the Oradell Dam in the 1920s. Located upstream of the Meadowlands, it greatly reduced freshwater flow

---

Hackensack Pirates

Around the time of the American Revolution, the Hackensack area was desolate and dangerous. It was a hangout for pirates and thieves who ambushed and raided stagecoaches and ferryboats. The states of New York and New Jersey planned a campaign against the so-called pirates of the cedar swamps, and they hunted the pirates from Hackensack to the town of Harrison. Armed boats patrolled the Passaic and Hackensack rivers, and naval boats armed with howitzers attacked the pirate boats in Newark Bay. The pirates retreated up the bay to the mouth of the Hackensack River.

Groups of armed men entered the creeks and marshes on foot in an attempt to find the remaining pirates. One group never returned, and the other group found no trace of the pirates. Their descriptions of the snake-infested wilderness ended further attempts to penetrate the meadows, and eventually the pursuers set fire to the woods and meadows. They burned for several days, driving the pirates to higher ground, where most of them were captured or killed by the armed patrols.

and allowed more salt water from Newark Bay to flow up the Hackensack River. Dams along the river impeded the migration of fishes such as American shad, alewife, and blueback herring, which migrate into fresh water to breed.

Decline of Water Quality

The growing urban population in the New York–New Jersey metropolitan area used the Hackensack Meadowlands as a place to dispose of its wastes. Throughout the 1950s and 1960s, the Meadowlands were devastated by uncontrolled dumping of millions of tons of garbage at twenty-four garbage dumps that covered twenty-five hundred acres. Garbage trucks and railroad cars filled with trash from many New Jersey municipalities and New York City were unloaded into the wetlands. In those days, since no distinction was made between household waste and "hazardous waste," all sorts of toxic materials were mixed with the garbage being dumped in the estuary. By the early 1970s the Meadowlands were being filled with thirty thousand tons of waste a week. Filling the marshes with garbage was thought to be a solution to waste disposal and also a way to raise the level of the marsh and "reclaim" it for future development. Fires would spontaneously combust on the dumps and some of them burned underground for years. Smoke from these burning heaps choked the skies and further fouled waters that were already contaminated from the waste that had been leaching into the wetlands, mudflats, and creeks. Waterborne diseases became rampant, made worse by industrial development that included paint, textile, petroleum, chemical, plastics, and pharmaceutical factories that all dumped their waste products directly into the wetlands and waterways.

As early as the 1920s, people complained about the poor fishing and about the pollution generated by sewage and industry, and several towns banned bathing in the river. To add insult to injury, the river was also filled with pig waste from rendering plants, hot water from power plants, and oil slicks. There were thirteen active sewage plants discharging effluents into the Hackensack River and, until the late 1960s, most of the sewage was untreated. The area smelled bad, liquids of various colors could be seen being discharged from factories into the water, and the water itself was topped with an oily sheen. Several huge power plants warmed up the water, which reduced the amount of dissolved oxygen, and aquatic life dwindled down to very few hardy species. Fisheries and river-based recreation basically ended. Children occasionally went into the swamps to look at animals, and duck hunters and trappers of muskrat and raccoons still searched for the remaining wildlife. Even in the worst of times muskrats could be trapped in large numbers by local trappers, but for most people, the Meadowlands was justifiably considered an unpleasant wasteland. More fresh water enters the Meadowlands from sewage treatment plants than flows in from the Oradell Dam, further up the Hackensack River. This toxic legacy has left hotspots of chromium, polychlorinated biphenyl (PCB), mercury, and other contaminants throughout the marshes and river.

Superfund Sites

Superfund sites are an important element in understanding the development of the Meadowlands area since there are three Superfund sites draining into Berry's Creek, a major tributary of the Hackensack River. Superfund is the common name for the U.S. environmental law officially known as the Comprehensive Environmental Response, Compensation, and Liability Act (CERCLA), which was enacted by the U.S. Congress in response to the Love Canal disaster in 1978. The thirty-six-square-block neighborhood around the Love Canal in the Niagara Falls area of upper New York State was found to be sitting on top of a toxic waste landfill that was causing illness in the area's residents, and the Superfund law was created to protect people and the environment from toxic waste sites that have been abandoned.

The law set up the National Priority List (NPL), which allowed states to recommend sites that were highly contaminated and in need of cleanup, and it assessed a tax on the chemical and oil industries to pay for toxic waste cleanups at sites where no other parties could be identified and held responsible. CERCLA authorizes two kinds of responses: short-term actions taken to address sites posing an immediate risk and requiring prompt response, such as abandoned drums leaking hazardous substances, and longer-term remedial actions that permanently reduce the risks associated with hazardous substances that are not posing an immediate threat.

In addition to establishing the sites on the priority list, CERCLA established the principle that "the polluter pays"—people are responsible for their releases of hazardous waste. Four classes of parties, termed "potential responsible parties" (PRPs), may be liable for contamination at a Superfund site: the current owner or operator of a site, the owner or operator of a site at the time that disposal of a hazardous substance occurred, a person who arranged for the disposal of a pollutant at a site, and a person who transported a hazardous substance to a site.

There are seven Superfund sites in or near the Meadowlands that contaminate the area, including Berry's Creek, mentioned above, which is one of the most mercury-contaminated sites in the nation. Just outside the borders of the district is the area of the lower Passaic River that is one of the most dioxin-contaminated sites in the country. One can still see places with ooze dripping into the river from abandoned factories as well as yellow chromium-laden soil near the shell of the factory that once refined this metal. Other debris can be seen falling into the river from former landfills. There are seven sewage treatment plants, thirty-two combined sewer overflows, and twelve emergency outflows in the Meadowlands District, so toxic contamination clearly remains a continuing problem. In addition to chromium and mercury, contaminants of concern in the system include PCBs, dioxins, chlorinated pesticides, polycyclic aromatic hydrocarbons (PAHs), and lead, according to the EPA (see http://www.epa.gov/region02/superfund/npl/0200674c.pdf).

The NPL helps the Environmental Protection Agency prioritize sites for cleanup. The list is updated periodically, and the identification of a site for the NPL is intended primarily to guide the EPA in determining which sites warrant further investigation to assess the extent of the human health and environmental risks. They identify what remedial actions may be appropriate, notify the public of sites that warrant further investigation, and serve notice to potentially responsible parties that EPA may initiate remedial action. Inclusion of a site on the NPL does not in itself require potentially liable parties to clean up the site, nor does it assign liability to any person.

The Superfund law lacks sufficient funds to clean up even a small number of the sites. The EPA will typically order PRPs to clean up the site themselves. If a party fails to comply, it may be fined up to twenty-five thousand dollars for each day that noncompliance continues. A party that spends money to clean up a site may sue other PRPs. As an example of what can result, a site like Berry's Creek in the Meadowlands, designated over thirty years ago as a site that needed to be cleaned up, has been in litigation ever since and has not received any remediation.

Loss of the Wetlands

In 1868, New Jersey state geologist George Cook reasoned that, because the marshes occupied a large area of land near the developing urban areas of Newark, Elizabeth, and Jersey City, "they must soon be reclaimed, so as to be fit either for cultivation, or for occupation with buildings," according to Stephen Marshall (2004). His advice was taken with enthusiasm, and remote sensing studies and historical maps show that of the approximately twenty thousand acres of wetlands that were present in George Cook's time, only about fifty-five hundred to seven thousand acres remained by 1995. (The varying estimates depend on whether drained wetlands are included in the count.)

Up until the 1950s losses were about one hundred acres per year, but the greatest wetland losses occurred in the 1960s and 1970s when annual losses averaged three hundred acres. From the 1970s to 1980s, losses declined to about two hundred acres per year, and currently only about twenty acres per year are lost. The wetlands remaining in the 1950s and 1960s were blocked with dams and tidal gates to stop the flow of water, and they were used as disposal sites for household garbage, old automobiles, liquid and solid industrial waste, and, possibly, Jimmy Hoffa.

Construction of Newark airport started in 1928 on marshland just south of the Hackensack Meadowlands proper. In order to build an airport on the marshland, enormous amounts of sand taken from Newark Bay were pumped into the area to raise the level of the marsh and to make it firm enough for runways. By 1930 it was the busiest airport in the country, and it was serving New York City before La Guardia and Kennedy airports were built on filled marshland in the borough of Queens in New York City. The smaller Teterboro airport was built in 1941 on 550 acres of former marshes in the Meadowlands. A regional plan in the late 1920s envisioned filling acres of "mosquito-infested New Jersey swampland," according to Marshall, with two hundred million cubic yards of dirt, dredging and straightening out the river, and building a city larger than New York (fig. 8.2), but not all the planned projects were completed.

The first roads built across the marshes in colonial times were made of planks of cedar wood that were very durable, and one road today is still called Paterson Plank Road, although these roads were eventually replaced by paved surfaces of concrete and asphalt. The New Jersey Turnpike, built in the 1950s, was probably the largest construction job affecting the Meadowlands, and it drastically altered the ecological integrity of the system. The vast *berms* (raised level areas) interrupted the tidal action of the estuary, and the traffic released tons of debris and pollutants including lead, copper, and rubber into the marshes. The turnpike is the site from which most people have a chance to look at the Meadowlands as they drive between Newark and areas further north.

The Hackensack Meadowlands Development Commission (HMDC)

The Hackensack Meadowlands Development Commission was established by an act of the New Jersey legislature in 1969 to provide for the reclamation, planned development, and redevelopment of the Hackensack Meadowlands, which at that time covered thirty-two square miles in Bergen and Hudson counties. HMDC was given the three-fold job of

A Magic City from a Swamp

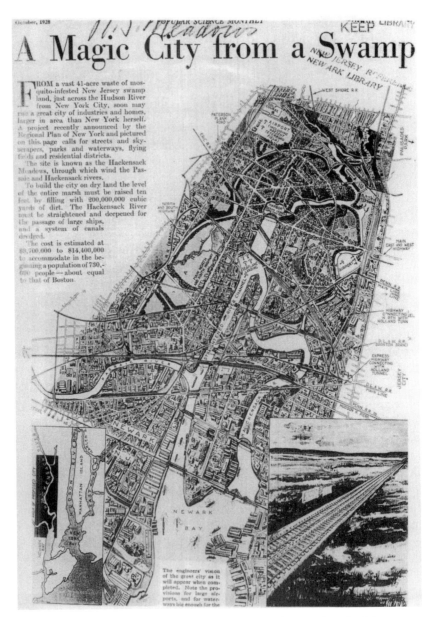

FROM a vast 41-acre waste of mosquito-infested New Jersey swamp land, just across the Hudson River from New York City, soon may rise a great city of industries and homes, larger in area than New York herself. A project recently announced by the Regional Plan of New York and pictured on this page calls for streets and skyscrapers, parks and waterways, flying fields and residential districts.

The site is known as the Hackensack Meadows, through which wind the Passaic and Hackensack rivers.

To build the city on dry land the level of the entire marsh must be raised ten feet, by filling with 200,000,000 cubic yards of dirt. The Hackensack River must be straightened and deepened for the passage of large ships, and a system of canals dredged.

The cost is estimated at $8,700,000 to $14,400,000 to accommodate in the beginning a population of 730,000 people—about equal to that of Boston.

The engineers' vision of the great city as it will appear when completed. Note the provisions for large airports, and for waterways big enough for the

Fig 8.2. A 1928 plan for the Hackensack Meadowlands. *From* Popular Science Monthly.

The Newark Meadows

The southern one-third of the original Meadowlands was located west of Newark Bay in Newark and Elizabeth, but this area has been largely filled and is home to one of the nation's largest and most diverse areas of transportation infrastructure. Only small remnant patches of the original tidal wetlands remain around parts of the airport and around Newark Bay. The area now contains Port Newark-Elizabeth, the birthplace of containerization, the site of world's first container terminal, and the center of containerization-induced urban waterfront abandonment. The growth of containerization at this port is a major cause of the decline of the nearby Port of New York. The area also contains Newark (Liberty) International Airport, the first major airport in the New York City–New Jersey metropolitan area, built in the late 1920s.

New Jersey Transit and the remaining Conrail rail facilities funnel commuters and travelers into the region, and the area is a major hub of highways. Originally, cars and trucks leaving the nation's largest city were unceremoniously dumped out of the western end of the Holland Tunnel onto local roads wending their way through the New Jersey (Newark) Meadowlands, but Jersey City mayor Frank Hague, head of the Hudson County political machine, was a prime mover behind the building of the country's first superhighway designed to connect New York City to the rest of the country. The New Jersey Turnpike and Routes 22, 1, and 9 now receive the New York City traffic and distribute it to the rest of the country. The construction of the Pulaski Skyway is a story of its own, an epic battle between big labor and big politics.

waste management, development, and conservation, which are at best difficult to balance. They first closed down and capped unregulated landfills, in many cases leaving the legacy of decades of toxic contaminants under a layer of dirt, so that leachate continues to ooze out of the dumpsites into the river. They also decreased illegal dumping activities, prohibited New York garbage from coming into the Meadowlands, and cleaned up remaining landfills, all of which reduced both the release of contaminants into the air and the amount of leachate oozing into the river and wetlands. Then they turned their attention to improving the wetlands.

The commission bought thousands of acres of wetlands and rezoned them for preservation, but they also permitted hundreds of development projects; and, by 1989, privately funded developments worth more than one billion dollars had been permitted. As the river got cleaner and the polluting factories were closed, the area became more attractive and many acres of wetlands were filled for the construction of warehouses, hotels, residences, and office buildings. Filling wetlands required permits under section 404 of the Clean Water Act, and they were easy to obtain from the Army Corps of Engineers. Although not under the control of the commission, a 750-acre sports complex, which includes the Meadowlands Racetrack, Continental Airlines Arena (now the Izod Center), Giants Stadium, and tens of thousands of paved parking spaces, was approved by the state legislature and built on wetlands in the 1970s. By this time, much of the acreage in the Meadowlands was owned by large developers who built industrial parks with warehouses and distribution centers. Although many hundreds of acres of wetlands were filled, because it was regulated development guided by the HMDC, it was an improvement over the indiscriminate dumping and haphazard land use and abuse that occurred in the 1950s and 1960s.

Renaissance: Water Quality

Filled with garbage, poisoned with industrial waste, drained, paved over, burned, mined, and deforested, America's most stubborn and unexpected wetlands are recovering from decades of abuse. Where else can you canoe down a marshy creek with a view of the Empire State Building?

—"Swamps of Jersey: The Meadowlands," *National Geographic*, February 2001

At the time the HMDC was established, the Hackensack River was nearly dead, and the Meadowlands' wetlands were being used as a disposal site for 30 to 40 percent of New Jersey's garbage. Since 1969 there have been dramatic improvements in this ecosystem, with the result that the water quality has greatly improved and wildlife has returned.

The founding of HMDC occurred shortly before the passage of the federal Clean Water Act in 1970. That act required permits to discharge materials into the water and stimulated communities to upgrade and build effective sewage treatment plants that greatly reduced the inflow of sewage wastes into the water. Changes in the region's economic base also helped improve the environmental quality as polluting industries closed and non-polluting service and information-technology businesses were established. This was the beginning of the turnaround of the Meadowlands.

As the water quality in the Hackensack River has improved dramatically, there have been striking increases in the numbers of fish, bird, and invertebrate species. More than fifty species of fishes now use the estuary for parts of their life cycles, and despite the fact that sediments remain contaminated with industrial pollutants and consumption of fishes and crabs from the area is prohibited, the lower Hackensack River system has been declared an essential fish habitat by the National Marine Fisheries Service, an action mandated by Congress (2006) for each federally managed fish species. An essential fish habitat is defined by Congress as "those waters and substrate necessary to fish for spawning, breeding, feeding, or growth to maturity." For the Meadowlands, this designation covers six species: red hake (*Urophycis chuss*), black sea bass (*Centropristis striata*), Atlantic butterfish (*Peprilus triacanthus*), and three flounders (in the families *Pleuronectidae* and *Bothidae*). Designation is pending for bluefish (*Pomatomus saltatrix*) and Atlantic herring (*Clupea harengus*). The Sustainable Fisheries Act requires cooperation among the National Marine Fisheries Service (NMFS), the Fishery Management Councils, and other agencies to work together to protect, conserve, and enhance these designated areas.

Low dissolved oxygen (DO) and other water quality problems still reduce species diversity, especially in marsh creeks and ponds. A survey of fishes in the late 1980s by Mark Kraus and A. Brett Bragin found many species of brackish, freshwater, and migratory fishes, but the small, tolerant killifish were far more numerous than any other species, comprising 85 percent of the total catch. A repeat survey in the early 2000s by Brett Bragin and colleagues found that the diversity of fishes had increased greatly and that killifish no longer comprised such a major component. There were more large predators, and the increase in numbers of white perch was particularly striking.

About 75 percent of the bird species seen in New Jersey use the Meadowlands, and the area is known as an important habitat for rare and vulnerable species of waterfowl and wading birds (fig. 8.3). Over 60 bird species are considered to be residents, and about 260 species of birds have been counted. The Meadowlands provides foraging habitat for migratory waterfowl, wading birds, and neotropical songbirds, as well as wintering grounds for raptors. As early as the 1970s, the New Jersey Audubon Society began surveys in the Meadowlands, and their Christmas Bird Count has found up to 73 overwintering species. Egrets and herons are seen foraging, moorhens, ducks, and American coots are present, and if you are very lucky you may spot a reclusive rail among the reeds. Endangered northern harrier and yellow-crowned night heron nest in the Meadowlands, and ospreys and peregrine falcons use the marshes as hunting grounds.

In the 2007 survey, the most commonly seen endangered species was the northern harrier, which breeds in the Meadowlands, and the most common threatened species included osprey, black-crowned night heron, and Savannah sparrow. The common moorhen was the most abundant marsh

Fig. 8.3. Egrets live in the *Phragmites* marshes of the Hackensack Meadowlands, a few miles from the Empire State Building. *Photo from Hackensack Riverkeeper.*

species, along with red-winged blackbirds. Herring gulls, ring-billed gulls, and great black-backed gulls were the most common colonial waterbirds, while mallards and Canada geese were the most abundant waterfowl. The most common raptor was the red-tailed hawk, while semipalmated sandpiper and ruddy duck had the highest numbers overall. Though not very common, up to five bald eagles were seen regularly. Shorebirds like sandpipers were found to use the area mostly as a stopover during their southern migration, while waterfowl such as the ruddy duck and green-winged teal were found primarily in the winter, and Canada geese, mallards, gadwalls, red-winged blackbirds, starlings, and song sparrows were found year round. Insectivores like marsh wrens, barn swallows, and tree swallows were present in the spring and summer during their breeding season when their prey is abundant. As expected, the Meadowlands was a critical foraging area for herons and egrets. Open water areas had 91 species, the high marsh had 87 species, and *Phragmites* had 81 species, supporting the ecological role of this plant.

The Environmental Protection Agency identified the Meadowlands as an "Aquatic Resource of National Importance" in 2002. In 2004, the state of New Jersey designated the entire upper watershed as "Category One" waters, which is the highest level of protection in the United States. Municipalities were required to manage their storm water, and several landfills were capped, preventing twelve billion gallons of leachate from entering the river over the next thirty years. Cleanups took place in a number of areas where hundreds of volunteers removed tons of trash from river and stream banks.

The Meadowlands is now an area of calm and open space in the midst of the urban bustle, and it provides a sense of wilderness and natural landscape for the twenty million residents of the surrounding urban area. The average motorist driving along the New Jersey Turnpike, scanning the reeds waving in the breeze, has no idea of the thriving life below. Sawmill Creek marsh is the healthiest within the system (fig. 8.1). It had been diked for mosquito control in the early 1900s, but in 1950 a storm destroyed the dikes and reopened the creek to tidal flow. The increased tidal flow may be one reason why it is the healthiest in the system, which reinforces the idea of the importance of tides to the survival of brackish marshes. Also, Sawmill Creek is not located very near to severely contaminated sites. Once the tidal flow was restored, cordgrass returned after low-lying common reeds died out in this now well-flushed area, and *Spartina* has been gradually taking over territory from the reeds ever since. The area is home to striped bass, diamondback terrapin, great blue heron, least bittern, black-crowned night heron, skimmers and osprey, and other animals. Visitors paddle in kayaks and canoes, retreating from the frenetic pace of urban life in the quiet creeks.

Duck hunting and fishing are popular, and there is a catch-and-release fishery. Despite the environmental improvements, the fishery was set up as catch and release because the fishes are too contaminated to eat safely. Half of the white perch tested exceeded the federal mercury guidelines for one meal per month, and nearly all showed PCB levels ten times the maximum levels recommended by the Environmental Protection Agency. There is concern that contamination could have adverse effects on new restoration projects because fishes and wildlife might now be exposed to newly released contaminants that had previously been stored in buried sediments. Continuing to identify the sources of the contaminants and eliminating them are goals of the New York–New Jersey Estuary Program.

Renaissance: Marsh Conservation and Restoration

The initial step in the restoration of the Meadowlands was a marginally successful enhancement project. The Harmon Cove condominiums were built on the shore of the river in Secaucus in the late 1980s by the Hartz

Mountain Corporation. They were permitted to fill in many acres of wetlands by HMDC as long as the company would mitigate the impact of the development by constructing a sixty-three-acre brackish marsh elsewhere. The mitigation site, the first in the Meadowlands, was less than half the size of the filled wetlands, but the new marsh was intended to be of much higher ecological value. Mitigation projects like this can cost over fifty thousand dollars per acre (in 1988 dollars).

The brackish marsh ecosystem restored by Hartz Mountain on Mill Creek in Secaucus, New Jersey, was considered a degraded marsh with poor water quality. It was dominated by tall, dense stands of common reed whose elevation severely limited tidal inundation. At the time, little was known about the ecological value of the reed, and the dense stands were not considered to be of any value to waterfowl, marsh mammals, or wading shorebirds. What was known was that the reed dries the marsh soil, reduces water flow, and increases site elevation through accumulation of organic matter and sediments. The mitigation goals were to enhance wildlife diversity and abundance by converting the site to a cordgrass marsh, removing the reeds, and lowering the elevation to increase tidal inundation. An effort was made to construct a more diverse habitat that included open water and raised areas.

The site was initially sprayed with the herbicide Rodeo® to kill the reeds, and then it was shaped and graded to produce the elevations required by cordgrass. The high marsh was shaped into channels and open water, lower-elevation intertidal zones and raised berms. But the trees, shrubs, and herbaceous vegetation that were planted in higher areas died due to the high salt content of the soil. Cordgrass did become established on much of the intertidal zone, but to this day it remains patchy and is found on elevated hummocks with low bare areas between them, which is not its normal distribution in natural marshes. Some native marsh plants, such as fleabane, rushes, and sedges, have reappeared naturally on higher parts of the site. The water quality has improved because of the creation of more channels which provide greater water surface area for oxygen exchange and greater tidal flushing. There are more bird species on the mitigation site than on the unrestored site.

It remains a problem that the level of coliform bacteria is still elevated, due in all likelihood to the proximity of a municipal sewage treatment plant, and the benthic community is comprised mostly of a few pollution-tolerant species, indicating that the ecosystem is still stressed. Changing the vegetation growing on the marsh cannot eliminate the legacy of toxic materials stored in the sediments.

Because there was no attempt to re-create the particular ecosystem

Personal Study in the Meadowlands

I have known about the Meadowlands for many years. Initially, they seemed to be a totally wrecked environment with nothing to interest an estuarine biologist like me, even though I am interested in pollution. Except for one short study in that area, my efforts during the 1970s and 1980s were focused mainly on other, somewhat less-contaminated brackish wetland areas just south of Newark Bay, where I felt the marshes had some organisms to study.

I passed by the Meadowlands often while driving on the New Jersey Turnpike or while on the train to New York City. I also flew over them on occasion, when I was on a plane landing at Newark Airport. In the late 1980s, when the first restoration project took place in the Meadowlands, the positive publicity surrounding it and the fact that a former graduate student of mine had worked on the project finally sparked my interest.

In the 1990s, the Meadowlands Commission set up a program, the Meadowlands Environmental Research Institute (MERI), designed to stimulate more research in their marshes. I responded and set up a number of research projects in the marsh and got to know the area, and I eventually made these wetlands the focus of most of the research done in my lab. I was interested in whether the common reed, which so dominates this system, is really ecologically as useless as some developers claimed. Did it have any value as habitat for marsh animals? Did its detritus have any food value? How did reed compare with cordgrass as food or as habitat? How did it deal with metal contaminants compared with cordgrass? I was also interested in how fishes and crabs in this system dealt with the stresses in their environment.

I interacted with other scientists who were also turning their attention to this abused ecosystem, as well as with environmental groups who were fighting to preserve it. The story of this urban wetland deserves telling. It is in some ways a worst-case scenario, but it is also a story with a happy ending (at least thus far, as the story hasn't really ended).

---

that existed on the site prior to the degradation of the Meadowlands, strictly speaking, the project was a habitat enhancement and conversion, not a restoration. Where there once probably was a high marsh of salt hay and spikegrass, there now is an intertidal marsh with mud flats and raised islands of woody vegetation. There is no evidence that this kind of ecosystem ever existed there before, and because of the limited scope of the project, it had no real impact on the overall ecological quality of the Meadowlands.

An increase in the presence of wildlife species is a promising indication that ecological health is returning, but it is insufficient evidence for declaring that restoration has occurred. Ecological integrity, structure, function, and ecosystem processes also need to be restored before the project can be declared a success as measured against reference sites (see chapter 7). The urban nature of the Meadowlands presents a major challenge in identifying reference sites since there are no similar, undisturbed sites nearby.

Additional wetland areas in the Meadowlands have been mitigated or improved in Skeetkill Marsh, Harrier Meadows, upper Mill Creek, Anderson Creek marsh, and other locations. A two-hundred-acre private mitigation bank was built to compensate for areas filled in the district, and the remediation of many acres of abandoned landfills is progressing. Restoration is also ongoing in upland areas, where a major project is underway to cap over one thousand acres of former landfills. This venture involves putting down a thick layer of soil and replanting vegetation. The cap will be made up of over three million cubic yards of dredged soils and nearly one million cubic yards of other recycled material. It will take several years to cap the four landfills that were never properly closed, but once the dumps are capped, a skirt of impermeable plastic or a steel barrier wall will be put in place with drains that collect any leachate that seeps through and pump it to a sewage plant for treatment. The former landfills will be revegetated for the benefit of wildlife and people. While they cannot ever be marshes again, they can become functional upland habitats.

The Role of Non-governmental Organizations

Throughout the 1990s, new players entered the scene. Environmental groups became active in working to conserve the Meadowlands and to call for the end of filling in wetlands for development. The New Jersey Audubon Society began regular bird surveys in the 1970s, and Andrew Willner began the work of the New York–New Jersey Baykeeper and pressed HMDC to stop development, fragmentation, and degradation of the remaining wetlands. Bill Sheehan, a former taxi dispatcher, was a volunteer with New York–New Jersey Baykeeper's Boating Auxiliary before founding the Hackensack Riverkeeper organization, which has become the leading advocate for conservation in the Meadowlands. Other local advocacy groups were founded to fight for environmental preservation in particular sites and to ensure public input. They were instrumental in stopping development on hundreds of acres. HMDC was considered a villain that took the side of developers.

The Battle of the SAMP, Mills Corporation, and the Empire Tract

The SAMP (Special Area Management Plan) was an outgrowth of the federal Coastal Zone Management Act. The act permits a SAMP to be written, ostensibly to protect sensitive habitats, but with the goal of helping the state and federal governments to balance environmental protection with economic development and to compromise on the amount of wetlands to be developed. Despite some sections on wetlands protection, the Meadowlands SAMP, written in the 1990s, was a lengthy plan that would speed up wetland fill permits by bringing together federal (EPA, Army Corps of Engineers, etc.), state (N.J. Department of Environmental Protection), and local (HMDC) regulatory agencies. The Draft Environmental Impact Statement (DEIS) for the entire 7,000 acres of remaining wetlands in the Meadowlands would have eliminated the need for federal review of large-scale development projects and would have allowed for the issuance of General Permits, which require no public review at all, for filling wetlands of 15 acres or less. Its supporters said it was a unique vision that would mesh together the interests of the economy and environment.

The SAMP initially allowed development on 2,200 acres, an even larger area than the 1,800 acres allowed in a master plan written fifteen years earlier in the less environmentally aware era. Environmental groups were furious that the no-net-loss policy was not being followed, the Fish and Wildlife Service would not agree to the SAMP, and many of the municipalities opposed it. After intense opposition led by Hackensack Riverkeeper and New York–New Jersey Baykeeper, the amount of proposed wetland fill was reduced from 2,200 to 435 acres. However, as Baykeeper Andy Willner said, "The problem was that they failed to acknowledge that two-thirds of the Meadowlands were already gone and that the time for compromise was over," as quoted by Hugh Carola in the *Hackensack Riverkeeper Newsletter* (see http://www.hackensackriverkeeper.org/newsletters/Winter2002/004_Winter_2002.htm).

The Mills Corporation proposed to build an enormous complex containing stores, entertainment facilities, and offices on 206 of the acres in the 592-acre Empire Tract (fig. 8.1) that was included in the SAMP. They proposed to pave over wetlands they considered degraded, full of reeds they deemed useless, and the compensation they proposed was to destroy additional acres of *Phragmites* elsewhere for mitigation projects that they hoped would eventually become *Spartina* marshes. In addition to the outright destruction of this huge area of wetlands, the mall and its parking lots would have produced a lot of air pollution and runoff, carrying grease and metals into nearby wetlands and creeks. A permit to fill the wetlands would have to be obtained from the Army Corps of Engineers, which received nine thousand public comments on this application, 85 percent of which strongly objected to the project. The EPA joined with acting New Jersey Governor Donald Di Francesco, the U.S. Fish and Wildlife Service, and the National Marine Fisheries Service in opposing this plan because of its severe impacts on the Meadowlands ecosystem, as well as because suitable alternative sites were available in nearby cities that were in need of urban renewal.

The HMDC held a series of public meetings on the Mills Corporation's proposal, and advocates of the project argued that economic benefits would accrue to the local economy from such a major construction project and that destroying degraded wetlands was worthwhile because of the need for more retail and office space. Union representatives wanted the jobs that would be created by the massive project.

Opponents of the project stressed that filling in the 465 acres would destroy vital marsh habitat and fragment the region's largest remaining open space. They pointed out that it would also be the largest wetland fill allowed since passage of the Clean Water Act in 1972, and they argued that the SAMP would harm the quality of life by increasing traffic, causing flooding, and eroding the health, including the financial health, of local downtowns. They questioned the need for yet another mall in northern New Jersey, the need for another truck parking lot in wetlands, and the reasons that such a project should not be created instead to redevelop an urban center, where the same jobs could be created. Municipal officials were split in their opinions; some supported the project for economic reasons while others opposed it due to concerns about flooding and competition with local retailers in their towns. At a meeting we attended, hundreds of union members, wearing caps to identify themselves, reacted loudly to proponents of the project by cheering and to opponents by booing. In a bizarre twist, at the stroke of 7:30 p.m. they all simultaneously stood up and left because, as we later learned, they had only been paid to stay until that hour.

On January 23, 2002, the Hackensack Meadowlands Development Commission, with Robert Ceberio as its new executive director, formally withdrew its support for the SAMP and for the Mills Corporation's proposed development of the Empire Tract. By a unanimous vote, the six commissioners put an end to the plan. Without a local sponsor, the SAMP died, a major victory for the environment. (Postscript: the mall, Xanadu, is being built on land filled in years ago for the sports complex at the Continental Airlines Arena site.)

A New Era for the Meadowlands Commission

In the past, the HMDC has approved the development of substantial wetland acreage, and it set a precedent of trading wetland development for wetland enhancement, with a resulting net loss of marsh acreage. In January 2004, the agency was re-named the New Jersey Meadowlands Commission, deleting the word *development* from its title. A master plan was adopted that called for permanent preservation of the remaining 8,400-acre ecosystem for the Meadowlands Estuary Reserve. Under their new executive director, the commission has developed a new appreciation for the oasis they manage in the middle of this highly populated region. They support the use of science to inform decision making, and they utilize the results of research sponsored by the Meadowland Environmental Research Institute (MERI) that was set up a few years earlier. Their goals include the following:

- Clean up contaminated sites;
- Acquire, preserve, and restore undeveloped land;
- Open up remaining tide gates to allow for normal tidal flow;
- Preserve and restore vegetated wetland and upland areas; and
- Control invasive and exotic species.

The New Jersey Meadowlands Commission has already re-zoned over one thousand acres, changing their designation from redevelopment zones to marshland preservation zones. Some of the restorations will include remediation of highly contaminated Superfund sites, and some are compensatory mitigation for the loss of other wetland sites. The projects are being undertaken by different government agencies, non-governmental organizations, and private businesses, although the NJMC is involved in them as well. Complicated agreements and funding arrangements are common.

In 2006, the New Jersey Audubon Society published a free booklet, *Guide for Birding and Wildlife Trails in the Meadowlands and More* (http://www.njaudubon.org/BWT/NJmeadowlands.html). Congressman Steve Rothman, whose district includes the Meadowlands, said at an area conference in 2003, "What people now realize is that we already have so much developed space that is abandoned, underutilized and in need of renovation, that jobs can be redirected toward revitalizing those sites. . . . Paving over precious open space degrades our quality of life. Instead, we are improving our quality of life both by saving our precious open space and by developing already developed space in order to create jobs for the

working families of our area" (see http://www.rothman.house.gov/index
.php?option=com_content&task=view&id=474&Itemid=1).

The Future

Despite the long history of abuse and misuse of its lands and waters, the
Meadowlands remains one of the largest and most productive brackish
marsh systems in the northeastern United States. Despite the loss of many
species due to damage done in the past, a lot of biodiversity remains and
more is expected in the future. Biological communities are still at some
risk from existing contamination, and recovery will require remediation
of contaminants such as mercury, PCBs, and dioxin. Restoration activities
are planned with a goal of increasing diverse vegetative communities of
native species.

Social and recreational uses of the Meadowlands are increasing and
provide many benefits to urban populations, including better health and
quality of life, along with an increasing awareness and appreciation of the
environment and local wildlife. To supplement existing recreational facilities such as parks, trails, river overlooks, boardwalks, and wildlife observation sites, an environmental park offering eco-canoe trips, nature walks,
bird watching, and an environmental center for children is being planned
in the midst of this densely populated region just three miles from Manhattan. Miracles can happen.

The Mills Corporation, which owned the Empire Tract, agreed to give
the tract to the Meadowlands Conservation Trust and to provide up to
twenty-five million dollars for the remediation and restoration of those
592 acres. The area has been renamed the Richard P. Kane Natural Area,
after the former vice president of the New Jersey Audubon Society. Miracles can happen.

The Meadows Path is a twenty-five-mile pedestrian trail planned
along the western side of the Hackensack River. A waterfront greenway is
planned through Secaucus and Jersey City on the east side of the river. The
Blue Water Trail is a canoe trail that connects the parks within the district,
including several restoration sites and the Sawmill Creek Wildlife Management Area. NJMC is setting up a 1,600-acre wildlife preservation zone
and will continue open-space acquisition to create a Meadowlands Estuary Preserve. There will be free public access for boating, birding, fishing,
paddling, walking, and other recreational activities. The preservation zone
will be administered by the Meadowlands Conservation Trust, a public-
private partnership. "Captain Bill" Sheehan, the Hackensack Riverkeeper,
leading environmental advocate, and former chief enemy of the HMDC,

was named chairman of the Meadowlands Conservation Trust, and NJMC is a partner with a seat on the board of directors. Miracles can happen.

People can go on eco-tours within sight of the Manhattan skyline. A reporter for the *New York Times* wrote in an article on July 16, 2005, that the eco-cruises on the Hackensack River offer "biodiversity, a great comeback story and practical lessons in preservation." Miracles do happen.

Appendix

List of Species Discussed in the Text

Bacteria

BTI (*Bacillus thuringensis israelensis*)

Fungus

Fusarium sp.

Microalgae: Phytoplankton

Alexandrium spp.
Karenia brevis
Pfiesteria spp.

Macroalgae: Seaweeds

Dead Man's Fingers (*Codium fragile*)
Enteromorpha
Eucheuma
Feather caulerpa (*Caulerpa taxifolia*)
Rockweed (*Fucus* spp.)
Sea lettuce (*Ulva lactuca*)

Macrophytes: Higher Plants

Alkali heath (*Frankenia salina*)
Arrowgrass (*Triglochin maritima*)
Atlantic white cedar (*Chamacyparis thyoides*)
Blackgrass (*Juncus gerardii*)
Baltic rush (*Juncus balticus*)
Bushy shoregrass (*Monanthochloe littoralis*)
Cattail (*Typha angustifolia* and *T. latifolia*)
Common reed (*Phragmites australis*)
Cordgrass (*Spartina alterniflora*)
Cordgrass on West Coast (*Spartina foliosa*)
Dodder (*Cuscuta salina*)

Eelgrass (*Zostera marina*)
Glasswort, pickleweed, or saltwort (*Salicornia* spp.)
Glasswort (*Sarcocornia* spp.)
Groundsel Tree (*Baccharis halimifolia*)
Gumplant (*Grindelia stricta*)
Humboldt Bay owl's clover (*Castilleja ambigua*)
Jaumea (*Jaumea carnosa*)
Lyngbye's sedge (*Carex lyngbyei*)
Marsh elder (*Iva frutescens*)
Needle rush (*Juncus roemeranius*)
Pink gerardia (*Gerardia maritime*)
Purple loosestrife (*Lythrum salicaria*)
Rush or bullrush (*Scirpus* spp.)
Salt bush (*Atriplex patula*)
Saltgrass or spikegrass (*Distichlis spicata*)
Salt hay (*Spartina patens*)
Salt-marsh aster (*Aster tenuifolius*)
Salt-marsh bird's beak (*Cordylanthus maritimus*)
Salt rush (*Juncus leseurii*)
Saltwort (*Salicornia*)
Sand spurrey (*Spergularia macrotheca* and *S. canadensis*)
Sea arrowgrass (*Triglochin maritime*)
Sea blite (*Suaeda californica*)
Sea lavender (*Limonium californicum* or *L. nashii*)
Sea milkwort (*Glaux maritima*)
Sea plantain (*Plantago maritime*)
Seaside goldenrod (*Solidago sempervirens*)
Switchgrass (*Panicum virgatum*)
Three-cornered grass (*Scirpus olneyi*)
Widgeon grass (*Ruppia maritima*)

Mollusks

Gastropods

Common periwinkle (*Littorina littorea*)
Mud snail (*Ilyanassa obsoleta*)
Northern rough (marsh) periwinkle (*L. saxatilis*)
Salt-marsh snail (*Melampus* spp.)
Slipper shell or boat shell (*Crepidula fornicata*)
Southern or gulf periwinkle (*Littoraria irrorata*)

Bivalves

Asian clam (*Corbicula fluminea* or *Potamocorbula amurensis*)
Asian oyster (*Crassostrea ariakensis*)
Atlantic Bay scallop (*Argopecten irradians*)
Baltic macoma (*Macoma balthica*)

Blue mussel (*Mytilus edulis*)
Oyster (*Crassostrea virginica*)
Quohog or hard clam (*Mercenaria mercenaria*)
Ribbed mussel (*Geukensia demissa*)
Soft shell (or steamer) clam (*Mya arenaria*)
Zebra mussel (*Dreissena polymorpha*)

Polychaete Annelids (Segmented Worms)

Bloodworm (*Glycera* spp.)
Clam worm (*Nereis* spp.)

Arthropods

Horseshoe crab (*Limulus polyphemus*)

Crustaceans

Acorn barnacle (*Balanus* spp.)
Beach flea (*Orchesia* and *Uhlorchestia*)
Beach hopper (amphipod) (*Gammarus palustris*)
Estuarine isopod (*Cyathura polita*)
Pillbug (*Armadillium* sp.)
Salt-marsh isopod (*Sphaeroma* spp.)
Woodlouse (*Porcellio* and *Philoscia*)

Crabs
Asian shore crab (*Hemigrapsus sanguineus*)
Blue crab (*Callinectes sapidus*)
Chinese mitten crab (*Erocheir sinensis*)
Dungeness crab (*Cancer magister*)
Fiddler Crabs: brackish water (red-claw) fiddler (*Uca minax*), mud fiddler
    (*Uca pugnax*), and sand fiddler (*Uca pugilator*)
Green (or shore) crab (*Carcinus maenas*)
Marsh mud crab (*Sesarma reticulatum* and *Armases cinereum*)
Mud crab (*Panopeus* spp. and *Eurypanopeus* spp.)
Mud fiddler (*Uca pugnax*)
Sand fiddler (*Uca pugilator*)
Hermit Crabs: flat-clawed hermit crab (*Pagurus pollicaris*) and long-clawed
    hermit crab (*Pagurus longicarpus*)

Shrimp
Grass shrimp (*Palaemonetes pugio*)
Sand shrimp (*Crangon septemspinosa*)

Fishes

Alewife (*Alosa pseudoharengus*)
American eel (*Anguilla rostrata*)

American shad (*Alosa sapidissima*)
Atlantic butterfish (*Peprilus triacanthus*)
Atlantic herring (*Clupea harengus*)
Atlantic silversides (*Menidia menidia*)
Bay anchovy (*Anchoa mitchelli*)
Black sea bass (*Centropristes striata*)
Blueback herring (*Alosa aestivalis*)
Bluefish (*Pomatomus saltatrix*)
Bluegill sunfish (*Lepomis macrochirus*)
Chinook salmon (*Oncorhynchus tshawytscha*)
Chum salmon (*Oncorhynchus keta*)
Coho salmon (*Oncorhynchus kisutch*)
Common killifish or mummichog (*Fundulus heteroclitus*)
English sole (*Pleuronectes vetulis*)
Menhaden (*Brevoortia tyrannus*)
Mosquitofish (*Gambusia affinis*)
Northern pipefish (*Syngnathus fuscus*)
Red hake (*Urophycis chuss*)
Sheepshead minnow (*Cyprinodon variegatus*)
Spot (*Leiostomus xanthurus*)
Striped bass (*Morone saxatilis*)
Striped killifish (*Fundulus majalis*)
Summer flounder or fluke (*Paralichthys dentatus*)
Three-spined stickleback (*Gasterosteus aculeatus*)
Tidewater silverside (*Menidia beryllina*)
White perch (*Morone americana*)
Winter flounder (*Pseudopleuronectes americanus*)

Insects

Deerfly (*Chrysops* spp.)
Greenhead fly (*Tabanus* spp.)
Midge or "no-see-um" (*Culicoides* spp.)
Salt-marsh grasshopper (*Orchelium fidicinium*)
Salt-marsh mosquito (*Aedes sollicitans*)

Reptiles

Alligator (*Alligator mississippiensis*)
Diamond-backed terrapin (*Malaclemys terrapin*)
Snapping turtle (*Chelydra serpentina*)

Birds

American bittern (*Botaurus lentiginosus*)
American Oystercatcher (*Haematopus palliates*)

American widgeon (*Anas americana*)
Bald eagle (*Haliaeetus leucocephalus*)
Barn swallow (*Hirundo rustica*)
Belted kingfisher (*Megaceryle alcyon*)
Black-crowned night heron (*Nycticorax nycticorax*)
Black duck (*Anas rubripes*)
Black skimmer (*Rynchops niger*)
Canada goose (*Branta canadensis*)
Canvasback duck (*Aythya valisineria*)
Clapper rail (*Rallus longirostris*)
Common moorhen (*Gallinula chloropus*)
Double-crested cormorant (*Phalacrocorax auritus*)
Egret, snowy (*Egretta thula*)
Gadwall (*Anas strepera*)
Glossy ibis (*Plegadis falcinellus*)
Great black-backed gull (*Larus marinus*)
Great blue heron (*Ardea herodias*)
Green-backed heron (*Butorides striatus*)
Green-winged teal (*Anas crecca*)
Herring gull (*Larus argentatus*)
King rail (*Rallus elegans*)
Laughing gull (*Larus atricilla*)
Least bittern (*Ixobrychus exilis*)
Least tern (*Sternula antillarum*)
Mallard duck (*Anas platyrhynchos*)
Marsh hawk (harrier) (*Circus cyaneus*)
Marsh wren (*Telmatodytes palustris*)
Mute swan (*Cygnus olor*)
Osprey or fish hawk (*Pandion haliaetus*)
Pintail (*Anas acuta*)
Red knot (*Calidris canutus*)
Red-tailed hawk (*Buteo jamaicensis*)
Red-winged blackbird (*Agelaius phoeniceus*)
Ruddy duck (*Oxyura jamaicensis*)
Ruddy turnstone (*Arenaria interpres*)
Sanderling (*Calidris alba*)
Savannah sparrow (*Passerculus sandwichensis*)
Seaside sparrow (*Ammodramus maritimus*)
Semipalmated sandpiper (*Calidris pusilla*)
Sharp-tailed sparrow (*Ammodramus caudacutus*)
Snow goose (*Chen caerulescens*)
Snowy egret (*Egretta thula*)
Sora rail (*Porzana carolina*)
Starling (*Sturnus vulgaris*)
Swamp sparrow (*Melospiza georgiana*)
Tern (*Sterna* spp.)

Tree swallow (*Tachycineta bicolor*)
Virginia rail (*Rallus limicola*)
Willet (*Catoptrophorus semipalmatus*)
Wood duck (*Aix sponsa*)

Mammals

Harvest mouse (*Reithrodontomys* spp.)
Marsh rabbit (*Sylvailagus palustris*)
Meadow mouse or meadow vole (*Microtus pennsylvanicus*)
Mink (*Mustela vison*)
Moose (*Alces alces*)
Muskrat (*Ondatra zibethica*)
Nutria (*Myocastor coypus*)
Otter (*Lutra canadensis*)
Raccoon (*Procyon lotor*)
Rice rat (*Oryzomys palustris*)
Shrew (*Sorex* spp.)
Swamp rabbit (*Sylvailagus aquaticus*)
White-footed mouse (*Peromyscus leucopus*)
White-tailed deer (*Odocoileus virginianus*)

References

Chapter 1: Salt-Marsh Basics, and
Chapter 2: Primary Producers

Bertness, M. D. 1992. The ecology of a New England salt marsh. *American Scientist* 80: 260–268.

———. 1999. *The ecology of Atlantic shorelines.* Sunderland, Mass.: Sinauer Associates.

Bertness, M. D., S. D. Gaines, and M. E. Hay, eds. 2001. *Marine community ecology.* Sunderland, Mass.: Sinauer Associates.

Carson, R. 1941. *Under the sea wind.* 1991 edition. New York: Dutton.

Carson, R. 1955. *The edge of the sea.* Boston, Mass.: Houghton Mifflin.

Castro, P., and M. E. Huber. 2007. *Marine biology.* 7th edition. New York: McGraw Hill.

Coulombe, D. 1984. *The seaside naturalist: A guide to study at the seashore.* New York: Simon & Schuster.

De la Cruz, A. A. 1973. The role of tidal marshes in the productivity of coastal waters. *Association of Southeast Biologists* 20:147–156.

Foote, A. L., and K. A. Reynolds. 1997. Decomposition of saltmeadow cordgrass (*Spartina patens*) in Louisiana coastal marshes. *Estuaries* 20:579–588.

Gallagher, J., et al. 1988. Persistent differences in two forms of *Spartina alterniflora*: A common garden experiment. *Ecology* 69:1005–1008.

Gosner, K. L. 1978. *A field guide to the Atlantic seashore: From the Bay of Fundy to Cape Hatteras.* The Peterson field guide series. Boston, Mass.: Houghton Mifflin.

Gosselink, J. 1980. *Tidal marshes: The boundary between land and ocean.* Baton Rouge, La.: Center for Wetlands Resources, Louisiana State University.

Hedgepeth, J. W. 1962. *Introduction to seashore life of the San Francisco Bay region and the coast of Northern California.* Berkeley, Calif.: University of California Press.

Held, G. 2007. *Aftermath* from /Grounded. Finishing Line Press. http://www.amazon.com/dp/1932755896?tag=writal-20&camp=0&creative=0&linkCode=as1&creativeASIN=1932755896&adid=1DAXFRSZC0TTCB01665C&.

Keatts, H. 1995. *Beachcomber's guide: From Cape Cod to Cape Hatteras.* Houston, Tex.: Gulf Publishing.

Kieran, J. 1959. *Natural history of N.Y. City.* Boston, Mass.: Houghton Mifflin.

Lippson, A. J., and R. Lippson. 1984. *Life in the Chesapeake Bay.* Baltimore, Md.: Johns Hopkins Press.

Little, C. 2000. *The biology of soft shores and estuaries.* New York: Oxford University Press.

Mann, K. H. 2000. *Ecology of coastal waters with implications for management.* Malden, Mass.: Blackwell Science.

Niering, W. A., and R. S. Warren. 1980. Vegetation patterns and processes in New England salt marshes. *BioScience* 30:301–306.

Nixon, S. W. 1980. Between coastal marshes and coastal water: A review of twenty years of speculation and research on the role of salt marshes in estuarine productivity and water chemistry. In *Estuarine and wetland processes,* ed. P. Hamilton and K. MacDonald, 437–525. New York: Plenum Publishers.

———. 1982. *The ecology of New England high salt marshes: A community profile.* FWS/OBS-81/55. Washington, D.C.: U.S. Department of the Interior, Fish and Wildlife Service, Office of Biological Services.

Nixon, S. W., and C. A. Oviatt. 1973. Ecology of a New England salt marsh. *Ecological Monographs* 43:463–498.

Nybakken, J. W., and M. D. Bertness. 2004. *Marine biology: An ecological approach.* San Francisco, Calif.: Pearson/Benjamin Cummings.

Redfield, A. C. l972. Development of a New England salt marsh. *Ecological Monographs* 42:201–237.

Reid, G. K. 1961. *Ecology of inland waters and estuaries.* New York: Reinhold.

Roberts, M. F. 1979. *The tidemarsh guide.* New York: E. P. Dutton.

Rudloe, J. 1988. *The wilderness coast: Adventures of a Gulf Coast naturalist.* New York: E. P. Dutton.

Silberhorn, G. M. 1982. *Common plants of the mid-Atlantic coast: A field guide.* Baltimore, Md.: Johns Hopkins University Press.

Teal, J. 1986. *The ecology of regularly flooded salt marshes of New England: A community profile.* Biology Report 85(7.4). Washington, D.C.: U.S. Fish and Wildlife Service.

Teal, J., and M. Teal. 1969. *Life and death of the salt marsh.* New York: Audubon/Ballantyne Books.

Tiner, R. W. 1987. *A field guide to coastal wetland plants of the northeastern United States.* Amherst: University of Massachusetts Press.

Watling, L., J. Fegley, and J. Moring. 2003. *Life between the tides.* Gardiner, Maine: Tilbury House.

Weinstein, M., and D. A. Kreeger, eds. 2000. *Concepts and controversies in tidal marsh ecology.* Dordrecht, The Netherlands: Kluwer Academic Publishers.

Wetlands: Their Use and Regulation. 1984. OTA-O-206. Washington, D.C.: United States Congress, Office of Technology Assessment.

White, C. 1989. *Chesapeake Bay: A field guide.* Centreville, Md.: Tidewater Publishers.

Whitlatch, R. B. 1982. *The ecology of New England tidal flats: A community profile.* FWS/OBS-81/01. Washington, D.C.: U.S. Fish and Wildlife Service, Biological Services Program.

Chapter 3: Animals of the Salt Marsh

Bigelow, H. B., and W. C. Schroeder. 1953. *Fishes of the Gulf of Maine.* Washington, D.C.: U.S. Government Printing Office.

Boesch, D. F., and R. E. Turner. 1984. Dependence of fishery species on salt marshes: the role of food and refuge. *Estuaries* 7:460–468.

Botton, M. L. 1984. Diet and food preferences of the adult horseshoe crab *Limulus polyphemus* in Delaware Bay, New Jersey, USA. *Marine Biology* 81:199–207.

Brockmann, H. J., and D. Penn. 1992. Male mating tactics in the horseshoe crab, Limulus polyphemus. *Animal Behaviour* 44:653–665

Christy, J. H., and M. Salmon. 1991. Comparative studies of reproductive behavior in mantis shrimps and fiddler crabs. *American Zoologist* 31:329–337.

Coulombe, D. 1984. *The seaside naturalist: A guide to study at the seashore.* New York: Simon & Schuster.

Daiber, F. C. 1982. *Animals of the tidal marsh.* New York: Van Nostrand Reinhold.

Ehrlich, P. R., D. S. Dobkin, and D. Wheye. 1988. *The birder's handbook: A field guide to the natural history of North American birds.* New York: Simon & Schuster.

Elphick, C., J. B. Dunning, Jr., and D. A. Sibley, eds. 2001. *The Sibley Guide to Bird Life and Behavior.* National Audubon Society. New York: Alfred A. Knopf.

Gosner, K. L. 1978. *A field guide to the Atlantic seashore: From the Bay of Fundy to Cape Hatteras.* The Peterson field guide series. Boston, Mass.: Houghton Mifflin.

Hedgepeth, J. W. 1962. *Introduction to seashore life of the San Francisco Bay region and the coast of Northern California.* Berkeley: University of California Press.

Kalm, P. 1751. *Travels in North America.* London: T. Lowndes.

Keatts, H. 1995. *Beachcomber's guide: From Cape Cod to Cape Hatteras.* Houston, Tex.: Gulf Publishing.

Kieran, J. 1959. *Natural History of N.Y. City.* Boston, Mass.: Houghton Mifflin.

Kneib, R. T. 1994. Nekton use of vegetated marsh habitats at different stages of tidal inundation. *Marine Ecology Progress Series* 106:227–238.

———. 1997. Early life stages of resident nekton in intertidal marshes. *Estuaries* 20:214–230.

Levinton, J. S., and J. R. Waldman, eds. 2006. *The Hudson River Estuary.* New York: Cambridge University Press.

Lippson, A. J., and R. Lippson. 1984. *Life in the Chesapeake Bay.* Baltimore, Md.: Johns Hopkins Press.

Little, C. 2000. *The biology of soft shores and estuaries.* New York: Oxford University Press.

Marshall, N. B. 1966. *The life of fishes.* New York: Universe Books.

McIvor, C. C., and W. E. Odum. 1988. Food, predation risk, and microhabitat selection in a marsh fish assemblage. *Ecology* 69:1341–1351.

O'Connor, N., and B. T. Van. 2006. Adult fiddler crabs *Uca pugnax* (Smith) enhance sediment-associated cues for molting of conspecific megalopae. *Journal of Experimental Marine Biology and Ecology* 335:123–130.

Pollock, L. W. 1998. *A practical guide to the marine animals of northeastern North America.* New Brunswick, N.J.: Rutgers University Press.

Rehder, H. 1981. *National Audubon Society field guide to shells.* New York: Alfred A. Knopf.

Robins, C. R., and G. C. Ray. 1986. *Atlantic coast fishes: North America.* The Peterson field guide series. Boston, Mass.: Houghton Mifflin.

Rountree, R. A., and K. W. Able. 1992. Fauna of polyhaline subtidal marsh creeks in southern New Jersey: Composition, abundance and biomass. *Estuaries* 15:171–185.

Rozas, L. P., C. C. McIvor, and W. E. Odum. 1988. Intertidal rivulets and creekbanks: Corridors between tidal creeks and marshes. *Marine Ecology Progress Series* 47:303–307.

Rudloe, J. 1988. *The wilderness coast: Adventures of a Gulf Coast naturalist.* New York: E. P. Dutton.

Schwab, R., and H. J. Brockmann. 2007. The role of visual and chemical cues in the mating decisions of satellite males horseshoe crabs, *Limulus polyphemus. Animal Behaviour* 74:837–846.

Silliman, B. R., and M. D. Bertness. 2002. A trophic cascade regulates salt marsh primary production. *Proceedings of the National Academy of Sciences* 99:10500–10505.

U.S. Fish and Wildlife Service. 1983. Species profiles: Life histories and environmental requirements of coastal fishes and invertebrates. Biology Report 82(11), U.S. Army Corps of Engineers, TR EL-82-7-4. Washington, D.C.: U.S. Fish and Wildlife Service.

Watling, L., J. Fegley, and J. Moring. 2003. *Life between the tides.* Gardiner, Maine: Tilbury House.

Weis, J. S., and P. Weis. 2004. Behavior of four species of fiddler crabs, genus *Uca* in Southeast Sulawesi, Indonesia. *Hydrobiologia* 523:47–58.

Weisberg, S., and V. Lotrich. 1982. The importance of an infrequently flooded intertidal marsh surface as an energy source for the mummichog *Fundulus heteroclitus:* An experimental approach. *Marine Biology* 66:307–310.

White, C. 1989. *Chesapeake Bay: A field guide.* Centreville, Md.: Tidewater Publishers.

Whitlatch, R. B. 1982. The ecology of New England tidal flats: A community profile. FWS/OBS-81/01. D.C.: U.S. Fish and Wildlife Service, Biological Services Program.

Wolcott, T. G., and A. H. Hines. 1990. Ultrasonic telemetry of small-scale movements and microhabitat selection by molting blue crabs (*Callinectes sapidus*). *Bulletin of Marine Sciences* 46:83–94.

Chapter 4: Physical Alterations

Bertness, M. D., P. Ewanchuck, and B. Silliman. 2002. Anthropogenic modification of New England salt marsh landscapes. *Proceedings of the National Academy of Sciences* 99:1305–1308.

Cahoon, D. R. 1994. Recent accretion in two managed marsh impoundments in coastal Louisiana. *Ecological Applications* 4:160–176.

Chapman, M. G. 2003. Paucity of mobile species on constructed seawalls: Effects of urbanization on biodiversity. *Marine Ecology Progress Series* 264: 21–29.

Costanza, R., and J. Farley, eds. 2007. Ecological economics of coastal disasters. Special ed. *Ecological Economies* 63, nos. 2–3.

Day, J., et al. 2007. Restoration of the Mississippi Delta: Lessons from hurricanes Katrina and Rita. *Science* 315:679–684.

Desbonnet, A., et al. 1994. *Vegetated buffers in the coastal zone: A summary review and bibliography.* Coastal resources center technical report 2064. Narragansett: University of Rhode Island Graduate School of Oceanography.

Donnelly, J. P., and M. D. Bertness. 2001. Rapid shoreward encroachment of salt marsh cordgrass in response to accelerated sea-level rise. *Proceedings of the National Academy of Sciences* 98:14218–14223.

McKee, K., I. Mendelssohn, and M. Materne. 2004. Acute salt marsh dieback in the Mississippi River deltaic plain: A drought-induced phenomenon? *Global Ecology and Biogeography* 13:65–73.

Montezuma Wetlands Project. On the Web site California Wetlands Information System: http://ceres.ca.gov/wetlands/projects/montezuma.html, accessed July 5, 2008.

Morris, J. T., et al. 2002. Responses of coastal wetlands to rising sea level. *Ecology* 83:2869–2877.

Niering, W. A., and R. M. Bowers. 1966. Our disappearing tidal marshes—their present status. *Connecticut Arboretum Bulletin* 12:1–4.

National Oceanic and Atmospheric Administration (NOAA). 2008. http://www.nmfs.noaa.gov/habitat/habitatprotection/wetlands/index.htm.

Ramsar convention on wetlands of international importance especially as waterfowl habitat. 1971. U.N. treaty series 14583. Ramsar, Iran: United Nations.

Ramsar Convention on Wetlands meeting. 1996. http://www.ramsar.org/about/about_wetland_loss.htm.

Schneider, R. W., and J. P. Jones. 2001. Determining the role of plant pathogens in the coastal marsh dieback: Lessons from agriculture and forestry. In *Coastal marsh dieback in the northern Gulf of Mexico: Extent, causes, consequences, and remedies,* ed. R. E. Stewart Jr., C. E. Profftt, and T. M. Charron, 17–18. USGS Information and Technology Report USGS/BRD/ITR—2001—2003. Washington, D.C.: U.S. Government Printing Office.

Schwartz, A. 2008. Saving Arlington Marsh. On the Web site *Gotham Gazette:* http://www.gothamgazette.com/article/parks/20071030/14/2333, accessed March 10, 2008.

Silliman, B. R., and M. D. Bertness. 2003. Shoreline development drives invasion of *Phragmites australis* and the loss of plant diversity on New England salt marshes. *Conservation Biology* 18:1424–1434.

U.S. Environmental Protection Agency. 2004. *Protecting water resources with smart growth.* EPA 231-R-04–002. Washington, D.C.: U.S. Environmental Protection Agency.

Chapter 5: Pollution

Bauer, M., ed. 2006. Harmful algal research and response: A human dimensions strategy. Woods Hole, Mass.: National Office for Marine Biotoxins and Harmful Algal Blooms, Woods Hole Oceanographic Institution.

Bergey, L., and J. S. Weis. 2008. Aspects of population ecology in two populations of fiddler crabs, *Uca pugnax. Marine Biology* 154: 435–442.

Bertness, M. D., et al. 2008. Eutrophication and consumer control of New England salt marsh primary productivity. *Conservation Biology* 22:131–139.

Bortone, S., and R. P Cody. 1999. Morphological masculinization in poeciliid females from a paper mill effluent receiving tributary of the St. Johns River, Florida, USA. *Bulletin of Environmental Contamination and Toxicology* 63:150–156.

Breitburg, D. L., et al. 1997. Varying effects of low dissolved oxygen on trophic interactions in an estuarine food web. *Ecological Monographs* 67:489–507.

Brown, S. B., et al. 2004. Contaminant effects on the teleost fish thyroid. *Environmental Toxicology and Chemistry* 23:1680–1701.

Bryan, G. W., et al. 1986. The decline of the gastropod *Nucella lapillus* around southwest England: Evidence for tributyltin from antifouling paints. *Journal of the Marine Biological Association of the UK* 66:611–640.

Burkholder, J. M., H. B. Glasgow Jr., and C. W. Hobbs. 1995. Fish kills linked to a toxic ambush-predator dinoflagellate: Distribution and environmental conditions. *Marine Ecology Progress Series* 124:43–61.

Candolin, U., J. Engström-Öst, and T. Salesto. 2008. Human-induced eutrophication enhances reproductive success through effects on parenting ability in sticklebacks. *Oikos* 117:459–465.

Cape May to Montauk: A coastal report card. 2002. New York: Natural Resources Defense Council.

Carson, R. 1950. *The sea around us.* 1961 edition. New York: Oxford University Press.

———. 1962. *Silent spring.* New York: Houghton Mifflin.

Colborn, T., and C. Clement. 1992. *Chemically-induced alterations in sexual and functional development: The wildlife/human connection.* Vol. 21, *Advances in modern environmental toxicology.* Princeton, N.J.: Princeton Scientific Publishing.

Colborn, T., D. Dumanski, and J. P. Meyers. 1996. *Our stolen future.* New York: Penguin Group.

Culbertson, J., et al. 2007. Long-term biological effects of petroleum residues on fiddler crabs in salt marshes. *Marine Pollution Bulletin* 54:955–962.

Diaz, R. J. 2001. Overview of hypoxia around the world. *Journal of Environmental Quality* 30:275–281.

Flanders, M., and D. Swann. 1963. Bedstead men. In *At the drop of another hat.* London: EMI Records Ltd.

Gambrell, R. P. 1994. Trace and toxic metals in wetlands: A review. *Journal of Environmental Quality* 23:883–891.

Guillette, L., et al. 1994. Developmental abnormalities of the gonad and abnormal sex hormone concentrations in juvenile alligators from contaminated and control lakes in Florida. *Environmental Health Perspectives* 102:680–688.

Harwell, M. A., and J. H. Gentile. 2006. Ecological significance of residual exposures and effects from the Exxon Valdez oil spill. *Integrated Environmental Assessment and Management* 2:204–246.

Hayes, T. B., et al. 2002. Hermaphroditic, demasculinized frogs after exposure to the herbicide atrazine at low ecologically relevant doses. *Environmental Health Perspectives* 99:5476–5480.

Jordan, T. W., et al. 1991. Long-term trends in estuarine nutrients and chlorophyll, and short-term effects of variation in watershed discharge. *Marine Ecology Progress Series* 75:121–132.

Kennish, M., and K. Townsend, eds. 2007. Eutrophication of estuarine and shallow coastal marine systems. *Ecological Applications* 17: Supplement.

Kime, D. E. 1998. *Endocrine disruption in fish.* Boston, Mass.: Kluwer Academic Publishers.

Krebs, C., and K. Burns. 1977. Long-term effects of an oil spill on populations of the salt marsh crab *Uca pugnax. Science* 19:484–487.

Levinton, J., et al. 2003. Rapid loss of genetically based resistance to metals after the cleanup of a Superfund site. *Proceedings of the National Academy of Sciences* 100:9889–9891.

McClelland, J., and I. Valiela. 1998. Linking nitrogen in estuarine producers to land-derived sources. *Limnology and Oceanography* 43:577–585.

Nacci, D., et al. 1999. Adaptation of wild fish populations to dioxin-like environmental contamination. *Marine Biology* 134:9–17.

National Research Council. 2000. *Clean coastal waters: Understanding and reducing the effects of nutrient pollution.* Washington, D.C.: National Academy Press.

Newman, M. C., and M. A. Unger. 2003. *Fundamentals of ecotoxicology.* Boca Raton, Fla.: CRC Press.

Peterson, C. H., et al. 2003. Long term ecosystem response to the Exxon Valdez oil spill. *Science* 302:2082–2086.

Rabalais, N., R. E. Turner, W. Wiseman Jr. 2002. Gulf of Mexico hypoxia, AKA "The dead zone." *Annual Review of Ecology and Systematics* 33:235–263.

Ryther, J. H., and W. M. Dunstan. 1971. Nitrogen, phosphorus, and eutrophication in the coastal marine environment. *Science* 17:1008–1013.

Samson, J., S. Shumway, and J. S. Weis. 2008. Effects of the toxic dinoflagellate, *Alexandrium fundyense,* on three species of larval fish: A food-chain approach. *Journal of Fish Biology* 72:168–188.

Sanders, H. L., et al. 1980. Anatomy of an oil spill: Long term effects from the barge *Florida* off West Falmouth. *Journal of Marine Research* 38:265–380.

Santiago Bass, C., S. Bhan, G. Smith, and J. Weis. 2001. Some factors affecting size distribution and density of grass shrimp (*Palaemonetes pugio*) populations in two New Jersey estuaries. *Hydrobiologia* 450:231–241.

Smith, G., and J. Weis. 1997. Predator-prey relationships in mummichogs (*Fundulus heteroclitus*): Effects of living in a polluted environment. *Journal of Experimental Marine Biology and Ecology* 209.75–87.

U.S. Environmental Protection Agency. 1989. *Saving bays and estuaries. A primer for establishing and managing estuary projects.* Washington, D.C.: EPA Office of Water.

U.S. Environmental Protection Agency. 1998a. *Condition of the mid-Atlantic estuaries.* USEPA-NHEERL-NAR-1822. Narragansett, R.I. .: U.S. EPA.

U.S. Environmental Protection Agency. 1998b. Endocrine Disruptor Screening and Testing Advisory Committee (EDSTAC) final report. Washington, D.C.: U.S. EPA.

Valiela, I., and N. Y. Persson. 1976. Production and dynamics of experimentally enriched salt marsh vegetation: Belowground biomass. *Limnology and Oceanography* 21:245–252.

Valiela, I., D. Ruteki, and S. Fox. 2004. Salt marshes: Biological controls of food webs in a diminishing environment. *Journal of Experimental Marine Biology and Ecology* 300:131–159.

Valiela, I., and J. M. Teal. 1974. Nutrient limitation in salt marsh vegetation. In *Ecology of halophytes,* ed. R. J. Reimold and W. H. Queens, 547–563. New York: Academic Press.

Vines, C. A., et al. 2000. The effects of diffusible creosote-derived compounds on development in Pacific herring (*Clupea pallasi*). *Aquatic Toxicology* 51:225–239.

Weis, J. S., et al. 2001. Effects of contaminants on behavior: Biochemical mechanisms and ecological consequences. *BioScience* 51:209–218.

Weis, J. S., and P. Weis. 1989. Tolerance and stress in a polluted environment: The case of the mummichog. *BioScience* 39:89–95.

———. 1994. Impacts of xenobiotics on estuarine ecosystems. In *Basic Environmental Toxicology,* ed. B. Shane and L. Cockerham, 385–407. Boca Raton, Fla.: CRC Press.

———. 1995. Environmental effects of chromated copper arsenate (CCA)-treated wood in the aquatic environment. *Ambio* 24:269–274.

Zhou, T., H. John-Alder, P. Weis, and J. Weis. 1999. Thyroidal status of mummichogs (*Fundulus heteroclitus*) from a polluted vs. reference habitat. *Environmental Toxicology and Chemistry* 18:2817–2823.

Chapter 6: Biological Alterations

Able, K. W., and S. M. Hagan. 2000. Effects of common reed (*Phragmites australis*) invasion on marsh surface macrofauna: Response of fishes and decapod crustaceans. *Estuaries* 23:633–646.

Bart, D., and J. M. Hartman. 2000. Environmental determinants of *Phragmites australis* expansion in a New Jersey salt marsh: An experimental approach. *Oikos* 89:59–69.

Benoit, L. K., and R. A. Askins. 1999. Impact of the spread of *Phragmites* on the distribution of birds in Connecticut tidal marshes. *Wetlands* 19:194–208.

Carlton, J. T. 2001. *Introduced species in U.S. coastal waters: Environmental impacts and management priorities.* Arlington, Va.: Pew Oceans Commission.

Chambers, R. M., L. A. Meyerson, and K. Saltonstall. 1999. Expansion of *Phragmites australis* into tidal wetlands of North America. *Aquatic Botany* 64:261–273.

Cohen, A. N., and J. T. Carlton. 1998. Accelerating invasion in a highly invaded estuary. *Science* 279:555–558.

Elton, C. 1958. *The ecology of invasions by animals and plants.* Chicago, Ill.: University of Chicago Press.

Franke, J. M. 2008. *The invasive species cook book.* Wauwatosa, Wisc.: Bradford Street Press.

Goreau, T. 2008. Fighting algae in Kaneohe Bay. *Science* 319:157.

He, W., R. Feagin, J. Liu, W. Liu, Q. Yan, and Z. Xie. 2007. Impacts of introduced *Spartina alterniflora* along an elevation gradient at the Jiuduansha Shoals in Yangtze Estuary, suburban Shanghai, China. *Ecological Engineering* 29:245–248.

Kane, R. 2001. Phragmites *use by birds in New Jersey.* Bernardsville, N.J.: New Jersey Audubon Society.

Lavoi, D. M., L. D. Smith, and G. M. Ruiz. 1999. The potential for intracoastal transfer of nonindigenous species in the ballast water of ships. *Estuarine, Coastal and Shelf Science* 48:551–564.

MacDonald, J., et al. 2007. The invasive green crab and Japanese shore crab: Behavioral interactions with a native crab species, the blue crab. *Biological Invasions* 9:837–848.

National Sea Grant Program. 2000. *Aquatic nuisance species report: An update on Sea Grant research and outreach projects.* National Sea Grant Program. Columbus: Ohio State University.

Paynter, K., J. Goodwin, M. Chen, N. Ward, M. Sherman, D. Merritt, and S. Allen. 2008. *Crassostrea ariakensis* in Chesapeake Bay: Growth, disease, and mortality in shallow subtidal environments. *Journal of Shellfish Research* 27:509–515.

Robertson, T., and J. S. Weis. 2005. A comparison of epifaunal communities associated with stems of the salt marsh grasses *Phragmites australis* and *Spartina alterniflora. Wetlands* 251–257.

Rooth, J., J. C. Stevenson, and J. C. Cornwell. 2003. The influence of 5- and 20-yr old *Phragmites* populations on rates of accretion in an oligohaline tidal marsh of Chesapeake Bay. *Estuaries* 26:475–483.

Roudez, R., T. Glover, and J. Weis. 2008. Learning in an invasive and a native predatory crab. *Biological Invasions.* 10.1007/s10530-007-9195-9.

Saltonstall, K. 2002. Cryptic invasion by a non-native genotype of *Phragmites australis* into North America. *Proceedings of the National Academy of Sciences* 99:2445–2449.

U.S. Fish and Wildlife Service. 2003. Draft Environmental Impact Report for the San Francisco Estuary. *Federal Register* 68(75), April 18.

Valega, M., et al. 2008. Long-term effects of mercury in a salt marsh: Hysteresis in the distribution of vegetation following recovery from contamination. *Chemosphere* 71:765–772.

Wainwright, S. C., et al. 2000. Relative importance of benthic microalgae, phytoplankton, and the detritus of smooth cordgrass (*Spartina*) and the common reed (*Phragmites*) to brackish marsh food webs. *Marine Ecology Progress Series* 200:77–91.

Warren, R. S., et al. 2001. Rates, patterns, and impacts of *Phragmites australis* expansion and effects of experimental *Phragmites* control on vegetation, macroinvertebrates, and fish within tidelands of the lower Connecticut River. *Estuaries* 24:90–107.

Weis, J. S., and P. Weis. 2003. Is the invasion of the common reed, *Phragmites australis*, into tidal marshes of the Eastern US an ecological disaster? *Marine Pollution Bulletin* 46:816–820.

———. 2004. Metal uptake, transport, and release by wetland plants: Implications for phytoremediation and restoration. *Environment International* 30:685–700.

Weis, J. S., L. Windham, and P. Weis. 2002. Growth, survival and metal content in marsh invertebrates fed diets of detritus from *Spartina alterniflora* and *Phragmites australis* from metal-polluted and clean sites. *Wetlands Ecology and Management* 10:71–84.

Windham, L., and R. Lathrop. 1999. Effects of *Phragmites australis* (common reed) invasion on above-ground biomass and soil properties in brackish tidal marshes of the Mullica River, New Jersey. *Estuaries* 22:927–935.

Windham, L., J. S. Weis, and P. Weis. 2001. Patterns and processes of mercury release from leaves of two dominant salt marsh macrophytes, *Phragmites australis* and *Spartina alterniflora*. *Estuaries* 24:787–795.

———. 2003. Uptake and distribution of metals in two dominant salt marsh macrophytes, *Spartina alterniflora* (cordgrass) and *Phragmites australis* (common reed). *Estuarine and Coastal Shelf Science* 56:63–72.

———. 2004. Metal dynamics of plant litter of *Spartina alterniflora* and *Phragmites australis* in metal-contaminated marshes. Part 1: Patterns of decomposition and metal uptake. *Environmental Toxicology and Chemistry* 23:1520–1528.

Zedler, J. B., and S. Kercher. 2004. Causes and consequences of invasive plants in wetlands: Opportunities, opportunists, and outcomes. *Critical Reviews in Plant Sciences* 23:431–452.

Chapter 7: Marsh Restoration and Management for Environmental Improvement

Able, K., D. Nemerson, and T. Grothues. 2004. Evaluating salt marsh restoration in Delaware Bay: Analysis of fish responses at former salt hay farms. *Estuaries* 27:57–69.

Batty, L., D. Hooley, and P. Younger. 2008. Iron and manganese removal in wetland treatment systems: Rates, processes, and implications for management. *Science of the Total Environment* 394:1–8.

Burdick, D. N., et al. 1997. Ecological responses to tidal restorations of two northern New England salt marshes. *Wetlands Ecology and Management* 4:129–144.

Craft, C. 1999. Twenty-five years of ecosystem development of constructed *Spartina alterniflora* marshes. *Ecological Applications* 9:1405–1419.

Craft, C., and J. Sacco. 2003. Long-term succession of benthic infauna communities on constructed *Spartina alterniflora* marshes. *Marine Ecology Progress Series* 257:45–58.

Craft, C., et al. 2003. The pace of ecosystem development of contructed *Spartina alterniflora* marshes. *Ecological Applications* 13:1417–1432.

Fernandez, J. B., and F. G. Novo. 2007. High-intensity versus low-intensity restoration alternatives of a tidal marsh in Guadalquivir estuary, SW Spain. *Ecological Engineering* 30:112–121.

Havens, K. J., L. M. Varnell, and B. D. Watts. 2002. Maturation of a constructed tidal marsh relative to two natural reference tidal marshes over 12 years. *Ecological Engineering* 18:305–315.

Howard, R. J., S. E. Travis, and B. A. Sikes. 2008. Rapid growth of a Eurasian haplotype of *Phragmites australis* in a restored brackish marsh in Louisiana, USA. *Biological Invasions* 10:369–379.

Lafferty, K. D., A. P. Dobson, and A. M. Kuris. 2006. Parasites dominate food web links. *Proceedings of the National Academy of Sciences* 103: 11211–11216.

LaSalle, M. W., M .C. Landin, and J. G. Sims. 1991. Evaluation of the flora and fauna of a *Spartina alterniflora* marsh established on dredge material in Winyah Bay, South Carolina. *Wetlands* 11:191–208.

Minello, T. J., R. J. Zimmerman, and R. Medina. 1994. The importance of edge for natant macrofauna in a created salt marsh. *Wetlands* 14:184–198.

Minton, M. D. 1999. Coastal wetland restoration and its potential impact on fishery resources in the northeastern United States. *American Fisheries Society Symposium* 22:405–420.

National Research Council. 1991. *Restoration of aquatic ecosystems: Science, technology and public policy.* Washington,D.C.: National Academy Press.

———. 2001. *Compensating for wetland losses under the Clean Water Act.* Washington, D.C.: National Academy Press.

Neckles, H. A., et al. 2002. A monitoring protocol to assess tidal restoration of salt marshes on local and regional scales. *Restoration Ecology* 10:556–563.

Raskin, I., and B. D. Ensley, eds. 2000. *Phytoremediation of toxic metals: Using plants to clean up the environment.* New York: Wiley Inter-science.

Restore America's estuaries: A national strategy to restore coastal and estuarine habitat. 2002. 156 pp. Washington, D.C.: U.S. GPO.

Richardson, C., and N. Hussain. 2006. Restoring the Garden of Eden: An ecological assessment of the marshes of Iraq. *BioScience* 56:477–489.

Roman, C. T., W. A. Niering, and R. S. Warren. 1984. Salt marsh vegetation change in response to tidal restriction. *Environmental Management* 8:141–150.

Roman, C. T., et al. 2002. Quantifying vegetation and nekton response to tidal restoration of a New England salt marsh. *Restoration Ecology* 10:450–460.

Streever, W. J. 2000. *Spartina alterniflora* marshes on dredged material: A critical review of the ongoing debate over success. *Wetlands Ecology and Management* 8: 295–316.

Swamy, V. 2002. Macroinvertebrate and fish populations in a restored impounded salt marsh 21 years after the reestablishment of tidal flooding. *Environmental Management* 29:516–530.

Terry, N., and G. Banuelos, eds. 1999. *Phytoremediation of contaminated soil and water.* Boca Raton, Fla.: CRC Press.

Thayer, G. W., et al., eds. 2005. *Science-based restoration monitoring for coastal habitats*. Vol. 2: *Tools for monitoring coastal habitats*. NOAA coastal ocean program decision analysis series no. 23. Silver Spring, Md.: NOAA National Centers for Coastal Ocean Science.

U.S. Environmental Protection Agency. 1999. *Phytoremediation Resource Guide*. EPA 542-B-99-003. Washington, D.C.: U.S. EPA.

Warren, R. S., et al. 2002. Salt marsh restoration in Connecticut: 20 years of science and management. *Restoration Ecology* 10:497–513.

Weinstein, M. P., et al. 1997. Success criteria and adaptive management for a large-scale wetland restoration project. *Wetlands Ecology and Management* 4:111–127.

Weis, J. S., and P. Weis. 2004. Metal uptake, transport and release by wetland plants: Implications for phytoremediation and restoration. *Environment International* 30:685–700.

Whigham, D. F. 1999. Ecological issues related to wetland preservation, restoration, creation and assessment. *Science of the Total Environment* 240:31–40.

Zedler, J. B. 1993. Canopy architecture of natural and planted cordgrass marshes: Selecting habitat evaluation criteria. *Ecological Applications* 6:38–56.

———. 2000. Progress in wetland restoration ecology. *Trends in Ecology and Evolution* 15:402–407.

———. 2005. Restoring wetland plant diversity: A comparison of existing and adaptive approaches. *Wetland Ecology and Management* 13:1572–9834.

Zedler, J. B., and J. C. Callaway. 1999. Tracking wetland restoration: Do mitigation sites follow desired trajectories? *Restoration Ecology* 7:69–73.

———. 2000. Evaluating the progress of engineered tidal wetlands. *Ecological Engineering* 15:211–225.

Chapter 8: Death and Rebirth of an Urban Wetland

Bragin, A. B., et al. 2005. *A fishery resource inventory of the lower Hackensack River within the Hackensack Meadowlands District: A comparative study, 2001–2003 versus 1987–1988*. Lyndhurst, N.J.: New Jersey Meadowlands Commission and Meadowlands Environmental Research Institute.

Carola, H. 2002. Meadowlands Commission declares SAMP dead. *Hackensack Riverkeeper Newsletter*. http://www.hackensackriverkeeper.org/newsletters/Winter2002/004_Winter_2002.htm.

Hackensack Meadowlands Development Commission. 1975. *Wetland bio-zones of the Hackensack Meadowlands: An inventory*. Lyndhurst, N.J.: Hackensack Meadowlands Development Commission.

Kiviat, E., and K. MacDonald. 2004. Biodiversity patterns and conservation in the Hackensack Meadowlands, New Jersey: History, ecology, and restoration of a degraded urban wetland. *Urban Habitats* 2:28–61.

Kraus, M., and A. B. Bragin. 1988. *Inventory of fishery resources of the Hackensack River within the jurisdictional boundary of the Hackensack Meadowlands Development Commission from Kearny, Hudson County, to Ridgefield, Bergen County, New Jersey*. Lyndhurst, N.J.: Hackensack Meadowlands Development Commission.

Marshall, S. 2004. The Meadowlands before the commission: Three centuries of human use and alteration of the Newark and Hackensack Meadows. *Urban Habitats* 2:4–27.

Mutz, H. A. 1976. *Harrison: The history of a New Jersey town.* Harrison, N.J.: Bicentennial Committee.

Quinn, John R. 1997. *Fields of sun and grass: An artist's journal of the New Jersey Meadowlands.* New Brunswick, N.J.: Rutgers University Press.

Sullivan, R. 1998. *The Meadowlands: Wilderness adventures at the edge of a city.* New York: Simon & Schuster.

Tiner, R. W., J. Q. Swords, and B. J. McClain. 2002. *Wetland status and trends for the Hackensack Meadowlands. Assessment report,* National Wetlands Inventory Program. Hadley, Mass.: U.S. Fish and Wildlife Service.

U.S. Congress. 2006. Sustainable Fisheries Act. Public Law 104-297.

U.S. Fish and Wildlife Service. 2007. *The Hackensack Meadowlands Initiative: Preliminary Conservation Planning.* Pleasantville, N.J.: U.S. Fish and Wildlife Service.

Weis, J. S. 2005. Diet and food web support of the white perch, *Morone americana* in the Hackensack Meadowlands. *Environmental Biology of Fishes* 74:109–113.

Weis, P., et al. 2005. Studies of a contaminated brackish marsh in the Hackensack Meadowlands of northeastern New Jersey: An assessment of natural recovery. *Marine Pollution Bulletin* 50:1405–1415.

Index

Page numbers in italics refer to figures

About the Authors

The authors were classmates at the Bronx High School of Science, and after graduation they went their separate ways. They were reunited inadvertently after many years by their editor, Doreen Valentine, who invited them to write this book together, unaware that their paths had crossed in the distant past. They each have two adult children, a girl and a boy in both cases.

Judith S. Weis, Ph. D., is a professor of biology at Rutgers University in Newark and has been studying salt marshes and their inhabitants for most of her career. Most of her work has been in northern New Jersey, but she has also studied estuaries and salt marshes from as far north as Massachusetts to Florida and mangrove swamps in Indonesia and Madagascar. She has served on advisory committees to the National Academy of Sciences, the National Oceanic and Atmospheric Administration, and the Environmental Protection Agency. She has published about two hundred scientific research articles, but this is her first book. She spends as much time as possible in the summers enjoying the salt marshes near Accabonac Harbor in eastern Long Island (location of many of the photos in this book) and also loves watching the recovery going on in the Hackensack Meadowlands.

Carol A. Butler, Ph. D., is a psychoanalyst in private practice in Manhatten, working with individual adults and couples. Her work with couples led to her decision to train as a divorce mediator, which led to her first book, *The Divorce Mediation Answer Book*. She is an adjunct assistant professor at New York University in the Department of Applied Psychology and a docent at the American Museum of Natural History. She is co-authoring a series of question-and-answer trade paperbacks about animals. *Do Butterflies Bite?* is currently available. *Do Bats Drink Blood?* is due out shortly, and *Why Do Bees Buzz?* and *Do Hummingbirds Hum?* will be published in 2010.